Study Guide
for use with

FOUNDATIONS
OF Financial
MANAGEMENT
SIXTH CANADIAN EDITION

Stanley B. Block
Texas Christian University

Geoffrey A. Hirt
DePaul University and Mesirow Financial

J. Douglas Short
Northern Alberta Institute of Technology

Prepared by

Dwight C. Anderson
Louisiana Tech University

J. Douglas Short
Northern Alberta Institute of Technology

Toronto Montréal Boston Burr Ridge, IL Dubuque, IA Madison, WI New York
San Francisco St. Louis Bangkok Bogotá Caracas Kuala Lumpur Lisbon London
Madrid Mexico City Milan New Delhi Santiago Seoul Singapore Sydney Taipei

McGraw-Hill
Ryerson Limited

A Subsidiary of The McGraw·Hill Companies

Study Guide for use with
Foundations of Financial Management
Sixth Canadian Edition

ISBN: 0-07-089763-8

1 2 3 4 5 6 7 8 9 10 CP 0 9 8 7 6 5 4 3

Printed and bound in Canada

Care has been taken to trace ownership of copyright material contained in this text; however, the publisher will welcome any information that enables them to rectify any reference or credit for subsequent editions.

Vice President and Editorial Director: Pat Ferrier
Senior Sponsoring Editor: Lynn Fisher
Developmental Editor: Maria Chu
Marketing Manager: Kelly Smyth
Supervising Editor: Anne Macdonald
Production Coordinator: Andree Davis
Printer: Canadian Printco, Ltd.

To the Student:

The purpose of this book is to assist you in your study of the *Foundations of Financial Management*. To maximize the assistance provided by the *Study Guide*, you should formulate a plan of study. A suggested plan follows:

1. Read the summary of the textbook chapter provided in the *Study Guide*. The summary is a succinct statement of the major issues covered in the corresponding chapter of the textbook.

2. Read through the outline of the text chapter that follows the summary in the *Study Guide*. The outline includes the most significant components of the chapter.

3. Carefully read the text chapter. Be especially attentive to the chapter components identified in the *Study Guide* outline.

4. Quickly review the textbook chapter by again reading the summary and outline in the *Study Guide*.

5. Test your knowledge of the chapter concepts by answering the multiple-choice questions in the *Study Guide*. If you incorrectly answer several questions, the text chapter should be read again.

6. Work the problems in the *Study Guide*. It is suggested that you thoroughly attempt to solve the problems before referring to the solutions provided. If your answers differ from the solutions, study the solutions to detect the errors (yours or mine) and rework the problems correctly.

7. Work the end of chapter problems in *Foundations of Financial Management*. You should strive to solve the problems without referring to the author's examples. If you cannot do so, reread the applicable portion of the text.

A study guide can be a valuable learning aid when used properly. Remember--it should be used as a supplement to the textbook, not as a substitute.

Dwight C. Anderson
J. Douglas Short

Contents

Chapter 1

The Goals and Functions of Financial Management

Summary: This chapter traces the evolution and interrelationships of finance as a field of study and the role of the financial manager in a dynamic economy. The chapter stresses financial markets as key to capital allocation.

I. **Financial management is critical for a firm's success. [p. 2]**

   A. Rapidly changing global economics continually revalue the asset values of the firm.

II. **The Field of Finance. [p. 3]**

   A. Economics provides structure to decision making and helps us to understand the economic environment in which the financial manager operates. Decision areas include:

      1. risk analysis
      2. price theory
      3. comparative return analysis

   B. Accounting provides the financial data needed for financial decision making.

   C. The demand for financial management skills exists in many sectors of our society, including corporate management, financial institutions and consulting.

III. **Finance as a field of study has evolved over time in response to changing business management needs. [p. 3-5]**

   A. Finance achieved recognition as a separate field of study from economics at the turn of this century.

   B. Initially, finance concentrated on institutional detail, defining stocks, bonds, and institutions such as the markets, with little or no systematic analysis.

   C. With the Depression, emphasis shifted to preservation of capital, maintenance of liquidity, reorganization, and bankruptcy. Government intervention in business financial affairs resulted in:

      1. The development of securities regulations
      2. Published financial data on corporate performance and eventual analysis of that data

   D. The most significant step in the evolution of contemporary financial management began in the mid-1950s. Emphasis was placed on the analytically determined employment of resources within the firm. The decision-making nature of financial management was manifested in the enthusiasm for the study of:

      1. Capital asset management: capital budgeting
      2. Efficient utilization of current assets
      3. Capital structure composition
      4. Dividend policy

   E. In the 1960s into the 1980s, these theories migrated to corporate boardrooms with a focus on the risk/return relationship, accompanied by portfolio management theories that led firms to diversification strategies. By the 1990s diversification strategies were challenged in theory and in practice with firms refocusing on core businesses.

   F. The sharpened focus on financial objectives, it has been critically suggested, has left Canadian managers too adverse to risk and concentrating too much on the short term.

   G. The derivatives market, developing from theory, has allowed management to reduce financial risks.

Technological advances have increased business efficiencies and risks.

    H.   In large corporations, the hired management acts as agents for owners. The study of the relationship between owners and managers as well as other agent relationships is referred to as **agency theory**. Institutional investors are playing a more significant role.

IV.   The Goals of Financial Management. [p. 5-12]

    A.   Shareholders' wealth maximization, the goal of the firm, is measured by the highest possible market price of the firm's shares.

    B.   Financial decision-making analysis is always predicated on this goal: to increase value to shareholders within a risk-return framework.

    C.   Shareholders' wealth maximization (a valuation concept) incorporates:

        1.   The risk associated with future earnings (cash flows).
        2.   The timing of benefits.
        3.   Market judgment on accuracy of profit measurement.

    D.   Maximizing profits is not the same as maximizing shareholder wealth. Profit or earnings per share has drawbacks because;

    E.   The efficiency of the capital market dictates that, with a given level of risk, capital will flow to those firms "promising" the highest return.

    F.   Management interests and risk perceptions may conflict with the goal of shareholder wealth maximization. This is the agency relationship. There is to some degree ownership concentration in Canada.

    G.   Maximization of shareholder wealth is tempered by social responsibility.

V.   Functions of Financial Management: A financial manager is responsible for financing an efficient level and composition of assets by obtaining financing through the most appropriate means. [p. 12-13]

    A.   Daily financial management activities

        1.   Credit management
        2.   Inventory control
        3.   Receipt and disbursement of funds

    B.   Less-routine activities

        1.   Sale of stocks and bonds
        2.   Capital budgeting
        3.   Dividend decisions

    C.   Forms of organization: The finance function may be carried out within a number of different forms of organizations. **[p. 13-15]**

        1.   Sole proprietorship
            a.   Single ownership
            b.   Simplicity of decision making
            c.   Low organizational and operating costs
            d.   Unlimited liability
            e.   Earnings are taxed as personal earnings of the individual owner

2. Partnership
   a. Two or more partners
   b. Usually formed by articles of partnership agreement
   c. Unlimited liability for all partners unless a limited partnership is formed which provides limited liability for one or more partners. At least one partner must be a general partner.
   d. Earnings are taxed as personal earnings of partners

3. Corporation
   a. Most important form of business in terms of revenue and profits
   b. Legal entity
   c. Formed by articles of incorporation
   d. Shareholders (owners) have limited liability
   e. Easy divisibility of ownership
   f. Managed by the board of directors
   g. Double taxation of earnings: Earnings of the corporation are subject to the corporate income tax; dividends (distributed net income) are subject to personal taxation. The dividend tax credit attempts to reduce the double taxation effect.

VI. **The Role of Financial Markets: Wealth maximization depends on the perception expectations of the market. The market through daily share price changes of each publicly traded company provides managers with a performance report card. [p. 15]**

A. Structure and Functions of the Financial Markets: Money markets (Chapter 7) and Capital markets (Chapter 14) are more fully presented in later chapters but students may find that current examples from the *Globe and Mail* will create a sense of realism about this course.

   1. **Financial markets** are the meeting places for people, corporations, and institutions that either need money or have money to lend or invest.
   2. Financial markets may be classified as:
      a. Markets that focus on short-term securities that have a life of a year or less are called **money markets**.
      b. **Capital markets** are defined as markets where securities have a life of more than one year. Capital markets are further classified as **intermediate** (1-10 years) and **long-term** (more than 10 years).

B. Allocation of Capital: Students need to understand how the market price reflects risk and return expectations and how a company's ability to raise funds is influenced by its financial performance and corporate behavior. The markets determine value. [p. 16]

   1. Financial markets allocate capital to the highest bidder within a risk-return framework. Individuals possessing capital seek to earn the highest rate of return at a given level of risk. Prices of securities in the market reflect the collective judgement of all participants. Securities price movements provide feedback to corporate managers indicating the markets' evaluation of their activities. Corporations raise capital by selling new securities in the **primary market**. Securities previously sold by corporations, trade in the **secondary market** between investors.

C. Reliance on Debt: The typical firm makes extensive use of debt financing. The government has been a heavy user of debt markets, although this is changing. [p. 17]

D. Interest Rates: The market interest rates are a key to determining required rates of return. Interest rates are volatile. See figure 1-2. [p. 18-19]

E. Internationalization of the Financial Markets: Emphasis is on the globalization of the capital markets and the worldwide pool of capital available to many companies. Modern corporate financial managers must understand international capital flows, electronic funds transfer, foreign currency hedging strategies, the Euro and many other global trading factors. [p. 19]

VII. Outline of the Text. [p. 20-21]

A. Introduction: An examination of the goals of financial management within an analytical framework.

B. Financial analysis and planning:

1. Review of accounting relationships with finance
2. Ratio analysis
3. Construction of budgets and pro forma statements
4. Operating and financial leverage

C. Working capital management: Techniques for managing the levels of current assets and short-term financing in a risk-return context.

D. Capital budgeting and related valuation concepts:

1. Time value of money
2. Cost of capital
3. Capital budgeting techniques

E. Long-term financing: An analysis of the characteristics of the structure, participants, and instruments of the capital markets.

F. Corporate growth through mergers: An integration of financial management concepts within the framework of corporate growth strategy.

G. International financial management: An examination of the complex, risky environment of international finance.

Chapter 1: Multiple Choice Questions

1. Profits of a sole proprietorship are: [p. 14]
   a. Taxed as income of the individual owner.
   b. Taxed as business income and again as personal income of the proprietor.
   c. Not taxed if retained in the business.
   d. Taxed at the same rates as earnings of corporations.
   e. None of the above are correct

2. Corporate managers: [p. 9-10]
   a. Ignore the desires of shareholders.
   b. May make decisions that are contrary to the interests of shareholders.
   c. Are sensitive to investor's risk-return preferences when pursuing the goals of financial management.
   d. Are insensitive to the desires of shareholders.
   e. Both *b* and *c* are correct.

3. The goal of financial management is: [p. 8]
   a. To maximize profit.
   b. To maximize cash flow.
   c. To maximize revenues (sales).
   d. To maximize shareholders' wealth.
   e. To maximize earnings per share.

4. Which of the following business forms exposes all owners to unlimited liability? [p. 13-15]
    a. Partnerships
    b. Proprietorships
    c. Corporations
    d. Limited partnerships
    e. Both *a* and *b* are correct

5. Valuation of assets utilizes: [p. 7]
    a. The present value model and future expected cash flows.
    b. The balance sheet and earnings.
    c. The summation of future expected cash flows.
    d. The present value model and recorded cash flows.
    e. Earnings and risk.

6. Daily activities of the financial manager include: [p. 13]
    a. Credit management..
    b. Inventory control.
    c. Capital budgeting.
    d. Receipt of funds.
    e. Answers *a*, *b*, and *d* are correct

7. Insider trading: [p. 12]
    a. Contributes to market efficiency because all information is reflected in the price of securities.
    b. Is illegal.
    c. Is protected against by the CDIC.
    d. Has no negative impact on shareholders.
    e. None of the above are correct

8. The financial markets determine value and allocate capital based on [p. 16]
    a. Reported earnings.
    b. Agency theory.
    c. The firm's capital budgeting projects.
    d. The firm's capital structure.
    e. It's most productive use.

9. New common stock is sold by firms in the _____ market and individuals trade securities in the _____ market. [p. 16]
    a. Money; primary
    b. Secondary; capital
    c. Primary; secondary
    d. International; domestic
    e. Government; corporate

10. Select the pair of terms that indicates a correct match. [p. 13-15]
    a. Corporation; limited partnership
    b. Partnership; articles of incorporation
    c. Proprietorship; limited liability
    d. Proprietorship; personal taxation only
    e. Partnership; double taxation

Multiple Choice Answer Key: Chapter 1

| 1. | a | 2. | e | 3. | d | 4. | e | 5. | a |
| 6. | e | 7. | b | 8. | e | 9. | c | 10. | d |

Chapter 2

Summary: An understanding of financial statements is a prerequisite for financial management decision making. In this chapter the characteristics of three basic financial statements--**income statement**, **balance sheet**, and **statement of cash flows**--are presented. The impact of income tax provisions on financial decisions is also examined.

I.   **Financial Statements**

    A. The Income Statement **[p. 27]**

        1. The income statement begins with the aggregate amount of sales (revenues) that are generated within a specific period of time.

        2. The various expenses that occur in generating the sales are subtracted in stair-step fashion to arrive at the net income for the defined period.

        3. The separation of the expense categories such as cost of goods sold, selling and administrative expenses, amortization, interest and taxes enables the management to assess the relative importance and appropriateness of the expenditures in producing each level of sales.

        4. The "bottom line" value, net income, is the aggregate amount available to the owners.

        5. Valuation from the Income Statement:

           a. The EPS is a measurement of the return available to providers of equity capital to the firm. The return to the providers of debt capital, interest, appears earlier in the income statement as a tax-deductible expense.

$$Earnings\ per\ share\ (eps) = \frac{Earnings\ available\ to\ common\ shareholders}{Number\ of\ shares\ outstanding} \qquad (2-1;\ page\ 29)$$

           b. Shareholders are interested in the percentage of earnings paid as dividends.

$$Payout\ ratio = \frac{Dividend\ per\ share}{Earnings\ per\ share} \qquad (2-2;\ page\ 29)$$

           c. The earnings per share may be converted to a measure of current value through application of the price/earnings (P/E) ratio. The P/E ratio is best used as a relative measure of value because the numerator, price, is based on the future and the denominator, earnings, is a current measure.

$$P/E\ ratio = \frac{Market\ per\ share}{Earnings\ per\ share} \qquad (2-3;\ page\ 29)$$

           d. Part of the investor's return comes as dividends. This is related to the value of the investment.

$$Dividend\ yield = \frac{Dividends\ per\ share}{Market\ share\ price} \qquad (2-4;\ page\ 31)$$

        6. The income statement reflects only income occurring to the individual or business firm from verifiable transactions as opposed to the economist's definition of income, which reflects changes in real worth.

        7. Income does not necessarily indicate cash available to shareholders.

    B.   Balance Sheet **[p. 32]**

        1. Whereas the income statement provides a summary of financial transactions for a period of time, the balance sheet portrays the cumulative results of transactions at a point in time. The balance sheet may present the position of the firm as a result of transactions for six months, twenty-five years, or other periods.

        2. The balance sheet is divided into two broad categories. The assets employed in the operations of the firm compose one category while the other, liabilities and net worth, is composed of the sources of financing for the employed assets.

3. Within the asset category, the assets are listed in their order of liquidity.
   a. Cash (including demand deposits)
   b. Marketable securities: investments of temporarily excess cash in highly liquid securities
   c. Accounts receivable
   d. Inventory
   e. Prepaid expenses: future expense items that have already been paid
   f. Investments: investments in securities and other assets for longer than one operating cycle
   g. Plant and equipment adjusted for accumulated amortization

4. The various sources of financing of a firm are listed in their order of maturity. Those sources that mature earliest, current liabilities, are listed first. The more permanent debt and equity sources follow.
   a. Accounts payable
   b. Notes payable
   c. Accrued expenses: an obligation to pay is incurred but payment has not been made
   d. Long-term debt: principal to be paid beyond the current period
   e. Preferred stock
   f. Common stock accounts:
      i. Common stock
      ii. Contributed surplus (sometimes)
      iii. Retained earnings

5. Confusing balance-sheet-related terms
   a. Retained earnings: All of the assets of a firm are listed on the asset side of the balance sheet, yet many individuals envision a pile of money when the term retained earnings is used. Retained earnings is simply a cumulative total of the earnings of the firm since its beginning until the date of the balance sheet that have not been paid to the owners. Earnings that are retained are used to purchase assets, pay liabilities, throw a big party for the management, etc. Regardless, there is no money available from a "container" labeled retained earnings.
   b. Net worth or book value of the firm is composed of the various common equity accounts and represents the net contributions of the owners to the business.

6. Valuation from the balance sheet:
   a. Book value is a historical value and does not necessarily coincide with the market value of the shareholders equity.

   $$\frac{Market\ value}{Book\ value} = \frac{MV}{BV} = \frac{Market\ value\ per\ share}{Book\ value\ per\ share} \qquad (2-5;\ page\ 35)$$

7. Limitation of the balance sheet: Values are recorded at cost; replacement cost of some assets, particularly plant and equipment may greatly exceed their recorded value. The Canadian Institute of Chartered Accountants (CICA), in January 1983, recommended that large companies disclose inflation adjusted accounting data in their annual reports. However, the standard is no longer in force and the inclusion of inflation adjusted accounting data in financial reports is purely a voluntary act.

C. Statement of cash flows [p. 37]

1. In 1998, the CICA replace the statement of changes in financial position with the statement of cash flows to report changes in cash and cash equivalents.
2. The statement emphasizes the critical nature of cash flow to the operations of the firm.
3. The three primary sections of the statement are:
   a. cash flows from operating activities.
   b. cash flows from investing activities.
   c. cash flows from financing activities.

4. Income from operations may be translated from an accrual basis to a cash basis in two ways to obtain **cash flow from operations.**
   a. Direct method: each and every item on the income statement is adjusted from accrual

accounting to cash accounting.
- *b.* Indirect method: a less tedious process than the direct method is usually preferred. Net income is used as the starting point and adjustments are made to convert net income to cash flows from operations. Beginning with net income,
  - i. Add amortization for the current period, decreases in individual current asset accounts (other than cash) and increases in current liabilities;
  - ii. Subtract increases in current asset accounts (other than cash) and decreases in current liabilities.

5. **Cash flow from investing** is found by summing the changes of investment in securities and plant and equipment. Increases are uses of funds and decreases are sources of funds.
6. **Cash flow from financing activities** is found by summing the sale or retirement of corporate securities and dividends. The sale of securities is a source of funds and the retirement of securities and payment of dividends are uses of funds.
7. Cash flows from operations, cash flows from investing, and cash flows from financing are combined to arrive at the statement of cash flows. The net increase or decrease shown in the statement of cash flows will be equal to the change in the cash balance on the balance sheet.
8. In analyzing cash flow, one is examining the sources and uses of funds to evaluate the firm's solvency, liquidity and financial flexibility.

II. Amortization and Funds Flow [p. 44]

A. Amortization is an attempt to allocate an initial asset cost over its life.

B. Amortization is an accounting entry and does not involve the movement of funds.

C. As indicated in the statement of cash flows, amortization is added back to net income to arrive at cash flow.

III. Free cash flow. [p. 45]

A. Free cash flow is equal to cash flow from operating activities:
   Minus: Capital expenditures required to maintain the productive capacity of the firm.
   Minus: Dividends

B. The amount of free cash flow is often available for special financing activities such as leveraged buy-outs.

IV. Income Tax Considerations [p. 46]

A. Most financial decisions are influenced by federal and provincial income tax considerations.

1. Personal taxes at varying rates apply to earnings of proprietors, partners and individuals. Investment income is taxed differently as interest, dividends, or capital gains.
2. Corporate income is taxed at two levels-at the corporate level and at the personal level when received as dividends or as capital gain. Provincial tax rates also apply.

B. The aftertax cost of a tax-deductible business expense is equal to the (expense) × (1 – tax rate).

C. Although amortization is a noncash expense, it does affect cash flow by reducing taxes. Tax reduction in cash outflow for taxes resulting from amortization charges may be computed by multiplying the (amortization expense) × (tax rate).

V. Review of Formulas

See text page 51 or the insert card.

Chapter 2: Multiple Choice Questions

1. The financial statement that reflects the profitability of a firm over a period of time is the: [p. 31]
   a. Balance sheet
   b. Income statement
   c. Statement of cash flows
   d. Income tax return
   e. None of the above are correct

2. Assuming a tax rate of 30%, the aftertax cost of $1,000,000 in interest and $1,000,000 in dividends respectively is: [p. 48]
   a. $1,000,000; $1,000,000.
   b. $700,000; $1,000,000.
   c. $700,000; $700,000.
   d. $1,000,000; $700,000.
   e. None of the above are correct

3. If a firm has retained earnings of $1,500,000 on its balance sheet, which of the following statements is correct? [p. 37]
   a. The firm may get $1,500,000 in cash from retained earnings.
   b. The firm has a market value of at least $1,500,000.
   c. The firm has retained $1,500,000 of earnings since the firm's beginning until the date of the balance sheet.
   d. The assets of the firm are worth at least $1,500,000.
   e. All of the above are correct

4. Temporarily, excess cash will often be invested in: [p. 35]
   a. Inventory
   b. Accounts receivable
   c. Common stock
   d. Accounts payable
   e. Marketable securities

5. The amortization expense shown on the income statement: [p. 47]
   a. Is equal to the accumulated amortization on the balance sheet.
   b. Will reduce the tax liability of the firm.
   c. Is a noncash expense.
   d. Both b and c are correct.
   e. Answers a, b, and c are correct.

6. Assets on the balance sheet are listed in order of: [p. 35]
   a. Age.
   b. Amount.
   c. Importance.
   d. Liquidity.
   e. Market value.

7. The statement of cash flows is composed of cash flow from operations, cash flow from financing activities, and: [p. 39]
   a. Free cash flow.
   b. Cash from changes in working capital.
   c. Cash from amortization.
   d. Cash from investing activities.
   e. All of the above are correct

8. Which of the following appropriately describe the correct relationship between the book value and market value of a firm's assets? [p. 38]
   a. Market value will be greater than book value.
   b. Book value will be greater than market value.
   c. Market value will equal book value.
   d. Market value may be more or less than book value.
   e. None of the above are correct

9. Free cash flow is equal to cash flow from operations: [p. 47]
   a. Plus capital expenditures to maintain productive capacity and dividends.
   b. Minus dividends.
   c. Minus capital expenditures to maintain productive capacity and dividends.
   d. Minus amortization.
   e. Plus amortization and dividends.

10. The price earnings ratio of a firm is found by: [p. 32-32]
    a. Dividing the market price per share of stock by the earnings per share.
    b. Multiplying the market price per share of stock by the payout ratio.
    c. Dividing the earnings per share by the market price per share of stock.
    d. Dividing the market price per share of stock by the book value per share.
    e. Multiplying the P/E times E.

Multiple Choice Answer Key: Chapter 2

| 1. | b | 2. | b | 3. | c | 4. | e | 5. | d |
| 6. | d | 7. | d | 8. | d | 9. | c | 10. | a |

Chapter 2: Problems

2-1.   Given the information below, complete the income statement for Dalia Corporation.

Shares outstanding	100,000
Earnings per share	$6
Taxes	40%

DALIA CORPORATION
Income Statement
For the Year Ended December 31, 2002

Sales	$
Cost of goods sold	8,000,000
Gross profit	
Selling and administrative expense	1,150,000
Amortization expense	250,000
Operating profit	
Interest expense	200,000
Earnings before taxes	
Taxes	
Net profit	$.

2-2. Dalia Corporation (2-1) has 12,000 shares of preferred stock outstanding with an annual dividend of $4 per share. The firm also has 100,000 shares of common stock outstanding and follows a 50% payout policy.
   (a) Calculate the earnings per share and dividends per share for common shareholders of Dickens Corporation.
   (b) What was the increase in retained earnings for the year?

2-3. Sources (S) and Uses (U) information is provided below.
   (a) Construct the year-end 2002 balance sheet for the Kroll Corporation.

Assets	Year-End 2002	Year-End 2002	Change	Source (S) or Use (U)
Current Assets:				
Cash	$ 200,000		$ 20,000	S
Marketable securities	30,000		10,000	S
Accounts receivable (net)	440,000		50,000	U
Inventory	520,000		70,000	U
Prepaid expenses	35,000		5,000	S
Total Current Assets	1,225,000			
Investments	45,000		10,000	S
Plant and equipment	1,600,000			
Less: Accumulated amortization	600,000			
Net plant and equipment	1,000,000		200,000	U
Total Assets	$2,270,000			

Liabilities and Shareholders' Equity

	Year-End 2002	Year-End 2002	Change	Source (S) or Use (U)
Current Liabilities:				
Accounts payable	$ 352,000		$ 68,000	S
Notes payable	44,000		6,000	U
Accrued expenses	80,000		10,000	S
Total Current Liabilities	476,000			
Long-Term Liabilities:				
Bonds payable, 2022	330,000		---	
Total Liabilities	806,000			
Shareholders' Equity:				
Preferred stock	100,000		---	S
Common stock	575,000		150,000	S
Retained earnings	789,000		53,000	S
Total Shareholders' Equity	$1,464,000			
Total Liabilities and Shareholders' Equity	$2,270,000			

   (b) Prepare a Statement of cash flows for the Emery Corporation that reflects the following:

   i. Net income = $114,000
   ii. Dividends = $61,000
   iii. Gross additions to plant and equipment = $500,000
   iv. Amortization expense = $300,000

2-4.   Given the information below, prepare a balance sheet for Zhong Manufacturing as of December 31, 2003.

Total current assets	$11,800,000
Cash	?
Inventory	5,800,000
Accounts payable	4,200,000
Gross capital assets	15,000,000
Shareholders' equity	6,450,000
Accrued expenses	600,000
Notes payable	3,800,000
Taxes payable	200,000
Retained earnings	?
Accrued amortization	6,800,000
Long-term debt	4,750,000
Accounts receivable	3,600,000
Common stock	3,000,000
Marketable securities	2,000,000

2-5.   Using the information in (2-4 above), compute the following values for Zhong Manufacturing.

(a)   Book value per share (2 million shares).
(b)   Market value per share if the P/E ratio is 12 and Washer's total earnings are $5,000,000.
(c)   The ratio of market value per share to book value per share.

2-6.   Suppose the earnings of Zhong Manufacturing (2-5 above) rise to $6,000,000 but their P/E ratio declines to 10 ×.

(a)   What is the market value per share of common stock?
(b)   What is the total market value of the common stock of Washer Manufacturing?

2-7.   The FMA Corporation ended 2002 operations with the following balance sheet.

FMA CORPORATION
Balance Sheet
December 31, 2002

Current Assets		Current Liabilities	
Cash	$ 15,000	Accounts payable	$ 60,000
Marketable securities	20,000	Notes payable	50,000
Accounts receivable	50,000	Total current liabilities	110,000
Inventory	80,000		
Total current assets	165,000	Long-term bonds	75,000
Capital Assets		Shareholders' Equity	
Gross plant & equipment 250,000		Common stock	100,000
Less: Acc. amortization 75,000			
Net plant & equipment	175,000	Retained earnings	55,000
Total assets	$340,000	Total liabilities and equity	$340,000

FMA's sales in 2001 were $360,000 with cost of goods sold averaging 65% of sales. Selling and administrative expenses were $36,000 and amortization expense for the year was $50,000. On December 31, 2002, the firm paid the interest (10%) on its bank loan (notes payable) for the year and also renewed the loan after paying $10,000 on the principal balance. Interest at a 12% rate was paid to the firm's bondholders. During 2002, accounts receivable declined by 5%, but inventory increased by 10%. A rise of 12% in accounts payable provided financing for much of the added inventory. The firm purchased a new machine for $65,000 in October and paid a total cash dividend of $10,805 at the end of the year. The management elected not to raise any additional external capital in 2002, but all of the marketable securities were converted to cash and used for business operations. The firm is in a 22% tax bracket.

(a)   Prepare an income statement for 2002.
(b)   Prepare a balance sheet as of December 31, 2002.
(c)   Prepare a statement of cash flows for 2002.

Chapter 2: Solutions

2-1.

DALIA CORPORATION
Income Statement
For the Year Ended December 31, 2002

Sales	**$10,600,000**
Cost of goods sold	8,000,000
Gross profit	**2,600,000**
Selling and administrative expense	1,150,000
Amortization expense	250,000
Operating profit	**1,200,000**
Interest expense	200,000
Earnings before taxes	**1,000,000**
Taxes	**400,000**
Net profit	**$ 600,000**

Steps:
i.   Net profit = ($6)(100,000) = $600,000
ii.   Earnings before taxes = NPAT/.6 = $600,000 = $1,000,000
iii. Taxes = EBT - NPAT = $1,000,000 - $600,000 = $400,000
iv.   Operating profit = EBT + Interest expense = $1,000,000 + $200,000 = $1,200,000
v.   Gross profit = Operating profit + Selling and administrative expense + Amortization expense = $1,200,000 + $1,150,000 + $250,000 = $2,600,000
vi.   Sales = Gross profit + COGS = $2,600,000 + $8,000,000 = $10,600,000

2-2.

(a)   Preferred dividends = 12,000 × $4 = $48,000
Earnings available to common shareholders = net income minus preferred dividends
$600,000 – $48,000 = $552,000

$$Earnings\ per\ share = \frac{\$552,000}{100,000} = \textbf{\$5.52}$$

Total dividends = payout ratio times earnings available = .50 x $552,000 = $276,000

$$Dividends\ per\ share = \frac{\$276,000}{100,000} = \textbf{\$2.76}$$

(b)   Addition to retained earnings = earnings available to common shareholders minus dividends
$552,000 – $276,000 = **$276,000**

2-3. Sources (S) and Uses (U) information is provided below.
(a) Construct the year-end 2002 balance sheet for the Kroll Corporation.

Assets	Year-End 2001	Year-End 2002	Change	Source (S) or Use (U)
Current Assets:				
Cash	$ 200,000	$ 180,000	$ 20,000	S
Marketable securities	30,000	20,000	10,000	S
Accounts receivable (net)	440,000	490,000	50,000	U
Inventory	520,000	590,000	70,000	U
Prepaid expenses	35,000	30,000	5,000	S
Total Current Assets	$1,225,000	$1,310,000		
Investments	$ 45,000	35,000	10,000	S
Plant and equipment	1,600,000			
Less: Accumulated amortization	600,000			
Net plant and equipment	1,000,000	1,200,000	200,000	U
Total Assets	$2,270,000	$2,545,000		

Liabilities & Shareholders' Equity

	Year-End 2001	Year-End 2002	Change	Source (S) or Use (U)
Current Liabilities:				
Accounts payable	$ 352,000	$ 420,000	$ 68,000	S
Notes payable	44,000	38,000	6,000	U
Accrued expenses	80,000	90,000	10,000	S
Total Current Liabilities	$ 476,000	$ 548,000		
Long-Term Liabilities:				
Bonds payable, 2022	330,000	330,000	---	
Total Liabilities	$ 806,000	$ 878,000		
Shareholders' Equity:				
Preferred stock	$ 100,000	$ 100,000	---	S
Common stock	575,000	725,000	$150,000	S
Retained earnings	789,000	842,000	53,000	S
Total Shareholders' Equity	$1,464,000	$1,667,000		
Total Liabilities. & Share. Equity	$2,270,000	$2,545,000		

(b)

KROLL CORPORATION
Statement of cash flows
For the Year Ended December 31, 2002

Operating activities:

Net income		$114,000
Add items not requiring an outlay of cash:		
Amortization	$300,000	
Cash flow from operations		414,000
Decrease in marketable securities	10,000	
Increase in accounts receivable	(50,000)	
Increase in inventory	(70,000)	
Decrease in prepaid expense	5,000	
Increase in accounts payable	68,000	
Decrease in notes payable	(6,000)	
Increase in accrued expenses	10,000	
Net change in noncash working capital		(33,000)
Cash provided by operating activities		381,000
Investing activities:		
Decrease in investments	10,000	
Increase in plant and equipment	(500,000)	
Cash used in investing activities		(490,000)
Financing activities:		
Increase in common stock	150,000	
Dividends paid	(61,000)	
Cash provided by financing activities		89,000
Decrease in cash during year		(20,000)
Cash, beginning of year		200,000
Cash, end of year		$ 180,000

2-4.

ZHONG MANUFACTURING
Balance Sheet
For the Year Ended December 31, 2003

Assets

Current Assets:		
Cash		$ 400,000
Marketable securities		2,000,000
Accounts receivable (net)		3,600,000
Inventory		5,800,000
Total Current Assets		11,800,000
Capital Assets:		
Gross capital assets	$15,000,000	
Less: Accumulated amortization	6,800,000	
Net capital assets		8,200,000
Total Assets		$20,000,000

Liabilities and Shareholders' Equity

Current Liabilities:

Accounts payable	$ 4,200,000
Taxes payable	200,000
Notes payable	3,800,000
Accrued expenses	600,000
Total Current Liabilities	8,800,000
Long-Term Debt	4,750,000
Total Liabilities	13,550,000

Shareholders' Equity:

Common stock	3,000,000
Retained earnings	3,450,000
Total Shareholders' Equity	6,450,000
Total Liabilities and Shareholders' Equity	$20,000,000

NOTE: The cash and retained earnings balances are "plug" figures.

2-5.

(a)   Zhong Manufacturing

$$Book\ value\ per\ share = \frac{shareholders'\ equity}{number\ of\ common\ shares} = \frac{\$6,450,000}{2,000,000} = \mathbf{\$3.225}$$

(b) $$Earnings\ per\ share = \frac{earnings\ available\ to\ common\ shareholders}{number\ of\ shares\ outstanding} = \frac{\$5,000,000}{2,000,000} = \mathbf{\$2.50}$$

$$\begin{aligned} Market\ value\ per\ share\ &= P/E \times E \\ &= 12 \times \$2.50 \\ &= \mathbf{\$30} \end{aligned}$$

(c) $$\frac{Market\ value\ per\ share}{Book\ value\ per\ share} = \frac{MV}{BV} = \frac{\$30}{\$3.225} = \mathbf{9.3} \times$$

2-6.

(a)   The new EPS of Zhong would be:

$$Earnings\ per\ share = \frac{earnings\ available\ to\ common\ shareholders}{number\ of\ shares\ outstanding} = \frac{\$6,000,000}{2,000,000} = \mathbf{\$3.00}$$

The market value per share at the lower P/E ratio = 10 would be 10 x $3 = **$30**. The increase in EPS is offset by the decline in the P/E ratio.

(b)   The total market value of Washer's common stock = 2,000,000 x $30 = **$60,000,000**.

2-7.

(a)

FMA CORPORATION
Income Statement
For the Year Ended December 31, 2002

Sales..	$ 360,000
Cost of goods sold...	234,000
Gross profit..	126,000
Selling and administrative expense.......................................	36,000
Amortization expense...	50,000
Earnings before interest and taxes..................................	40,000
Interest expense..	14,000
Earnings before taxes...	26,000
Taxes...	5,720
Net income	$ 20,280

   i.   Cost of goods sold = ($360,000) (.65) = $234,000
   ii. Interest expense = ($50,000) (.10) + ($75,000)(.12) = $5,000 + $9,000 = $14,000
   iii. Taxes = ($26,000) (.22) = $5,720

(b)

FMA CORPORATION
Balance Sheet
December 31, 2002

Current Assets			*Current Liabilities*	
Cash		$ 21,175	Accounts payable	$ 67,200
Accounts receivable		47,500	Notes payable	40,000
Inventory		88,000	Total current liabilities	107,200
Total current assets		156,675		
			Long-term bonds	75,000
Capital Assets				
Gross plant & equipment	$315,000		*Shareholders' Equity*	
Less: Acc. amortization	125,000		Common stock	100,000
Net plant & equipment		190,000	Retained earnings	64,475
Total Assets		$346,675	Total liabilities & equity	$346,675

   i.   Accounts receivable = $50,000 - (.05)($50,000) = $47,500
   ii. Inventory = $80,000 + (.10)($80,000) = $88,000
   iii. Gross plant and equipment = $250,000 + $65,000 = $315,000
   iv. Accumulated amortization = $75,000 + $50,000 = $125,000
   v. Accounts payable = $60,000 + (.12)($60,000) = $67,200
   vi. Notes payable = $50,000 - $10,000 = $40,000
   vii. Retained earnings = previous retained earnings + addition to retained earnings
        [addition to retained earnings = net income – dividends]
        Retained earnings = $55,000 + $20,280 – $10,805 = $64,475
   viii. Cash = "plug" figure = $346,675 – $325,500 = $22,175

(c)

FMA CORPORATION
Statement of cash flows
For the Year Ended December 31, 2002

Operating activities:

Net income		$20,280
Add items not requiring an outlay of cash:		
Amortization	$50,000	
Cash flow from operations		70,280
Changes in noncash working capital:		
Decrease in marketable securities	20,000	
Decrease in accounts receivable................	2,500	
Increase in inventory	(8,000)	
Increase in accounts payable	7,200	
Decrease in notes payable	(10,000)	
Net change in noncash working capital		11,700
Cash provided by operating activities		81,980

Investing activities:

Increase in plant and equipment	($65,000)	
Cash used in investing activities		(65,000)

Financing activities:

Common stock dividends paid	(10,805)	
Cash used in financing activities		(10,805)

Increase in cash flows during the year		6,175
Cash, beginning of year		15,000
Cash, end of year		$ 21,175

i.   Net income from income statement
ii.   Amortization given
iii.   Dividends given
iv.   All other sources and uses were determined by comparing balance sheets of December 31, 2001, and December 31, 2002.

Summary: The thrust of this chapter is twofold. First, the use of financial ratios to evaluate the success of a firm is examined. Second, the distortions in financial reporting are explored and the impact on business operations is assessed.

I. **Ratio analysis [p. 64]**

A. Uses of ratios:
1. Provide a basis for evaluating the operating performance of a firm.
2. Facilitate comparison with other firms.

B. Overall considerations in using ratios
1. There are 13 basic ratios presented in the text.
2. We shall break them down into four categories.
3. Ratio analysis is like solving a mystery: What you learn from one ratio, you apply to another.
4. Sources include Dun & Bradstreet, Statistics Canada, Industry Associations, Robert Morris, and Financial Post Information Services.

C. Classification and computation **[p. 65]**
1. Profitability: Measures of returns on sales, total assets and invested capital Shareholders are primary users. **[p. 66]**
    a. Profit margin = Net income/Sales
    b. Return on assets (ROA) (investment) = Net income/ Total assets
    c. Return on equity (ROE) = Net income/Shareholders' equity = ROA × Equity multiplier (Equity multiplier = Total assets/ equity

2. Du Pont system **[p. 68]**
    a. The Du Pont Company was one of the first firms to stress the relationships of profitability.
    b. The profitability of a firm is determined by its ability to utilize its assets efficiently by generating profitable sales.
        Return on assets (ROA) (Investment) = Profit margin x Asset turnover
        $$\frac{Net\ income}{Total\ assets} = \frac{Net\ income}{Sales} \times \frac{Sales}{Total\ assets}$$
    c. Profit margin is the profit-per-dollar of sales.
    d. Asset turnover indicates the dollar sales generated per dollar of assets employed.

3. Asset utilization: Measures of the speed at which the firm is turning over accounts receivable, inventories, and longer term assets Management is primary user. **[p. 71]**.

    a. Receivables turnover = Sales/ Receivables
    b. Average collection period = Accounts receivable/ Average daily credit sales
    c. Inventory turnover = Sales/ Inventory or COGS/Inventory
    d. Inventory holding period = Inventory/ Average days COGS
    e. Accounts payable turnover = COGS/ Accounts payable
    f. Accounts payable period = Accounts payable/ Average daily purchases (COGS)
    g. Capital asset turnover = Sales/ Capital assets
    h. Total asset turnover = Sales/ Total assets

4. Liquidity ratios: Measures of the firm's ability to pay off short-term obligations as they come due Short-term creditors are primary users. **[p. 73]**.

    a. Current ratio = Current assets/ Current liabilities
    b. Quick ratio = Current assets minus inventory/ Current liabilities

5. Debt Utilization Ratios: Measures the prudence of the firm's debt management policies. **Long-term creditors are primary users. [p. 74]**.

   a. Debt to total assets = Total debt/ Total assets
   b. Times interest earned = EBIT/ Interest
   c. Fixed charge coverage = EBIT and fixed charges/ Fixed charges

6. Review the summary and evaluation of all ratios for the Saxton Company with conclusions.
7. Trend analysis is as important as industry comparisons **[p. 75]**.

D. Interpreting financial ratios **[p. 75-77]**.
   1. Individually, financial ratios convey little meaning.
   2. Collectively, financial ratios provide an evaluation for the firm's investors, creditors, and management.
   3. Ratios must be viewed in light of the fact that:
      a. they are based on historical information
      b. they are often prepared on the basis of financial information from only one point in time

E. Trend analysis consists of computing the financial ratios of a firm at various points in time to determine if the firm is improving or deteriorating.

F. Common size financial statements, as in Table 3-4, are sometimes prepared to identify relative changes in the components of the financial statements. **[p. 78]**

G. Comparative analysis provides the management and external evaluators with information as to how successful the firm is relative to other firm's in the industry.

II. **Distortion in Financial Reporting [p. 77-83]**

A. Inflationary impact
   1. First-in, first-out (FIFO) inventory valuation during inflation periods "understates" cost of goods sold and causes "inventory profits."
   2. The use of replacement cost accounting reduces income and interest coverage during inflationary periods, but lowers debt to assets.

B. Disinflation effect
   1. A leveling off of prices referred to as disinflation may cause a reduction in profits.

C. Valuation basics with changing prices **[p. 80]**
   1. Assets on the balance sheet are recorded at cost.
   2. The replacement cost of long-term assets may greatly exceed the reported values. Cash flows from the amortization process may be insufficient to replace assets as they wear out.
   3. Investors generally require higher rates of return during periods of inflation.
   4. Although earnings may drop because of disinflation, the declining rate of return demanded by investors may cause the value of a firm's securities to increase.
   5. The movement away from financial assets (stocks and bonds) into tangible assets (gold, silver,) by investors during periods of inflation makes it difficult and more expensive for firms to raise capital. Likewise the reverse trend during periods of disinflation enhances a firm's ability to issue securities.

D. Accounting discretion **[p. 81]**
   1. Revenue
      a. A conservative firm may recognize long-term installment sales revenues when payments are received, whereas other firms report the full amount of the sale as soon as possible.

   2. Expenses
      a. A firm may use LIFO, FIFO, or average cost for financial reporting purposes each giving different COGS figures.
      b. Research and development may receive varying treatment.

    3. Extraordinary gains/losses
        a. These are reported as additions/deductions from income by some firms but not shown as additions/deductions from income by others, based on discretion.

III.   **Review of Formulas**

    See text pages 83-84 or the insert card.

Chapter 3: Multiple Choice Questions

1. Share prices: [p. 80]
    a. Frequently rise during periods of rapid inflation.
    b. Are not affected by inflation.
    c. Frequently fall during periods of rapid inflation.
    d. Rise more than the price of tangible assets during periods of inflation.
    e. Answers *a* and *d* are correct.

2. Times interest earned is a: [p. 74]
    a. Profitability ratio
    b. Debt utilization ratio
    c. Asset utilization ratio
    d. Liquidity ratio
    e. Quick ratio

3. A firm may use _____ inventory valuation to reduce "inventory profits" during _____ periods. [p. 79; 81]
    a. LIFO; disinflation
    b. FIFO; inflation
    c. LIFO; stable cost/price periods
    d. LIFO; inflation
    e. LILO; inflation

4. Analyzing the financial condition of a firm over time is called: [p. 75]
    a. Comparative analysis
    b. Ratio analysis
    c. Trend analysis
    d. The Du Pont system
    e. Profitability analysis

5. A shift from investment in _____ assets into _____ assets such as gold and silver may occur during periods of inflation. [p. 80]
    a. Liquid; tangible
    b. Tangible; liquid
    c. Financial; tangible
    d. Capital; current
    e. Tangible; financial

6. Employing the Du Pont system, the ROA is determined by: [p. 69]
    a. Multiplying ROE by the net profit margin.
    b. Multiplying the net profit margin by the asset turnover.
    c. Dividing the gross profit by net profit.
    d. Multiplying ROA by the debt ratio.
    e. None of the above are correct

7. A firm that has a total asset turnover of 1.8: [p. 72
   a. Requires $1.80 in assets to produce $1 of sales.
   b. Is highly profitable.
   c. Will soon become bankrupt.
   d. Requires $1 in assets to produce $1.80 in sales.
   e. Should lower its investment in assets.

8. During periods of disinflation, investors may: [p. 80]
   a. Require lower rates of return.
   b. Bid the prices of securities up.
   c. Require higher rates of return.
   d. Invest heavily in financial assets.
   e. Ignore a firm's financial ratios.

9. A firm's return on equity (ROE) is calculated by: [p. 68]
   a. Dividing net income by shareholders' equity.
   b. Multiplying net income by shareholders' equity.
   c. Dividing return on assets by (1 – debt/assets).
   d. Dividing net income by total assets.
   e. Answers a and c are correct; either approach may be used.

10. The ability of a firm to pay off short-term obligations as they come due is indicated by: [p. 65]
    a. Profitability ratios
    b. Liquidity ratios
    c. Debt utilization ratios
    d. Asset utilization ratios
    e. My grade point average

Multiple Choice Answer Key: Chapter 3

1.	c	2.	b	3.	d	4.	c	5.	c
6.	b	7.	d	8.	c	9.	e	10.	b

Chapter 3: Problems

3-1.   Using the following information, construct the income statement of the Bulldog Corporation.

Times interest earned	5
Gross profit margin.................................	20%
Tax rate	30%

THE BULLDOG CORPORATION
Income Statement 2002

Sales...	$
Cost of goods sold..	1,600,000
Gross profit	
Selling and administrative expense	
Operating profit (EBIT)...	
Interest...	50,000
Earnings before taxes..	
Taxes	
Net income...	$_____

3-2. Without referring to the text or the preceding outline, complete the following:

Ratio	Computation	Primary Ratio Group
(a) Current ratio	$\dfrac{\text{Current Assets}}{\text{Current Liabilities}}$	
(b) Inventory turnover	$\dfrac{\rule{2cm}{0.4pt}}{\text{Inventory}}$	Asset utilization
(c) _____	$\dfrac{\text{EBIT}}{\text{Interest}}$	
(d) Average collection period	_____	
(e) _____	$\dfrac{\text{Net income}}{\text{Sales}}$	
(f) _____	$\dfrac{\text{Net income}}{\rule{2cm}{0.4pt}}$	Profitability
(g) Quick ratio	$\dfrac{\rule{2cm}{0.4pt}}{\text{Current Liabilities}}$	
(h) Fixed charge coverage	_____	
(i)* _____	_____	
(j)* _____	_____	

*In *i* and *j* indicate the name, computation, and grouping of two ratios not previously used.

3-3. The financial statements of the Salazar Company for 2000, 2001, and 2002 are given below.

THE SALAZAR COMPANY
Balance Sheets for Years 2000 - 2002

	2000	2001	2002
Assets			
Cash	$ 10,000	$ 8,000	$ 20,000
Accounts receivable	50,000	30,000	30,000
Inventories	44,000	68,000	50,000
Total Current Assets	104,000	106,000	100,000
Net property	50,000	50,000	52,000
Other assets	4,000	4,000	4,000
Total Assets	$158,000	$160,000	$156,000
Liabilities and Shareholders' Equity			
Accounts payable	$ 20,000	$ 24,000	$ 24,000
Notes payable (6%)	14,000	14,000	14,000
Accrued expenses	6,000	2,000	4,000
Total Current Liabilities	40,000	40,000	42,000
Long-term debt (8%)	30,000	30,000	30,000
Common stock (25,000 shares)	25,000	25,000	25,000
Retained earnings	63,000	65,000	59,000
Total Liabilities and Shareholders' Equity	$158,000	$160,000	$156,000

THE SALAZAR COMPANY
Income Statements for Years Ending December 31,
2000 - 2002

	2000	2001	2002
Sales	$240,000	$220,000	$260,000
Cost of goods sold	192,000	173,000	201,000
Gross profit	48,000	47,000	59,000
Selling and administrative expenses	39,000	38,500	37,500
Operating profit	9,000	8,500	21,500
Interest expense	3,240	3,240	3,240
Net income before taxes	5,760	5,620	18,260
Taxes (15%)	864	789	2,739
Net income	$ 4,896	$ 4,471	$ 15,521

Required: Fill in the blanks on the following page to show Phoenix's financial position.

THE SALAZAR COMPANY
Financial Ratios

	2000	2001	2002

1. Current Ratio = $\dfrac{\text{Current Assets}}{\text{Current Liabilities}}$ _____ _____ _____

2. Quick Ratio = $\dfrac{\text{Current Assets} - \text{Inventory}}{\text{Current Liabilities}}$ _____ _____ _____

3. (a) Inventory Turnover = $\dfrac{\text{Sales}}{\text{Inventory}}$ _____ _____ _____

3. (b) Inventory Turnover = $\dfrac{\text{Cost of Goods Sold}}{\text{Inventory}}$ _____ _____ _____

4. Average Collection Period = $\dfrac{\text{Accounts Receivable}}{\text{Average Daily Credit Sales}}$ _____ _____ _____

5. Capital Asset Turnover = $\dfrac{\text{Sales}}{\text{Capital Assets}}$ _____ _____ _____

6. Total Asset Turnover = $\dfrac{\text{Sales}}{\text{Total Assets}}$ _____ _____ _____

7. Debt to Total Assets = $\dfrac{\text{Total Debt}}{\text{Total Assets}}$ _____ _____ _____

8. Times Interest Earned = $\dfrac{\text{Earnings Before Interest \& Taxes}}{\text{Interest}}$ _____ _____ _____

9. Profit Margin = $\dfrac{\text{Net Income}}{\text{Sales}}$ _____ _____ _____

10. Return on Investment = $\dfrac{\text{Net Income}}{\text{Total Assets}}$ _____ _____ _____

11. Return on Equity = $\dfrac{\text{Net Income}}{\text{Shareholders' Equity}}$ _____ _____ _____

3-4. Using the data below, complete the balance sheet (round to the nearest $) and sales data for the Bienville Corporation.

BIENVILLE CORPORATION
Balance Sheet, December 31, 2002

Assets		*Liabilities & Shareholders' Equity*	
Cash	$_____ .	Accounts payable	$_____ .
Accounts receivable	_____ .	Long-term debt	_____ .
Inventory........................	250,000	Common stock	150,000
Plant & equipment...........	_____ .	Retained earnings	260,000
Total assets	_____ .	Total L & SE	_____ .
Sales	_____ .		
Cost of goods sold	_____ .		

All sales are credit sales.
Average collection period = 75 days
Credit purchases = 60% of sales
Accounts payable period = 73 days
Total asset turnover = 2
Quick ratio = 2.1
Inventory turnover (Sales/ inventory) = 5
Gross Profit Margin = .2

3-5. The Kolari Corporation currently has the following ratios:
Total asset turnover = 1.6
Total debt to total assets = .5
Current ratio = 1.7
Current liabilities = $2,000,000

(a)   If Kolari's sales are currently $16,000,000, what is the amount of total assets?

(b)   Of the total in (a) above, what amount is current assets?

(c)   What is the total debt of the firm?

(d)   If Kolari's sales are expected to increase by $6,400,000 and existing ratios remain unchanged, what is the amount of additional assets required?

3-6. The Sharpe Corporation is planning a major expansion. As a recently employed financial "wizard," you are expected to provide some guidance regarding financing the expansion. Using the information given, answer the questions that would likely be asked by your supervisor. (Assume all ratios remain the same after expansion unless directed otherwise.)

2002 operating and financial characteristics:

Sales = $100,000,000   Total debt to total assets = .4
Total assets = $125,000,000   Long-term debt to equity = .5
Capital assets = $70,000,000   Net profit margin = 5%

(a)   If Sharpe expects sales to increase by 80%, what amount of assets must the firm add (assuming all relationships are maintained)?

(b)   How much of the increase in assets will be financed by debt? How much will be financed by long-term debt?

3-7.   In *3-6* above, Sharpe Corporation must finance 60% of the increase in assets with equity (TD/ TA = 0.4).

   (a)   If Sharpe Corporation retains all earnings, will it be necessary to issue any new common shares?

   (b)   If Sharpe distributes 40% of earnings as dividends, what amount of new common share must be issued?

3-8.   Using the data below, complete the income statement and balance sheet for the Pennathur Corporation.

PENNATHUR CORPORATION
Income Statement
For the Year Ended December 31, 2002

Sales	$
Cost of goods sold	_____
Gross profit	
Selling & administrative expense.	2,000,000
Operating profit (EBIT)	
Interest	_____
Earnings before taxes	_____
Taxes	_____
Net income	$_____

PENNATHUR CORPORATION
Balance Sheet
December 31, 2002

Assets			*Liabilities & Shareholders' Equity*	
Cash		$ 500,000	Accounts payable	$2,000,000
Accounts receivable			Notes payable	
Inventory			Long-term debt	
Gross plant & equipment	$		Preferred stock	1,000,000
Less: Acc. amortization	3,000,000		Common stock	
Net plant & equipment			Retained earnings	_____
Total assets		$10,000,000	Total L & SE	$_____

Total asset turnover = 2
Gross profit margin = 25%
Times interest earned = 5
Tax rate = 34%
Current ratio = 2
All sales are on credit.
Average collection period = 45.6 days
Size of parking lot = 600 cars
Inventory turnover (using sales) = 10
Total debt to assets = .5
2001 balance sheet, retained earnings = $3,000,000
Goodling paid out 60% of 2002 earnings in dividends.

Chapter 3: Solutions

3-1.

THE BULLDOG CORPORATION
Income Statement, 2002

Sales	$2,000,000
Cost of goods sold	1,600,000
Gross profit	400,000
Selling and administrative expenses...............	150,000
EBIT	250,000
Interest expense	50,000
Earnings before taxes	200,000
Taxes	60,000
Net income...	$ 140,000

(a)

$$Gross\ profit\ margin = \frac{Gross\ profit}{Sales} = 0.2$$

$$\frac{Cost\ of\ goods\ sold}{Sales} + \frac{Gross\ profit}{Sales} = 1$$

$$\frac{\$1,600,000}{Sales} + 0.2 = 1 \qquad \frac{\$1,600,000}{Sales} = 0.8 \qquad Sales = \frac{\$1,600,000}{0.8} = \mathbf{\$2,000,000}$$

(b)   Sales – Cost of goods sold = Gross profit
$2,000,000 – $1,600,000 = **$400,000**

(c)

$$Times\ interest\ earned = \frac{EBIT}{Interest}$$

$$5 = \frac{EBIT}{\$50,000}$$

$$EBIT = 5 \times \$50,000 = \mathbf{\$250,000}$$

(d)   Gross profit – Selling and administrative expense = EBIT
$400,000 – Selling and administrative expense = $250,000
Selling and administrative expense = **$150,000**

(e)   Earnings before taxes = EBIT – Interest
Earnings before taxes = $250,000 - $50,000 = **$200,000**

(f)   Taxes = .30 x $200,000 = **$60,000**

(g)   Net income = earnings before taxes - taxes
Net income = $200,000 – $60,000 = **$140,000**

3-2.	Without referring to the text or preceding problems, complete the following:

	Ratio	Computation	Primary Ratio Group

(a)	Current ratio

$$\frac{\text{Current assets}}{\text{Current liabilities}}$$

Liquidity

(b)	Inventory turnover

$$\frac{\textbf{Sales}}{\text{Inventory}}$$

Asset utilization

(c)	**Times interest earned**

$$\frac{\text{EBIT}}{\text{Interest}}$$

Debt utilization

(d)	Average collection period

$$\frac{\textbf{Accounts receivable}}{\textbf{Average daily credit sales}}$$

Asset utilization

(e)	**Profit margin**

$$\frac{\text{Net income}}{\text{Sales}}$$

Profitability

(f)	**Return on investment**

$$\frac{\text{Net income}}{\textbf{Total assets}}$$

Profitability

(g)	Quick ratio

$$\frac{\textbf{Current assets – inventory}}{\text{Current Liabilities}}$$

Liquidity

(h)	Fixed charge coverage

$$\frac{\textbf{Earnings before fixed charges and taxes}}{\textbf{Fixed charges}}$$

Debt utilization

(i)*	_____	_____	_____

(j)*	_____	_____	_____

*In problems *i* and *j* indicate the name, computation, and grouping of two ratios not previously used.

3-3.

THE SALAZAR COMPANY
Financial Ratios

	2000	2001	2002
1. Current Ratio = $\frac{\text{Current Assets}}{\text{Current Liabilities}}$	2.60	2.65	2.38
2. Quick Ratio = $\frac{\text{Current Assets – Inventory}}{\text{Current Liabilities}}$	1.50	0.95	1.19
3. (a) Inventory Turnover = $\frac{\text{Sales}}{\text{Inventory}}$	5.45	3.23	5.20
(b) Inventory Turnover = $\frac{\text{Cost of Goods Sold}}{\text{Inventory}}$	4.36	2.54	4.02
4. Average Collection Period = $\frac{\text{Accounts Receivable}}{\text{Average Daily Credit Sales}}$	76 days	50 days	42 days
5. Capital Asset Turnover = $\frac{\text{Sales}}{\text{Capital Assets}}$	4.44	4.07	4.64

6. Total Asset Turnover = $\dfrac{\text{Sales}}{\text{Total Assets}}$	**1.52**	**1.38**	**1.67**
7. Debt to Total Assets = $\dfrac{\text{Total Debt}}{\text{Total Assets}}$	**0.44**	**0.44**	**0.46**
8. Times Interest Earned = $\dfrac{\text{Earnings Before Interest \& Taxes}}{\text{Interest}}$	**2.78**	**2.62**	**6.64**
9. Profit Margin = $\dfrac{\text{Net Income}}{\text{Sales}}$	**2.0%**	**2.0%**	**6.0%**
10. Return on Investment = $\dfrac{\text{Net Income}}{\text{Total Assets}}$	**3.1%**	**2.8%**	**9.9%**
11. Return on Equity = $\dfrac{\text{Net Income}}{\text{Shareholders' Equity}}$	**5.6%**	**5.0%**	**18.5%**

3-4.   Sales:

$$\frac{Sales}{Inventory} = 5$$

$$\frac{Sales}{\$250,000} = 5$$

$$Sales = \$250,000 \times 5 = \mathbf{\$1,250,000}$$

Cost of goods sold:
$Sales - COGS = Gross\ profit$
$Gross\ profit = 0.2 \times Sales$
$Gross\ profit = 0.2 \times \$1,250,000 = \$250,000$
$COGS = \$1,250,000 - \$250,000 = \mathbf{\$1,000,000}$

Total assets:

$$Total\ asset\ turnover = \frac{Sales}{Total\ assets} = 2$$

$$Total\ asset\ turnover = \frac{\$1,250,000}{Total\ assets} = 2$$

$$Total\ assets = \frac{\$1,250,000}{2} = \mathbf{\$625,000}$$

Total liabilities & shareholders' equity: Plug figure
$Total\ assets$ $= Total\ liabilities\ and\ Shareholders'\ equity$
$\$625,000$ $= \mathbf{\$625,000}$

Accounts receivable:

$$Average\ daily\ credit\ sales = \frac{Credit\ sales}{365} = \frac{\$1,250,000}{365} = \$3,424.66$$

$$Average\ collection\ period = \frac{Accounts\ receivable}{Average\ daily\ credit\ sales} = 75$$

$$Accounts\ receivable = Average\ daily\ credit\ sales \times Average\ collection\ period$$
$$= \$3,424.66 \times 75$$
$$= \mathbf{\$260,274}$$

Accounts payable:

$$\text{Average daily credit purchases} = \frac{\text{Credit purchases}}{365} = \frac{0.6 \times \$1,250,000}{365} = \$2,054.79$$

$$\text{Average payables period} = \frac{\text{Accounts payable}}{\text{Average daily purchases (COGS)}} = 73$$

$$\text{Accounts payable} = \text{Average daily credit purchases} \times \text{Average payables period}$$
$$= \$2,054.79 \times 73$$
$$= \mathbf{\$150,000}$$

Cash:

The only quick assets that the Bienville Corp. has are cash and accounts receivable.

$$\text{Quick ratio} = \frac{\text{Current assets - inventory}}{\text{Current liabilities}} = 2.1$$

$$= \frac{\text{Cash + Accounts receivable}}{\text{Current liabilities}} = 2.1$$

$$= \frac{\text{Cash} + \$260,274}{\$150,000} = 2.1$$

$$\text{Cash} + \$260,274 = 2.1 \times \$150,000$$
$$\text{Cash} = \$315,000 - \$216,274$$
$$= \mathbf{\$54,726}$$

Long-term debt: Plug figure
$$\$625,000 - \$150,000 - \$150,000 - \$260,000 = \mathbf{\$65,000}$$

Plant & Equipment: Plug figure
$$\$625,000 - \$54,726 - \$260,274 - \$250,000 = \mathbf{\$60,000}$$

BIENVILLE CORPORATION
Balance Sheet
December 31, 2002

Assets		*Liabilities & Shareholders' Equity*	
Cash	$ 54,726	Accounts payable	$ 150,000
Accounts receivable	260,274	Long-term debt	65,000
Inventory	250,000	Common stock	150,000
Plant & equipment	60,000	Retained earnings	260,000
Total Assets	$ 625,000	Total L & SE	$ 625,000

Sales	$1,250,000
Cost of goods sold	$1,000,000

3-5.   Kolari Corporation
         (a)
$$Total\ asset\ turnover = \frac{Sales}{Total\ assets} = \frac{\$16,000,000}{Total\ assets} = 1.6$$

$$Total\ assets = \frac{\$16,000,000}{1.6} = \textbf{\$10,000,000}$$

         (b)
$$Current\ ratio = \frac{Current\ assets}{Current\ liabilities} = 1.7$$

$$\frac{Current\ assets}{\$2,000,000} = 1.7$$

$$Current\ assets = 1.7 \times \$2,000,000 = \textbf{\$3,400,000}$$

         (c)
$$\frac{Total\ debt}{Total\ assets} = 0.5$$

$$\frac{Total\ debt}{\$10,000,000} = 0.5$$

$$Total\ debt = 0.5 \times \$10,000,000 = \textbf{\$5,000,000}$$

         (d)   The increase in total assets can be found by applying the total asset turnover ratio to the increase in sales.
$$Total\ asset\ turnover = \frac{\Delta\ Sales}{\Delta\ Total\ assets} = 1.6$$

$$\frac{\$6,400,000}{\Delta\ Total\ assets} = 1.6$$

$$\Delta\ Total\ assets = \frac{\$6,400,000}{1.6} = \textbf{\$4,000,000}$$

3-6.   Sharpe Corporation
         (a)   The increase in total assets can be found by applying the total asset turnover ratio to the increase in sales. (Assumes ratios maintained).
$$Total\ asset\ turnover = \frac{Sales}{Total\ assets} = \frac{\$100,000,000}{\$125,000,000} = 0.8$$

$$0.8 = \frac{\Delta\ Sales}{\Delta\ Total\ assets} = \frac{0.8 \times \$100,000,000}{\Delta\ Total\ assets}$$

$$\Delta\ Total\ assets = \frac{\$80,000,000}{0.8} = \textbf{\$100,000,000}$$

(b)

$$Total\ asset\ turnover = \frac{Total\ debt}{Total\ assets} = 0.4$$

$$\Delta\ Total\ debt = 0.4 \times \Delta\$100,000,000 = \$40,000,000$$

$$If\ \ \frac{Total\ debt}{Total\ assets} = 0.4, \quad then\ \ \frac{Total\ equity}{Total\ assets} = 0.6$$

$$and\ if\ \ \frac{Long\ term\ debt}{Equity} = 0.5, \quad then\ \ \frac{Long\ term\ debt}{Total\ assets} = 0.5 \times 0.6 = 0.3$$

$$\Delta\ long - term\ debt = 0.3 \times \$100,000,000 = \mathbf{\$30,000,000}$$

3-7.   Sharpe Corporation

(a)   Sixty percent of assets are financed with equity.
Additional equity financing needed is: .60 x $100,000,000 = $60,000,000.
New sales = 1.8 x $100,000,000 = $180,000,000
Net profit = net profit margin x sales = .05 x $180,000,000 = $9,000,000
If all earnings are retained, ($60,000,000 - $9,000,000) = **$51,000,000** in new common shares must be issued.

(b)   Dividends = .40 x $9,000,000 = $3,600,000
Addition to retained earnings = $9,000,000 - $3,600,000 = $5,400,000
Amount of new common shares to be issued is: $60,000,000 - $5,400,000 = **$54,600,000**

3-8.

PENNATHUR CORPORATION
Income Statement
For the Year Ended December 31, 2002

Sales	**$20,000,000**
Cost of goods sold	15,000,000
Gross profit	$ 5,000,000
Selling & administrative expense	2,000,000
Operating profit (EBIT)	$ 3,000,000
Interest	600,000
Earnings before taxes	$ 2,400,000
Taxes	816,000
Net income	**$ 1,584,000**

PENNATHUR CORPORATION
Balance Sheet
December 31, 2002

Assets			Liabilities & Shareholders' Equity	
Cash		$ 500,000	Accounts payable	$2,000,000
Accounts receivable		2,500,000	Notes payable	500,000
Inventory		2,000,000	Long-term debt	2,500,000
Gross plant & equipment	$8,000,000		Preferred stock	1,000,000
Less: Acc. amortization	3,000,000		Common stock	366,400
Net plant & equipment		5,000,000	Retained earnings	3,633,600
Total assets		$10,000,000	Total L & SE	$10,000,000

The solution to this problem requires a series of calculations that illustrate the relationships among ratios.

Sales
= total asset turnover x total assets
= 2 x $10,000,000
= **$20,000,000**

COGS
= sales – gross profit
= $20,000,000 – (.25)($20,000,000)
= $20,000,000 – $5,000,000 = **$15,000,000**

Operating profit (EBIT) = gross profit – selling and administrative expense
= $5,000,000 – $2,000,000 = **$3,000,000**

$$Times\ interest\ earned = \frac{EBIT}{Interest} = 5$$

$$Interest = \frac{EBIT}{5} = \frac{\$3,000,000}{5} = \mathbf{\$600,000}$$

Earnings before taxes
= EBIT – Interest
= $3,000,000 – $600,000
= **$2,400,000**

Taxes = .34 x $2,400,000 = **$816,000**

$$Average\ daily\ credit\ sales = \frac{Credit\ sales}{365} = \frac{\$20,000,000}{365} = \$54,794.92$$

$$Average\ collection\ period = \frac{Accounts\ receivable}{Average\ daily\ credit\ sales} = 45.6$$

$$Accounts\ receivable = Average\ daily\ credit\ sales \times Average\ collection\ period$$
$$= \$54,794.92 \times 45.6$$
$$= \mathbf{\$2,500,000}\ (rounded)$$

$$Inventory\ turnover = \frac{Sales}{Inventory} = 10$$

$$Inventory = \frac{Sales}{10} = \frac{\$20,000,000}{10} = \mathbf{\$2,000,000}$$

Net plant and equipment is a "plug" figure.
Total assets – current assets = net capital assets
$10,000,000 – ($500,000 + $2,500,000 + $2,000,000) = Net capital assets
Net capital assets = **$5,000,000**

Gross plant and equipment   = *Net capital assets + accumulated amortization*
         = $5,000,000 + $3,000,000 = **$8,000,000**

$$Current\ ratio = \frac{Current\ assets}{Current\ liabilities} = 2$$

$$= \frac{\$5,000,000}{Accounts\ payable + notes\ payable} = 2$$

$$= \frac{\$5,000,000}{\$2,000,000 + notes\ payable} = 2$$

Notes payable = **$500,000**

$$Debt\ to\ total\ assets = \frac{Current\ liabilities + long\text{-}term\ debt}{Total\ assets} = 0.5$$

$$= \frac{\$2,500,000 + long\text{-}term\ debt}{\$10,000,000} = 0.5$$

Long-term debt = **$2,500,000**

Addition to retained earnings in 2002 = *net income – dividends*
     Dividends = .60 x $1,584,000
     Dividends = $950,400

Addition to retained earnings   = $1,584,000 – $950,400
         = $633,600

Balance sheet retained earnings December 31, 2002:
     BS retained earnings December 31, 2001 + addition to retained earnings during 2002
     = $3,000,000 + $633,600
     = **$3,633,600**

Common stock = "plug" figure
Total liabilities and shareholders' equity = $10,000,000
     CS = $10,000,000 – $2,000,000 – $500,000 – $2,500,000 – $1,000,000 – $3,633,600
         = **$366,400**

Chapter 4

Summary: Financial planning is essential for a successful business firm. In this chapter the construction and use of various pro forma financial statements for financial forecasting are explained.

I. **Need for Financial Planning [p. 100]**

   A. Growth requires additions to assets; arrangements for financing such asset additions must be made in advance.

   B. Financial planning is necessary not only for success but for survival as well.

   C. Lenders frequently require evidence of planning prior to making funds available.

   D. Financial forecasting is part of the larger financial planning process, including capital structure and capital budgeting decisions and strategies.

II. **The most comprehensive means for doing financial planning is through the development of pro forma financial statements; namely the pro forma income statement, the cash budget, and the pro forma balance sheet.**

   A. Pro Forma Income Statement: A projection of how much profit a firm will make over a specific time period. **[p. 103]**

      1. Establish a sales projection (quantity demanded x price). **[p. 103]**
          a. Forecast economic conditions
          b. Survey sales personnel

      2. Determine production needs, cost of goods sold, and gross profits based on the sales forecast. **[p. 104]**
          a. Determine units to be produced.
                      Projected unit sales
                      Desired ending inventory
                      – Beginning inventory
                      Production requirements
          b. Determine the cost of producing the units.
              i.   Unit cost = materials + labour + overhead
              ii. Total costs = number of units to be produced × unit cost
          c. Compute cost of goods sold.
              i.   Estimate unit sales
              ii. Cost of goods sold = unit sales × unit cost (FIFO or LIFO)
          d. Compute gross profit.

      3. Compute value of ending inventory.
                      Beginning inventory
                      + Total inventory
                      Total inventory available for sale
                      – Cost of goods sold
                      Ending inventory

      4. Compute other expenses. **[p. 107]**
          a. General and administrative
          b. Interest expense

5. Finally construct the pro forma income statement. **[p. 107]**

> Sales revenue
> <u>– Cost of goods sold</u>
> Gross profit
> <u>– General and administrative expenses</u>
> Operating profit (EBIT)
> <u>– Interest expense</u>
> Earnings before taxes
> <u>– Taxes</u>
> <u>Earnings aftertaxes</u>
> <u>– Common stock dividends</u>
> <u>Increase in retained earnings</u>

B. Cash budget: A summary of expected cash receipts and disbursements for a specific period of time. **[p. 107]**

1. Estimate cash sales and collection timing of credit sales
2. Forecast cash payments
   a. Payments for materials purchase according to credit terms
   b. Wages
   c. Capital expenditures
   d. Principal payments
   e. Interest payments
   f. Taxes
   g. Dividends

3. Determine monthly cash flow (receipts minus payments). **[p. 109]**
4. Construct cash budget. **[p. 110]**

> Total receipts (for each month, week, etc.)
> <u>– Total payments (for each month, week, etc.)</u>
> Net cash flow (for the period)
> <u>+ Beginning cash balance</u>
> Cumulative cash balance

Note: The beginning cash balance for each period of the cash budget is equal to the cumulative cash balance of the previous period in the absence of borrowing or investing of cash balances.

5. Determine cash excess or need for borrowing. **[p. 112]**

> Cumulative cash balance (at end of period)
> <u>– Loan required or cash excess </u>(desired cash balance – cumulative cash balance)
> Ending cash balance

C. Pro Forma Balance Sheet: An integrated projection of the firm's financial position based on its existing position, forecasted profitability (from pro forma income statement), anticipated cash flows (cash budget), asset requirements and required financing. **[p. 112]**

1. Construction of pro forma balance sheet.
   a. Assets (source of information)
      i.   Cash: (cash budget)
      ii. Marketable securities: (previous balance sheet and cash budget)
      iii. Accounts receivable: (sales forecast, cash budget)
      iv. Inventory: (COGS computation for pro forma income statement)
      v.   Plant and equipment: (previous balance sheet + purchases – amortization)

     b. Liabilities and Net Worth
- i. Accounts payable: (cash budget work sheet)
- ii. Notes payable: (previous balance sheet and cash budget)
- iii. Long-term debt: (previous balance sheet plus new issues)
- iv. Common stock: (previous balance sheet plus new issues)
- v. Retained earnings: (previous balance sheet plus projected addition from pro forma income statement)

III. **Percent of sales method: Shortcut, less exact, alternative for determining financial needs. [p 115]**

  A Assume balance sheet accounts maintain a given relationship to sales

$$\% \text{ of sales} = \frac{Asset}{Current \ sales}$$

  B Project asset levels on basis of forecasted sales (percent of sales of each asset × forecasted sales)

  C Project spontaneous financing: Some financing is provided spontaneously when asset levels increase; for example, accounts payable increase when a firm buys additional inventory on credit.

  D Project internal financing from profit = profit margin × forecasted sales

  E Determine external financing = required new assets to support sales – spontaneous financing – retained earnings. The relationship is expressed as follows:

$$Required \ new \ funds = \frac{A}{S_1}(\Delta S) - \frac{L}{S_1}(\Delta S) - PS_2(1-D) \qquad \text{(4-1; page 116)}$$

    Where:

A/S_1	= percentage relationship of variable assets to sales
ΔS	= change in sales
L/S_1	= percentage relationships of variable liabilities to sales
P	= profit margin
S_2	= new sales level
D	= payout ratio.

  F **The need for external financing can is demonstrated by the use of a balance sheet on page 124 of the text. This method is a complement to the RNF formula.**

IV. **Sustainable growth rate. [p. 119]**

  A Assuming a company's debt ratio should remain the same, its growth rate is limited to

$$SGR = \frac{P(1-D)\left(1+\dfrac{D_T}{E}\right)}{\dfrac{A}{S_1}P(1-D)\left(1+\dfrac{D_T}{E}\right)} \qquad \text{(4-2; page 119)}$$

$$\frac{D_T}{E} = Debt/ \ equity \ ratio$$

V. **Review of Formulas**

  See text page 121 or insert card.

Chapter 4: Multiple Choice Questions

1. The beginning step in financial forecasting is the projection of: [p. 103]
    a. Net profit.
    b. Sales.
    c. Cash flows.
    d. Liabilities.
    e. Equity.

2. A cash budget is a summary of _____ for some specific time period. [p. 110]
    a. Revenues and expenses
    b. Asset and liabilities
    c. Expected cash receipts and disbursements
    d. Profit plus amortization
    e. Credit and cash sales

3. On a *pro forma* balance sheet, the primary source of information for the cash balance is: [p. 112]
    a. Income statement.
    b. Cash budget.
    c. Previous balance sheet.
    d. *Pro forma* income statement.
    e. None of the above are correct

4. A substantial portion of the increase in assets necessitated by rising sales may be automatically financed through: [p. 116]
    a. Accounts receivable.
    b. Retained earnings.
    c. Amortization.
    d. Spontaneous assets.
    e. Accounts payable.

5. Which of the following statements concerning the construction of a cash budget is (are) not true? [p. 107-112]
    a. Amortization expense is a primary consideration.
    b. A cash budget is a historical statement.
    c. The beginning step is a forecast of sales.
    d. Collection of receivables must be forecasted.
    e. Both *a* and *b* are not true.

6. The percent-of-sales method is a shortcut approach to constructing a: [p. 115]
    a. *Pro forma* income statement.
    b. Cash budget.
    c. Balance sheet.
    d. *Pro forma* balance sheet.
    e. Statement of cash flows.

7. Which of the following is not a step in preparing a *pro forma* income statement? [p. 103-107]
    a. Projection of sales
    b. Projection of cost of goods sold
    c. Projection of debt principal payments
    d. Projection of taxes
    e. Projection of gross profit

8. The forecasted addition to retained earnings is included in the required new funds formula as: [p. 117]
   a. $P\Delta S(1-D)$.
   b. $PS_2(D)$.
   c. PS_2.
   d. $P\Delta S$.
   e. $PS_2(1-D)$.

9. As an estimate of the financing required to support an asset expansion, the firm must: [p. 115-118]
   a. Add spontaneous assets and retention of earnings.
   b. Add variable assets and spontaneous financing.
   c. Subtract variable assets from the addition to retained earnings.
   d. Subtract spontaneous financing and projected retention of earnings from the projected increase in assets.
   e. None of the above are correct

10. The primary benefit(s) of a cash budget is (are): [p. 112]
    a. Enables a financial manager to forecast borrowing needs.
    b. Guarantees the success of the firm.
    c. Provides a forecast of temporarily excess cash balances.
    d. Answers a, b, and c are correct.
    e. Both a and c are correct.

Multiple Choice Answer Key: Chapter 4

1.	b	2.	c	3.	b	4.	e	5.	e
6.	d	7.	c	8.	e	9.	d	10.	e

Chapter 4: Problems

4-1. The marketing staff of Vallee Corporation has forecast a 20% increase in sales for 2003. Assist the firm's financial manager in projecting the required external financing to support the increase in sales. Use the relationships below to forecast needed funds.

   Variable assets/sales = 40%
   Net profit margin = 3%
   Payout ratio = 40%
   2002 sales = $60,000,000
   Spontaneous liabilities/sales = 25%

   (a)   Will Vallee Corporation need additional external financing to support the anticipated sales increase?

   (b)   Will Vallee need to arrange external financing if the spontaneous liabilities/sales = 30%?

4-2. Tough Stuff Manufacturing had credit sales of $1,000,000; $1,500,000; and $800,000 in October, November, and December 2002, respectively. The company's credit sales projections for January through March of 2003 are as follows: January - $3,000,000; February - $2,400,000; March - $2,000,000.

   Tough Stuff has normally collected 60% of its credit sales in the month following the sale, 30% in the second following month and 10% in the third month. Assuming this collection pattern continues, prepare a schedule of cash receipts from receivables collection for the period January through March of 2003.

4-3.   Using the following information, prepare a *pro forma* income statement for 2003 for Middle Fork Lumber Company:

Projected sales	$10,000,000
Cost of goods sold	60% of sales
Selling and administrative expenses	$100,000/month
Amortization expense	$140,000/month
Interest expense	$120,000
Tax rate	34%
Dividend payout rate	50%

4-4.

(a)   Using the income information above and the December 31, 2002 balance sheet for the Middle Fork Lumber Company, prepare a *pro forma* balance sheet for December 31, 2003. You should use the percent-of-sales method and assume that all long-term financing for Two-by-Four Lumber Company will be achieved from retention of earnings and borrowing. Sales for 2002 were $8,000,000.

(b)   Calculate the sustainable growth rate of Middle Fork Lumber Company if its debt ratio is to remain the same.

MIDDLE FORK LUMBER COMPANY
Balance Sheet
December 31, 2002

Assets		*Liabilities and Equity*	
Cash	$ 400,000	Accounts payable	$ 800,000
Accounts receivable	900,000	Long-term debt	1,500,000
Inventory	1,200,000	Common stock	1,800,000
Net plant & equipment	2,500,000	Retained earnings	900,000
Total Assets	$5,000,000	Total Liabilities & Equity	$5,000,000

4-5.   Using the following information, prepare a *pro forma* income statement for 2003 for Shongaloo, Inc.

Projected sales = $20,000,000
Cost of goods sold = 72% of sales
Selling and administrative expenses = estimated to be 15% of COGS
Amortization expense = $100,000 per month for January through March, $108,000 per month April through November and $117,000 in December
Interest expense is projected on the basis of the following: 10.5% on $10,000,000 bonds outstanding throughout the year and 9% on a 3-month bank loan of $2,500,000
Tax rate = 40%

4-6.   One of your first jobs as a new employee of the Zero Corporation is to prepare a cash budget for the period January 1 through June 30, 2003. Use the data below.

(a)   Eighty percent (80%) of all sales are credit sales; 80% of credit sales are collected in the following month; 15% and 4% of credit sales are collected 60 days and 90 days after sale, respectively; 1% of sales become bad debts and are never collected.

(b)   Purchases during each month equal 65% of the following month's estimated sales. Payment for purchases is made in the month following the purchase.

(c)   The firm seeks to maintain a minimum cash balance of $300,000. The January 1 cash balance is $300,000.

(d)   The firm anticipates delivery of new equipment in April. A payment of $400,000 will be made upon delivery.

(e)   A quarterly tax payment of $500,000 is anticipated in March and June.

(f)   Rent is $100,000 per month. Other cash expenses average 3% of current month's sales.

(g)   Amortization expense averages $150,000 monthly.

(h)   Labour costs paid monthly average 10% of the following month's sales.

(i)   The board of directors desires to maintain the firm's current dividend policy. A dividend payment of $450,000 is scheduled for June.

(j)   The company experienced sales of $3,000,000 in October **2002** and sales of $2,000,000 during each of the last two months of **2002**.

(k)   The projected sales schedule for the first seven months of 2003 is given below:

Sales Projections for January-July of 2003

January	$3,000,000
February	5,000,000
March	5,000,000
April	6,000,000
May	3,000,000
June	2,000,000
July	2,000,000

(l)   The firm must make a semiannual interest payment of $310,000 in June *2003*.

4-7.   Quasimodo Corporation has the following balance sheet/sales relationships.

Cash:	6%
Accounts receivable:	18%
Inventory:	22%
Net capital assets:	35%
Accounts payable:	20%
Accruals:	13%

Quasimodo's financial manager must formulate a plan to finance a projected 20% increase in sales in 2003. The firm has a net profit margin of 6% and the board of directors voted to pay out 40% of the firm's $3,000,000 net income in **2002**.

(a)   Assuming the firm was operating at full capacity to produce **2002** sales of $50,000,000, how much external capital will be needed to finance the sales expansion? The directors desire to maintain a 40% payout ratio, and no debt payments are due in 2003.

(b)   What amount of financing would be needed if the firm was operating considerably below capacity and no new capital assets would be required?

(c)   What amount of external financing will Quasimodo need if the payout ratio is lowered to 35% and a $5,000,000 long-term debt is retired? (Assume full-capacity operations in **2002**.)

(d)   Under the conditions of (*a*) above and assuming that all external financing will be achieved through issuing long-term bonds, prepare a *pro forma* balance sheet for December 31, 2003. The firm's long-term debt at the end of **2002** was $9,000,000 and its common stock and retained earnings balances were $7,000,000 and $8,000,000 respectively.

Chapter 4: Solutions

4-1.   Vallee Corporation

(a) $Required\ new\ funds = \dfrac{A}{S_1}(\Delta S) - \dfrac{L}{S_1}(\Delta S) - PS_2(1 - D)$

$\Delta S = .20\ (60,000,000) = \$12,000,000$

RNF = .4 ($12,000,000) – .25 ($12,000,000) – .03 ($72,000,000) (1 – .4)
RNF = $4,800,000 – $3,000,000 – $1,296,000
RNF = **$504,000**

(b)   RNF = .4 ($12,000,000) – .3 ($12,000,000) – .03 ($72,000,000) (1 – .4)
RNF = $4,800,000 – $3,600,000 – $1, 296,000
RNF = – **$96,000**.

No, spontaneous financing and retention of earnings is expected to provide more than sufficient financing.

4-2.

TOUGH STUFF MANUFACTURING
Schedule of Forecasted Cash Collections January-March 2003

	October	November	December	January	February	March
Credit Sales	$1,000,000	$1,500,000	$800,000	$3,000,000	$2,400,000	$2,000,000
Collections:						
60% of previous months' sales				480,000	1,800,000	1,440,000
30% of credit sales 2 months prior				450,000	240,000	900,000
10% of credit sales 3 months prior				100,000	150,000	80,000
Total forecasted cash collections				$1,030,000	$2,190,000	$2,420,000

4-3.

MIDDLE FORK LUMBER COMPANY
Pro Forma Income Statement
For the Year Ending December 31, 2003

Sales	$ 10,000,000
Cost of goods sold	6,000,000
Gross profit	4,000,000
Amortization expense	1,680,000
Selling and administrative expenses	1,200,000
Operating profit (EBIT)	1,120,000
Interest expense	120,000
Profit before taxes	1,000,000
Taxes (34%)	340,000
Net income	$ 660,000
Less dividends	330,000
Increase in retained earnings	$ 330,000

4-4.

(a)   PERCENT OF SALES (2002)

Assets as a percent of sales
    Cash/ sales = $400,000/ $8,000,000 =   .05
    Accounts receivable/ sales = $900,000/ $8,000,000 =   .1125
    Inventory/ sales = $1,200,000/ $8,000,000 =   .15
    Net plant and equipment/ sales = $2,500,000/ $8,000,000 = .3125
    Total assets/sales = $5,000,000/ $8,000,000 =   .625

Spontaneous financing
    Accounts payable/sales = $800,000/ $8,000,000 =   .10

Required assets to support projected sales = $10,000,000
    $10,000,000 × .625 = $6,250,000
    Present assets   5,000,000
    Addition to assets $1,250,000

Required financing
    New assets to be financed $1,250,000
    Spontaneous financing from accounts payable:
    .10 × $10,000,000 = $1,000,000
    Less existing accounts payable   800,000
                                          200,000
                                     1,050,000
    Less additions to retained earnings   330,000
    External financing required . . . . $ 720,000

MIDDLE FORK LUMBER COMPANY
Pro Forma **Balance Sheet**
For the Year Ending December 31, 2003

Assets		*Liabilities and Net Worth*	
Cash	$ 500,000	Accounts payable	$1,000,000
Accounts receivable	1,125,000	Long-term debt	2,220,000
Inventory	1,500,000	Common stock	1,800,000
Net plant & equipment	3,125,000	Retained earnings	1,230,000
	$6,250,000		$6,250,000

An alternative approach to determining needed external financing is:

$$Required\ new\ funds = \frac{A}{S_1}(\Delta S) - \frac{L}{S_1}(\Delta S) - PS_2(1 - D)$$

$$Required\ new\ funds = \frac{\$5,000,000}{\$6,000,000}(\$2,000,000) - \frac{\$800,000}{\$8,000,000}(\$2,000,000) - (0.066)(\$10,000,000)(.5)$$

$$= 0.625(\$2,000,000) - 0.10(\$2,000,000) - 0.66(\$10,000,000)(.5)$$

$$= \$1,250,000 - \$200,000 - \$330,000$$

$$= \mathbf{\$720,000}$$

(b)

$$SGR = \frac{P(1-D)\left(1 + \dfrac{D_T}{E}\right)}{\dfrac{A}{S_I} P(1-D)\left(1 + \dfrac{D_T}{E}\right)}$$

$$SGR = \frac{.06(1 - .5)\left(1 + \dfrac{3{,}250}{3{,}000}\right)}{\dfrac{5{,}000}{8{,}000} - .06(1 - .5)\left(1 + \dfrac{3{,}250}{3{,}000}\right)}$$

$$SGR = .1111 = 11.11\%$$

4-5.

SHONGALOO, INC.
Pro Forma Income Statement
For the Year Ended December 31, 2003

Sales	$20,000,000
Cost of goods sold	14,400,000
Gross profit	5,600,000
Amortization expense	1,281,000
Selling and administrative expenses	2,160,000
Operating profit (EBIT)	2,159,000
Interest expense	1,106,250
Taxable income	1,052,750
Taxes (40%)	421,100
Net income	$ 631,650

Calculations:

COGS   = 0.72 × $20,000,000
              = $14,400,000

Selling and administration expense = 0.15 × $14,400,000
                                 = $2,160,000

Amortization expense   = (3 × $100,000) + (8 × $108,000) +$117,000
                     = $1,281,000

Interest expense   = 0.105 ($10,000,000) + 0.09 ($2,500,000) × 3/ 12
                     = $1,050,000 + $56,250
                     = $1,106,250

Schedule of Forecasted Cash Receipts
(in thousands)

4-6.

	Oct.	Nov.	Dec.	Jan.	Feb.	Mar.	Apr.	May	June	July
Total sales	$3,000	$2,000	$2,000	$3,000	$5,000	$5,000	$6,000	$3,000	$2,000	$2,000
Credit sales	2,400	1,600	1,600	2,400	4,000	4,000	4,800	2,400	1,600	1,600
Cash sales	600	400	400	600	1,000	1,000	1,200	600	400	
Collections										
80% of previous month's credit sales	---	1,920	1,280	1,280	1,920	3,200	3,200	3,840	1,920	
15% of credit sales two months prior		---	360	240	240	360	600	600	720	
4% of credit sales 3 months prior				96	64	64	96	160	160	
Total cash receipts				$2,216	$3,224	$4,624	$5,096	$5,200	$3,200	

45

Schedule of Forecasted Monthly Cash Payments
(in thousands)

	Dec.	Jan.	Feb.	Mar.	Apr.	May	June
Monthly material purchase	$1,950	$3,250	$3,250	$3,900	$1,950	$1,300	$1,300
Payment for materials (prior month's purchases)		1,950	3,250	3,250	3,900	1,950	1,300
Monthly labour cost (10% of following month's sales)		500	500	600	300	200	200
Monthly rent		100	100	100	100	100	100
Other cash expenses (3% of current month's sales)		90	150	150	180	90	60
Interest expense							310
Capital expense					400		
Taxes				500			500
Dividends							450
Total payments		$2,640	$4,000	$4,600	$4,880	$2,340	$2,920

46

Monthly Cash Budget
January 1 – June 30, 2001

	Jan.	Feb.	Mar.	Apr.	May	June
Total cash receipts	$2,216	$3,224	$4,624	$5,096	$5,200	$3,200
Total payments	2,640	4,000	4,600	4,880	2,340	2,940
Net cash flow	(424)	(776)	24	216	2,860	280
Beginning monthly cash balance	300	(124)	(900)	(876)	(660)	2,200
Cumulative cash balance	(124)	(900)	(876)	(660)	2,200	2,480

Borrowing and Repayment Plan for Cash Budget

	Jan.	Feb.	Mar.	Apr.	May	June
Cumulative cash balance	$(124)	$(900)	$(876)	$(660)	$2,200	$2,480
Desired cash balance	300	300	300	300	300	300
Loans required (cumulative)	424	1,200	1,176	960	---	---
Additional loans required	424	776	*(24)	*(216)	*(960)	---
Ending cash balance	300	300	300	300	1,240	2,480
Available for investment	---	---	---	---	$940	$2,180

*The assumption is made that payments are made on the outstanding loan as soon as possible.

47

4-7.

(a) Variable assets as a percent of sales = 6% + 18% + 22% + 35% = 81%
Variable liabilities as a percent of sales = 20% + 13% = 33%
Projected increase in sales = (.2) ($50,000,000) = $10,000,000

$$Required\ new\ funds = \frac{A}{S_1}(\Delta S) - \frac{L}{S_1}(\Delta S) - PS_2(1-D)$$

$$Required\ new\ funds = (0.81)(\$10,000,000) - (0.33)(\$10,000,000) - (0.06)(\$60,000,000)(1-0.4)$$
$$= \$8,100,000 - \$3,300,000 - \$2,160,000$$
$$= \mathbf{\$2,640,000}$$

(b)

$$Required\ new\ funds = (0.81 - 0.35)(\$10,000,000) - (0.33)(\$10,000,000) - (0.06)(\$60,000,000)(1-0.4)$$
$$= \$4,600,000 - \$3,300,000 - \$2,160,000$$
$$= \mathbf{(\$860,000)}$$

No new external funds would be needed under these conditions. The firm would generate more than enough spontaneously and internally to finance the expansion.

(c)

$$Required\ new\ funds = (0.81)(\$10,000,000) - (0.33)(\$10,000,000) - (0.06)(\$60,000,000)(1-0.35) + \$5,000,000$$
$$= \$8,100,000 - \$3,300,000 - \$2,340,000 + \$5,000,000$$
$$= \mathbf{\$7,460,000}$$

(d)

QUASIMOTO CORPORATION
Pro Forma Balance Sheet
For the Year Ending December 31, 2003

Assets		Liabilities and Net Worth	
Cash	$ 3,600,000	Accounts payable	$12,000,000
Accounts receivable	10,800,000	Accruals	7,800,000
Inventory	13,200,000	Long-term debt	11,640,000
Net capital assets	21,000,000	Common stock	7,000,000
	$48,600,000	Retained earnings	10,160,000
			$48,600,000

i. Cash = (.06) ($60,000,000) = $3,600,000
ii. Accounts receivable = (.18) ($60,000,000) = $10,800,000
iii. Inventory = (.22) ($60,000,000) = $13,200,000
iv. Net capital assets = (.35) ($60,000,000) = $21,000,000
v. Accounts payable = (.2) ($60,000,000) = $12,000,000
vi. Accruals = (.13) ($60,000,000) = $7,800,000
vii. Common stock =   no change
viii. Retained earnings   = $8,000,000 + (.06) ($60,000,000) (1 - 4)
      = $8,000,000 + $2,160,000 = $10,160,000
ix. Long-term debt = plug figure or $9,000,000 + additional required funds
      = $9,000,000 + $2,640,000 = $11,640,000

Summary: This chapter examines the possible effects of a firm employing fixed cost factors for operating purposes or financing purposes. Operating leverage is associated with fixed production costs, and financial leverage results from using sources of financing to which a fixed return is paid.

I.   **Leverage: The use of fixed charge obligations with the intent of magnifying the potential return to the firm. [p. 134]**

   A.   Fixed operating costs: Those operating costs that remain relatively constant regardless of the volume of operations such as rent, amortization, property taxes, and executive salaries.

   B.   Fixed financial costs: The interest costs arising from debt financing that must be paid regardless of the level of sales or profits.

II. **Break-Even Analysis and Operating Leverage [p. 135-141]**

   A.   Break-even analysis: A numerical and graphical technique used to determine at what point the firm will break even.
      1.   Break-even point: the unit sales where total revenue = total costs
      2.   Break-even point formula:

$$BE = \frac{Fixed\ costs}{Contribution\ margin} = \frac{Fixed\ costs}{Price - variable\ costs\ per\ unit} = \frac{FC}{P - VC} \qquad \text{(5-1; page 138)}$$

Refer to Figures 5-1 & 5-2; text pages 137 & 140.

   3.   It may be desirable to calculate the break-even point in sales dollars rather than in units. Break-even sales may be calculated as follows:

$$BES = \frac{Fixed\ costs}{1 - \dfrac{TVC}{S}}$$

Where: TVC/ S = percentage relationship of total variable costs to sales.

   B.   Cash break-even analysis **[p. 141]**

      1.   Deducting non-cash fixed expenses such as amortization in the break-even analysis enables one to determine the break-even point on a cash basis.

      2.   Cash break-even point formula:

$$Cash\ BE = \frac{Fixed\ costs - (Non - cash\ fixed\ costs)}{P - VC} \qquad \text{(Page 141)}$$

      3.   Although cash break-even analysis provides additional insight, the emphasis in the chapter is on the more traditional accounting-data related break-even analysis.

C. **Operating leverage**: A reflection of the extent capital assets and fixed costs are utilized in the business firm. The employment of operating leverage causes operating profit to be more sensitive to changes in sales.

> For examples in this part **C**, refer to Table 5-2; text page 138.

1. The use of operating leverage increases the potential return but it also increases potential losses.
2. The amount of leverage employed depends on anticipated economic conditions, nature of the business (cyclical or noncyclical), and the risk aversion of management.
3. The sensitivity of a firm's operating profit to a change in sales as a result of the employment of operating leverage is reflected in its degree of operating leverage.
4. **Degree of operating leverage (DOL)** is defined as the ratio of percentage change in operating income in response to percentage change in volume.

$$DOL = \frac{\% \, \Delta \, in \, operating \, income}{\% \, \Delta \, in \, unit \, volume}$$

(5-2; page 141)

Example: In Table 5-2, if the firm's sales increased by 25% from 80,000 units to 100,000 units, operating profit increases by 66.67%. The DOL is:

$$DOL = \frac{66.7\%}{25\%} = 2.67$$

5. The DOL may also be computed using the formulation:

$$DOL = \frac{Q(P - VC)}{Q(P - VC) - FC}$$

(5-3a; page 142)

Where:
- Q = quantity at which DOL is computed
- P = price per unit
- VC = variable cost per unit
- FC = fixed costs

Illustration: Applying the DOL formula to the previous example, DOL at 80,000 units is:

$$DOL = \frac{80,000 \, (\$2.00 - \$0.80)}{80,000 \, (\$2.00 - \$0.80) - \$60,000} = 2.67$$

Interpretation: The percentage *change* in operating profit will be 2.67 times as large as the percentage change in sales from 80,000 units *in either direction*.

Also:

$$DOL = \frac{S - TVC}{S - TVC - FC}$$ (5 3b; page 143)   Or: $$DOL = \frac{Contribution \, margin}{Operating \, profit \, (EBIT)}$$

6. DOL and other measures of leverage always apply to the starting point for the range used in the computation.

The DOL for the example firm at 60,000 unit sales would be:

$$DOL = \frac{60,000 \, (\$2.00 - \$0.80)}{60,000 \, (\$2.00 - \$0.80) - \$60,000} = 6.0$$

7. The normal assumption in doing break-even analysis is that a linear function exists for revenue and costs as volume changes. This is probably reasonable over a reasonable range. However, for more extreme levels of operations, there may be revenue weakness and cost overruns. Some non-linearity may exist.

III. **Financial Leverage: A measure of the amount of debt used in the capital structure of the firm. [p. 145-150]**

> For examples in this part **III**, refer to Table 5-5; text page 146.

A. Two firms may have the same operating income but greatly different net incomes due to the magnification effect of financial leverage. The higher the financial leverage the greater the profits or losses at high or low levels of operating profit, respectively.

B. While operating leverage primarily pertains to the left-hand side of the balance sheet (assets and associated costs), and **capital budgeting** decisions. Financial leverage deals with the right-hand side of the balance sheet (liabilities and net worth) and **capital structure** decisions.

C. Financial leverage is beneficial only if the firm can employ the borrowed funds to earn a higher rate of return than the interest rate on the borrowed amount. The extent of a firm's use of financial leverage may be measured by computing its **degree of financial leverage (DFL)**. The DFL is the ratio of the percentage change in net income (or earnings per share) in response to a percentage change in EBIT.

$$DFL = \frac{\% \, \Delta \, in \, EPS}{\% \Delta \, in \, EBIT} \qquad \text{(5-4; page 147)}$$

In Table 5-5 the DFL for the conservative firm at an EBIT level of $12,000 is:

$$DFL = \frac{\frac{\Delta \, EPS}{EPS}}{\frac{\Delta \, EBIT}{EBIT}} = \frac{\frac{0.67 - 0.17}{0.17}}{\frac{36,000 - 12,000}{12,000}} = \frac{300\%}{200\%} = 1.5$$

D. The DFL may also be computed utilizing the following formula:

$$DFL = \frac{EBIT}{EBIT - I} \quad \text{(5-5; page 147)} \qquad \text{Or:} \qquad DFL = \frac{Operating \, profit}{Earnings \, before \, taxes \;\; (EBT)}$$

$$DFL = \frac{12,000}{12,000 - 4,000} = \frac{12,000}{8,000} = 1.5$$

Interpretation: Earnings per share will increase or decrease by a factor of 1.5 times the percentage increase or decrease in EBIT (operating profit).

E. The DFL is associated with a specific level of EBIT and changes as EBIT changes.

F. The purpose of employing financial leverage is to increase return to the owners but its use also increases their risk.

G. An indifference point, with respect to EPS impact, between two alternative financing plans can be calculated with the following formula:

$$EBIT^* = \frac{S_B \times I_A - S_A - I_B}{S_B - S_A} \qquad \text{(5-6; Page 149)}$$

Where: EBIT* = operating income at the indifference point
         I   = interest costs under plan A and B
         S   = shares outstanding under plan A and B

H. The use of financial leverage is not unlimited.

    1. Interest rates that a firm must pay for debt-financing rise as it becomes more highly leveraged.
    2. As the risk to the shareholders increases with leverage, their required rate of return increases and stock prices may decline.

IV. **Combined Leverage [p. 151-154]**

> For examples in this part **IV**, refer to Table 5-7; text page 153

A. Combining operating and financial leverage provides maximum magnification of returns-it also magnifies the risk.

B. The combined leverage effect can be illustrated through the income statement.

Sales
EBIT
}
   DOL
}
EBIT
}
   DFL
}
   DCL
Net Income

C. The **degree of combined leverage (DCL)** is a measure of the effect on net income as a result of a change in sales. The DCL is computed similar to DOL or DFL.

$$DCL = \frac{\% \, \Delta \, in \, EPS}{\% \Delta \, in \, sales} \qquad \text{(5-7; page 152)}$$

In Table 5-3 an increase in sales of 25% ($40,000/ $160,000) generates a 100% ($1.50/ $1.50) increase in EPS.

$$DCL = \frac{100\%}{25\%} = 4$$

Interpretation: Earnings per share will increase by 4% with each 1% increase in sales. Likewise, EPS will decrease by 4% with each 1% decline in sales.

D. The DCL may also be computed as follows:

$$DCL = \frac{Q(P-VC)}{Q(P-VC)-FC-I} \qquad \qquad DCL = \frac{S-TVC}{S-TVC-FC-I}$$

(5-8a; page 154)   or: (5-8b, page 154)

$$DCL = \frac{80,000\,(\$2.00 - \$0.80)}{80,000\,(\$2.00 - \$0.80) - \$60,000 - \$12,000} = \frac{\$96,000}{\$96,000 - \$60,000 - \$12,000} = 4$$

E. The DCL may also be found by multiplying DOL times DFL.

DCL   =   DOL   ×   DFL

$$\frac{\% \Delta \, in \, EPS}{\% \Delta \, in \, unit \, volume} = \frac{\% \, \Delta \, in \, EBIT}{\% \Delta \, in \, unit \, volume} \times \frac{\% \Delta \, in \, EPS}{\% \Delta \, in \, EBIT}$$

DCL   = 2.67 × 1.5   = 4

V. **Review of Formulas**

See text pages 155-156 or insert card.

Chapter 5: Multiple Choice Questions

1. At a firm's break-even point: [p. 138]
   a. Total costs = total revenues.
   b. Total contribution = total fixed costs.
   c. Contribution per unit = variable cost per unit.
   d. Both *a* and *b* are correct.
   e. Answers *a*, *b*, and *c* are correct.

2. A firm that has a DOL = 3 will experience what change in operating earnings if sales decrease from $100,000 to $80,000? [p. 142]
   a. 25%
   b. 20%
   c. 75%
   d. 60%
   e. 8.33%

3. Financial leverage is the result of having: [p. 145]
   a. Fixed financial costs.
   b. Amortization.
   c. Fixed operating costs.
   d. A low break-even point.
   e. None of the above are correct

4. Assuming no change in financing strategy, the substitution of machinery for labour: [p. 135]
   a. Decreases a firm's operating leverage.
   b. Increases a firm's financial leverage.
   c. Decreases operating and financial leverage.
   d. Increases operating leverage.
   e. Increases operating and combined leverage.

5. A firm's break-even point in sales dollars may be computed by which of the following? [SG, p. 49]
   a. DOL x DFL
   b. Fixed Costs/ (1 – TVC/ S)
   c. DOL/ DFL
   d. EBIT/ (EBIT – I)
   e. Q (P – VC)

6. Which of the following influence a firm's use of operating leverage? [p. 135-144]
   a. Nature of the business
   b. Anticipated economic conditions
   c. The desire to increase returns
   d. The risk aversion of management
   e. All of the above are correct

7. The DCL of a firm with a DOL = 1.5 and DFL = 1.2 is: [p. 152]
   a. 1.8
   b. 1.25
   c. 2.7
   d. 0.8
   e. Answer cannot be computed from the information given.

8. A firm currently has earnings per share of $2.72. If its DFL is 2.1 and operating earnings increase by 20%, what will be its new EPS? (Assume no change in the number of shares of stock.) [p. 148]
   a. $3.26
   b. $2.72
   c. $3.86
   d. $1.58
   e. $6.58

9. The DFL of a firm: [p. 145-150]
   a. Is invariant with the level of operations of the firm.
   b. Varies with the level of EBIT.
   c. Can easily be determined from the balance sheet.
   d. Is equal to the break-even point in units.
   e. All of the above are correct

10. Beyond the break-even point: [p. 136-141]
   a. All of the contribution per unit is profit.
   b. All of the contribution per unit is absorbed by fixed cost.
   c. All of the contribution per unit is absorbed by variable cost.
   d. There is no contribution per unit.
   e. None of the above are correct

Multiple Choice Answer Key: Chapter 5

1.	d	2.	d	3.	a	4.	e	5.	b
6.	e	7.	a	8.	c	9.	b	10.	a

Chapter 5: Problems

5-1.   A recently retired professor, Hy Dollar, plans to establish the Hot-Air Fan Company and manufacture circulating fans. He estimates the fixed costs of operations to be $250,000 annually. The variable cost of producing the fans is forecasted to be $75 per unit.

(a)   If the fans are priced at $100, how many must be sold to break even?

(b)   What is the cash break-even point if $100,000 amortization expense is included in fixed costs?

(c)   If Mr. Dollar seeks to earn $50,000 in profits, how many fans must be sold?

(d)   What would Hot-Air's degree of operating leverage be:
   i.   At a sales level of 11,000 units?
   ii.   At 15,000 units?

(e)   What would be the percentage loss of operating profit if Hot Air's sales tumbled to 12,000 from a high of 20,000 units?
   i.   Answer by computing the operating profit at each level of sales.
   ii.   Answer by using the DOL measure.

(f)   Construct a break-even chart on Figure 5-1. On the chart indicate the following:
i.   Total revenue.
ii.   Total cost.
iii.   Total fixed cost.
iv.   Profit area.
v.   Loss area.
vi.   Break-even point.

FIGURE 5-1

5-2.   Rock Industries has recently begun operations. The firm has estimated that 100,000 units can be sold by the third year of operation if their product can be reasonably priced. The firm has estimated that fixed operating costs will be $1,300,000 and the variable cost per unit will be approximately $6.

(a)   At what price must the units be sold if Rock is to break even in the third year?

(b)   If Rock sells 90,000 units, how much will its profit be?

(c)   How much profit will Rock have if 150,000 units are sold?

5-3.   Using the information in 5-2 above, answer the following questions.

(a)   Assuming that $195,000 of the fixed costs is amortization expense, what is the cash break-even point?

(b)   What is Rock's DOL at a sales level of 90,000 units?

(c)   What is Rock's DOL at a sales level of 200,000 units?

(d)   What is Rock's DOL at a sales level of 100,000 units?

5-4.

	A	B	C
Sale	$10,000,000	$10,000,000	$10,000,000
Fixed costs	1,000,000	1,300,000	405,000
Variable cost	6,000,000	6,875,000	9,000,000
Interest	1,000,000	525,000	193,000
Price/Unit	5.00	4.00	2.50

(a)   Which of the three companies above has the highest degree of operating leverage?

(b)   Which has the highest degree of financial leverage?

(c)   Which has the highest degree of combined leverage?

(d)   If Company C should experience a 20% decline in sales, how would its net income be affected?

5-5.   Professional Supply sells bags of manure to retail nurseries. The retired professors who own and manage the firm must decide whether to further mechanize their operation or continue on a labour intensive basis. The variable cost is currently $.50 per bag and fixed costs are $100,000. By employing more machinery, the firm can reduce variable costs to $.35 per bag although new fixed costs are estimated to be $126,000. The wholesale price of manure is expected to be $2 per bag regardless of the decision.

(a)   What is the current break-even point in units?

(b)   What will the break-even point be if the firm increases mechanization?

(c)   If the firm anticipates sales of 85,000 bags per year, should the firm increase mechanization?

(d)   How many bags must be sold for increased mechanization to be preferable?

(e)   If Professional Supply has annual interest payments of $15,000, calculate its degree of financial leverage at 75,000 and 90,000 units under current conditions?

5-6.   The officers of the Jekyll and Hyde Corporation are debating the merits of alternative capital structures. The more conservative officers prefer capital structure A, whereas other officers would prefer that capital structure B be established.

	A		B
Long-term debt (6%)	$ 3,500,000	Long-term debt (6%)	$ 5,000,000
Common shareholders' equity	6,500,000	Common shareholders' equity	5,000,000
	$10,000,000		$10,000,000

(a)   Compute the degree of financial leverage under each capital structure at the following levels of operating earnings:
i. $1,000,000
ii. $500,000
iii. $350,000

(b)   Compute the earnings per share under each structure for an EBIT of:
i. $2,000,000 and
ii. $300,000.
Assume 650,000 and 500,000 shares outstanding under structures A and B, respectively, and a 40% tax rate.

5-7.

BRET-MARK CORPORATION
Balance Sheet

Assets		*Liabilities & Shareholders' Equity*	
Current assets	$ 8,750,000	Current liabilities	$ 4,375,000
Capital assets	13,125,000	Long-term debt	5,000,000
Total	$21,875,000	Common equity	12,500,000
			$21,875,000

The Bret-Mark Corporation currently produces and sells 1,750,000 zippets per year at an average price of $50 per unit. The variable cost per unit is $35, and the firm's total fixed cost is $7,000,000.

The marketing and financial managers are considering a change in pricing strategy and capital structure. The two managers estimate that unit sales would increase by 20% if the price of a zippet is lowered to $45. Although variable cost per unit would not change, total fixed cost would rise to $8,000,000. The firm is operating at capacity, and an increase in assets would be necessary to support the additional sales.

The financial manager has suggested that additional long-term debt be used to finance the expansion of sales if the pricing change is made. Although using more long-term debt would cause the debt/equity ratio to rise, the financial manager thinks that the new long-term debt can be raised at a cost of 12%, only 2% above the cost of existing debt.

Using the abbreviated balance sheet and the information above, compute the following for B-M on a before and after expansion basis.

(a)   Break-even point.
(b)   Degree of operating leverage.
(c)   Degree of financial leverage.
(d)   Earnings per share (assume a 34% tax rate, a constant asset turnover ratio, and 2,000,000 shares of common stock outstanding).

Chapter 5: Solutions

5-1.

(a)

$$BE = \frac{Fixed\ costs}{Contribution\ margin} = \frac{FC}{P-VC} = \frac{\$250,000}{\$100-\$75} = \frac{\$250,000}{\$25} = \textbf{10,000}\ \ units$$

(b)

$$Cash\ BE = \frac{Fixed\ costs - (Non - cash\ fixed\ costs)}{P-VC} = \frac{\$250,000 - \$50,000}{\$100 - \$75} = \frac{\$150,000}{\$25} = \textbf{6,000}\ \ units$$

(c)   Units that must be sold to provide $50,000 profit:

$$BE + \$50,000 = \frac{FC + \$50,000}{P-VC} = \frac{\$300,000}{\$100 - \$75} = \frac{\$300,000}{\$25} = \textbf{12,000}\ \ units$$

(d)

i.

$$DOL = \frac{Q(P-VC)}{Q(P-VC) - FC} = \frac{11,000(\$100 - \$75)}{11,000(\$100 - \$75) - \$250,000} = \frac{\$275,000}{\$275,000 - \$250,000} = \textbf{11}$$

ii.

$$DOL = \frac{15,000(\$100 - \$75)}{15,000(\$100 - \$75) - \$250,000} = \frac{\$375,000}{\$375,000 - \$250,000} = \textbf{3}$$

(e)

i.

Sales (20,000 units)	=	$2,000,000
Total variable costs	=	1,500,000
Total contribution	=	$ 500,000
Fixed costs	=	250,000
Operating profit	=	$ 250,000

Sales (12,000 units)	=	$1,200,000
Total variable costs	=	900,000
Total contribution	=	$ 300,000
Fixed costs	=	250,000
Operating profit	=	$ 50,000

Percentage decline of profits = $200,000/ $250,000 = **80%**.

ii.

$$DOL\,(20,000\,units) = \frac{20,000\,(\$100 - \$75)}{20,000\,(\$100 - \$75) - \$250,000} = \frac{\$500,000}{\$500,000 - \$250,000} = 2$$

Percentage decline of sales = $800,000/ $2,000,000 = **40%**.

Percentage decline of profit = DOL × % decline of sales = 2 × 40% = 80%.

(f)

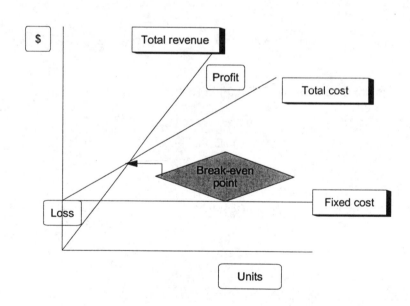

58

5-2. **Rock Industries**
  (a)

$$BE = \frac{Fixed\ costs}{Contribution\ margin} = \frac{FC}{P-VC} = \frac{\$1,300,000}{P-\$6} = \textbf{100,000} \quad units$$

$$100,000\,(P-\$6) = \$1,300,000$$
$$100,000\,P = \$1,900,000$$
$$P = \$1,900,000\,/\,100,000$$
$$P = \textbf{\$19}$$

  (b) TR – TVC – FC = profit
  90,000($19) – 90,000($6) – $1,300,000 = profit
  $1,710,000 – $540,000 – $1,300,000 = **– $130,000**

  (c) Since all contributions beyond break even goes to profits and 100,000 units is estimated to be the break-even point, profits at 150,000 units of sales would be:
  50,000($19 – $6) = **$650,000**

5-3. **Rock Industries (continued)**
  (a)

$$Cash\ BE = \frac{Fixed\ costs - (Non\text{-}cash\ fixed\ costs)}{P-VC} = \frac{\$1,300,000 - \$195,000}{\$19 - \$6} = \frac{\$1,105,000}{\$13} = \textbf{85,000} \quad units$$

  (b)

$$DOL = \frac{90,000\,(\$19-\$6)}{90,000\,(\$19-\$6)-\$1,300,000} = \frac{\$1,170,000}{\$1,170,000-\$1,300,000} = \textbf{-9}$$

  (c)

$$DOL = \frac{200,000\,(\$19-\$6)}{200,000\,(\$19-\$6)-\$1,300,000} = \frac{\$2,600,000}{\$2,600,000-\$1,300,000} = \textbf{2}$$

  (d)

$$DOL = \frac{100,000\,(\$19-\$6)}{100,000\,(\$19-\$6)-\$1,300,000} = \frac{\$1,300,000}{\$1,300,000-\$1,300,000} = \textbf{undefined}$$

  The break-even point for Rock Industries is 100,000 units. At break-even, profit equals zero. The percentage change from zero is not defined.

5-4.
  (a)

$$Company\ A\ (unit\ sales) = \frac{\$10,000,000}{\$5} = \textbf{2,000,000}$$

$$Company\ B\ (unit\ sales) = \frac{\$10,000,000}{\$4} = \textbf{2,500,000}$$

$$Company\ C\ (unit\ sales) = \frac{\$10,000,000}{\$2.50} = \textbf{4,000,000}$$

$$\text{Company A } (variable\ cost\ per\ unit) = \frac{\$6,000,000}{2,000,000} = \mathbf{\$3}$$

$$\text{Company B } (variable\ cost\ per\ unit) = \frac{\$6,875,000}{2,500,000} = \mathbf{\$2.75}$$

$$\text{Company C } (variable\ cost\ per\ unit) = \frac{\$9,000,000}{4,000,000} = \mathbf{\$2.25}$$

$$DOL\ (Company\ A) = \frac{2,000,000\,(\$5 - \$3)}{2,000,000\,(\$5 - \$3) - \$1,000,000} = \frac{\$4,000,000}{\$4,000,000 - \$1,000,000} = \mathbf{1.33}$$

$$DOL\ (Company\ B) = \frac{2,500,000\,(\$4 - \$2.75)}{2,500,000\,(\$5 - \$3) - \$1,300,000} = \frac{\$3,125,000}{\$3,125,000 - \$1,300,000} = \mathbf{1.712}$$

$$DOL\ (Company\ C) = \frac{4,000,000\,(\$2.50 - \$2.25)}{4,000,000\,(\$2.50 - \$2.25) - \$405,000} = \frac{\$1,000,000}{\$1,000,000 - \$405,000} = \mathbf{1.68}$$

(b) *EBIT(A)* = $10,000,000 – $1,000,000 – $6,000,000 = $3,000,000
EBIT (B) = $10,000,000 – $1,300,000 – $6,875,000 = $1,825,000
EBIT(C) = $10,000,000 – $405,000 – $9,000,000 = $595,000

$$DFL\ (Company\ A) = \frac{\$3,000,000}{\$3,000,000 - \$1,000,000} = \frac{\$3,000,000}{\$2,000,000} = \mathbf{1.50}$$

$$DFL\ (Company\ B) = \frac{\$1,825,000}{\$1,825,000 - \$525,000} = \frac{\$1,825,000}{\$1,300,000} = \mathbf{1.40}$$

$$DFL\ (Company\ C) = \frac{\$595,000}{\$595,000 - \$193,000} = \frac{\$595,000}{\$402,000} = \mathbf{1.48}$$

(c)

$$DCL\ (Company\ A) = \frac{2,000,000\,(\$5 - \$3)}{2,000,000\,(\$5 - \$3) - \$1,000,000 - \$1,000,000} = \frac{\$4,000,000}{\$2,000,000} = \mathbf{2.0}$$

$$DCL\ (Company\ B) = \frac{2,500,000\,(\$4 - \$2.75)}{2,500,000\,(\$5 - \$3) - \$1,300,000 - \$525,000} = \frac{\$3,125,000}{\$1,300,000} = \mathbf{2.4}$$

$$DCL\ (Company\ C) = \frac{4,000,000\,(\$2.50 - \$2.25)}{4,000,000\,(\$2.50 - \$2.25) - \$405,000 - \$193,000} = \frac{\$1,000,000}{\$402,000} = \mathbf{2.5}$$

(d) Percentage change in income
DCL × % change in sales
2.5 × 20% = 50%
Net income would decline by 50%.
An alternative approach to the solution would be as follows (assume a 34% tax rate):

	Present	20% Decline in Sales
Sales	$10,000,000	$8,000,000
Variable costs	9,000,000	7,200,000
	$ 1,000,000	$ 800,000
Fixed costs	405,000	405,000
EBIT	$ 595,000	$ 395,000
Interest	193,000	193,000
Taxable income	$ 402,000	$ 202,000
Taxes (34%)	136,680	68,680
Net Income	$ 265,320	$ 133,320

$132,000

$$\% \Delta \text{ of net income} = \frac{\$132,000}{\$265,000} = 0.50 = 50\%$$

5-5. **Professional Supply**

(a)
$$BE = \frac{Fixed\ costs}{Contribution\ margin} = \frac{FC}{P - VC} = \frac{\$100,000}{\$2.00 - \$0.50} = \frac{\$100,000}{\$1.50} = \mathbf{66,667}\ bags$$

(b)
$$BE = \frac{FC}{P - VC} = \frac{\$126,000}{\$2.00 - \$0.35} = \frac{\$126,000}{\$1.65} = \mathbf{76,364}\ bags$$

(c) All contribution beyond the break-even point is profit. Under current operations the profit at 85,000 units of sales would be:
(85,000 – 66,667) × ($1.50) = **$27,499.50**
Under increased mechanization, profit at 85,000 units would be:
(85,000 – 76,364) × ($1.65) = **$14,249**
The firm should continue current operations.

(d) There are several approaches to this question. The easiest approach is to use the break-even formula. Since the contribution per unit is $0.15 more per bag and the fixed costs are $26,000 more under mechanization,

$$BE = \frac{\Delta FC}{\Delta (P - VC)} = \frac{\$26,000}{\$0.15} = \mathbf{173,333}\ bags$$

Under current operations, profit at 173,333 bags would be:
Profit = 173,333($2 - $.50) - $100,000 = $159,999.50
Under mechanization profit would be:
Profit = 173,333($2 - $.35) - $126,000 = $159,999.45
Beyond 173,333 bags in sales, mechanization will provide greater profits.

(e) *EBIT @ 75,000 units*

$$EBIT = 75,000(\$2 - \$0.50) - \$100,000 = \$12,500$$

$$DFL = \frac{\$12,500}{\$12,500 - \$15,000} = \frac{\$12,500}{-\$2,500} = -5$$

EBIT @ 90,000 units
$$EBIT = 90,000(\$2 - \$.50) - \$100,000 = \$35,000$$

$$DFL = \frac{\$35,000}{\$35,000 - \$15,000} = \frac{\$35,000}{\$20,000} = 1.75$$

5-6. **Jekyll and Hyde Corporation**
(a)

$$DFL = \frac{EBIT}{EBIT - I} \qquad\qquad Or: \quad DFL = \frac{Operating\ profit}{Earnings\ before\ taxes\ \ (EBT)}$$

$$DFL(A) = \frac{\$1,000,000}{\$1,000,000 - \$210,000} = \frac{\$1,000,000}{\$790,000} = 1.27 \qquad DFL(B) = \frac{\$1,000,000}{\$1,000,000 - \$300,000} = \frac{\$1,000,000}{\$700,000} = 1.43$$

$$DFL(A) = \frac{\$500,000}{\$500,000 - \$210,000} = \frac{\$500,000}{\$290,000} = 1.72 \qquad DFL(B) = \frac{\$500,000}{\$500,000 - \$300,000} = \frac{\$500,000}{\$200,000} = 2.5$$

$$DFL(A) = \frac{\$350,000}{\$350,000 - \$210,000} = \frac{\$350,000}{\$140,000} = 2.5 \qquad DFL(B) = \frac{\$350,000}{\$350,000 - \$300,000} = \frac{\$350,000}{\$50,000} = 7.0$$

(b)
i.

A			B		
EBIT	=	$2,000,000	EBIT	=	$2,000,000
Interest	=	210,000	Interest	=	300,000
Taxable income	=	1,790,000	Taxable income	=	1,700,000
Taxes (40%)	=	716,000	Taxes (40%)	=	680,000
Net income	=	$1,074,000	Net income	=	$1,020,000

$$EPS\ (A) = \frac{\$1,074,000}{650,000} = \$1.65 \qquad EPS\ (B) = \frac{\$1,020,000}{500,000} = \$2.04$$

ii.

A			B		
EBIT	=	$300,000	EBIT	=	$300,000
Interest	=	210,000	Interest	=	300,000
Taxable income	=	90,000	Taxable income	=	0
Taxes (40%)	=	36,600	Taxes (40%)	=	0
Net income	=	$ 54,000	Net income	=	$ 0

$$EPS\ (A) = \frac{\$54,000}{650,000} = \$0.083 \qquad EPS\ (B) = \frac{\$0}{500,000} = \$0.00$$

5-7. **Bret-Mark Corporation**

(a)

$$BE \ (before) = \frac{FC}{P - VC} = \frac{\$7,000,000}{\$50 - \$35} = \frac{\$7,000,000}{\$15} = \textbf{466,667} \quad zippets$$

$$BE \ (after) = \frac{FC}{P - VC} = \frac{\$8,000,000}{\$45 - \$35} = \frac{\$8,000,000}{\$10} = \textbf{800,000} \quad zippets$$

(b)

$$DOL \ (before) = \frac{Q(P - VC)}{Q(P - VC) - FC} = \frac{1,750,000(\$50 - \$35)}{1,750,000(\$50 - \$35) - \$7,000,000} = \frac{\$26,250,000}{\$19,250,000} = \textbf{1.36}$$

Unit sales (after): 1,750,000 × 1.20 = 2,100,000

$$DOL \ (after) = \frac{Q(P - VC)}{Q(P - VC) - FC} = \frac{2,100,000(\$45 - \$35)}{2,100,000(\$45 - \$35) - \$8,000,000} = \frac{\$21,000,000}{\$13,000,000} = \textbf{1.62}$$

(c) Annual interest (before): $5,000,000 × 0.10 = $500,000
EBIT = sales − variable operating costs − fixed operating costs
EBIT = $87,500,000 − $61,250,000 − $7,000,000
EBIT = $19,250,000

$$DFL = \frac{EBIT}{EBIT - I} = \frac{\$19,250,000}{\$19,250,000 - \$500,000} = \frac{\$19,250,000}{\$18,750,000} = \textbf{1.03}$$

After: New sales = 2,100,000 ($45) = $94,500,000

If the total asset turnover ratio remains the same (this would depend upon the interrelationships of price, sales volume, and production characteristics), $87,500,000/ $21,875,000 = 4, then the new required asset level will be $94,500,000/ 4 = $23,625,000.

Additional assets required = $23,625,000 − $21,875,000 = $1,750,000
New long-term debt level = $5,000,000 + $1,750,000 = $6,750,000
Annual interest = $5,000,000 (.10) + $1,750,000 (.12) = $500,000 + $210,000 = $710,000
EBIT = $94,500,000 − $2,100,000($35) − $8,000,000
= $94,500,000 − $73,500,000 − $8,000,000 = $13,000,000

$$DFL = \frac{EBIT}{EBIT - I} = \frac{\$13,000,000}{\$13,000,000 - \$710,000} = \frac{\$13,0000,000}{\$12,290,000} = \textbf{1.06}$$

(d) *Before:* EPS = net income/ number of shares outstanding
Taxable income = EBIT − I = $19,250,000 − $500,000 = $18,750,000
Taxes = .34 ($18,750,000) = $6,375,000
Net income = $18,750,000 − $6,375,000 = $12,375,000

$$EPS = \frac{\$12,375,000}{2,000,000} = \textbf{\$6.19}$$

After: Taxable income = $13,000,000 − $710,000 = $12,290,000
Taxes = .34 ($12,290,000) = $4,178,600
Net income = $12,290,000 − $4,178,600 = $8,111,400

$$EPS = \frac{\$8,111,400}{2,000,000} = \textbf{\$4.06}$$

The change in pricing strategy of the firm would probably have a negative impact on the firm and should not be undertaken.

Chapter 6

Working Capital and the Financing Decision

Summary: Working capital management is concerned with the financing and management of the current assets of the firm. This chapter emphasizes the factors that the financial manager must consider in determining the mix between **temporary and permanent current assets** and the nature of the financing arrangement. The cash flow cycle and hedging in a risk-return framework are outlined. The term structure of interest rates is discussed.

I. **Working Capital Management [p. 172]**

    A. Management of working capital is the financial manager's most time-consuming function.

    B. Success in managing current assets in the short run is critical for the firm's long-run existence.

    C. Nature of asset growth

        1. Changes in current assets may be temporary (seasonal) or "permanent."
            a. Current assets by definition are those expected to become cash in one operating cycle, but the level of the current assets may be "permanent" or increasing.
            b. Businesses subject to cyclical sales may have temporary fluctuations in the level of current assets.

> Refer to Figure 6-7, text page 186.

Study Note: An illustration should clarify the concept of seasonal and permanent working capital. A department store that expands its selling area by 10,000 square feet must stock the shelves with additional merchandise. Although the individual items are not expected to remain on the shelf, the shelves must always be stocked. The company's *level* of inventory has risen. There is a minimum or permanent level of inventory that the firm must always maintain. As the firm grows, this permanent level of inventory also grows. Likewise, other current asset levels increase with growth. If the department store sells on credit, its level of accounts receivable should rise as a result of the expansion due to the added sales. Cash requirements are likely to increase also as cash registers are added to the new sales area, and additional bank balances are needed.

                Seasonal fluctuations also occur. During the Christmas shopping season, for example, the department store will place more merchandise than usual on its shelves. This temporary increase will not be replaced, however, at the end of the holiday season.

        2. The cash flow cycle can be used to describe how funds move in and out of the firm and influences the firm's liquidity. **[p. 179]**
            a. Calculation of the cash conversion cycle is described as:

                Time in inventory + time for collection – time allowed for payables

            b. This cycle can be described by the asset utilization formulas of chapter 3:

                Inventory holding period + average collection period – accounts payable period

        3. Matching sales and production
            a. Both accounts receivable and inventory rise when sales increase as production increases. When sales rise faster than production, inventory declines and receivables rise.
            b. Level production (matching production and sales over an entire cycle) may cause large buildups in current assets when sales are slack. These buildups drop rapidly during peak demand periods since sales exceed the level production output.

II. **Both seasonal and permanent increases in working capital must be financed. [p. 184]**

    A. Ideally, temporary increases in current assets are financed by short-term funds and permanent current assets are financed with long-term sources.

        1. Matching short-term funds with short-term assets allows the company to increase and decrease sources and uses of funds as the company's sales fluctuate.
        2. Many firms, however, choose or are forced to use plans that do not match up financing with asset needs.
        3. Financing a high percentage of short-term assets with long-term funds means the financial manager will have excess funds to invest at seasonal or cyclical troughs, in other words excess financing.
        4. Financing permanent current assets and some long-term assets with short-term funds is quite risky because short-term funds will be permanently needed and thus cost is highly volatile and sources of short-term funds are not always available in tight credit markets.
        5. Hedging is the matching of maturities of assets and liabilities to reduce risk. **[p. 187]**

III. **The term structure of interest rates indicates the relative cost of short and long-term financing and is important to the financing decision. [p. 189-193]**

    A. The relationship of interest rates at a specific point in time for securities of equal risk but different maturity dates is referred to as the term structure of interest rates.

    B. The **term structure of interest rates** is depicted by yield curves.

    C. There are three theories describing the shape of the yield curve.

        1. **Liquidity premium theory**: the theory states that long-term rates should be higher than short-term rates because long-term securities are less liquid and more price sensitive.
        2. **Segmentation theory**: the yield curve is "shaped" by the relative demand for securities of various maturities. Some institutions such as commercial banks are primarily interested in short-term securities. Others such as insurance companies manifest a preference for much longer-term securities.
        3. **Expectations hypothesis**: the expectations hypothesis says that long-term rates reflect the average of expected short-term rates over the time period that the long-term security is outstanding.

    D. Types of yield curves **[p. 193]**

> **Refer to Figure 6-12, text page 193.**

        1. Flat: Short- and long-term interest rates are roughly equal.
        2. Normal: upward sloping; shorter maturities have lower required yields.
        3. Inverted: downward sloping: short-term rates are higher than intermediate or long-term rates.

    E. Yield curves shift upward and downward in response to changes in anticipated inflation rates and other conditions of uncertainty.

IV. **A Decision Process [p. 194]**

    A. The composition of a firm's financing of working capital is made within the risk-return framework.

        1. Short-term financing is generally less costly but more risky than long-term financing.
        2. During tight money periods, short-term financing may be unavailable or very expensive. Short-term rates are more volatile.

    B. Applying probabilities of occurrence of various economic conditions, an expected value of alternative forms of financing may be computed and used as a decision basis.

V.   **Shift in Asset Structure [p. 197]**

   A. Risk versus return considerations also affect the composition of the left-hand side of the balance sheet.

   B. A firm may compensate for high risk on the financing side with high liquidity on the asset side or vice versa.

   C. Since the early 1960's, business firms have reduced their liquidity as a result of:

      1. Profit-oriented financial management.
      2. Better utilization of cash balances, through electronic funds transfer.

VI.   **Toward an Optimum Policy [p. 198]**

   A. An aggressive firm will borrow short term and carry high levels of inventory and longer term receivables. Panel 1 of Table 6-11 represents the firm's position.

   B. The conservative firm (panel 4) will maintain high liquidity and utilize more long-term financing.

   C. Moderate firms compensate for short-term financing with highly liquid assets (panel 2) or balance low liquidity with long-term financing (panel 3).

Refer to Table 6-11, text page 199.

Chapter 6: Multiple Choice Questions

1. Working capital management is concerned with: [p. 172]
    a. Management of current assets.
    b. Management of capital assets.
    c. Financing current assets.
    d. Management of seasonal assets.
    e. Both *a* and *c* are correct

2. An aggressive firm will utilize more _____ and maintain _____ liquidity than a conservative firm. [p. 198-199]
    a. Short-term debt; higher
    b. Long-term debt; lower
    c. Long-term debt; higher
    d. Short-term debt; lower
    e. None of the above are correct

3. Usually yield curves are _____ _____, but during peak periods of economic expansion yield curves may be _____ _____. [p. 192]
    a. Upward sloping; downward sloping
    b. Downward sloping; sharply peaked
    c. Downward sloping; upward sloping
    d. Upward sloping; normally humped
    e. None of the above are correct

4. The theory that the yield curve is "shaped" by the relative demand for securities of various maturities is the: [p. 191]
   a. Liquidity premium theory.
   b. Segmentation theory.
   c. Risk-return tradeoff.
   d. Short theory.
   e. Expectations hypothesis.

5. The "term structure of interest rates" is depicted by: [p. 189]
   a. The level of permanent current assets.
   b. The level of seasonal current assets.
   c. The yield curve.
   d. The ratio of current assets to capital assets.
   e. None of the above is correct.

6. A firm may compensate for _____ risk on the financing side with _____ liquidity on the asset side. [p. 198-199]
   a. Low; high
   b. High; low
   c. Low; low
   d. High; high
   e. All of the above are acceptable answers

7. The concept of "permanent" current assets refers to: [p. 173]
   a. Plant and equipment.
   b. Inventory.
   c. The minimum level of current assets.
   d. Accounts receivable plus cash.
   e. Total assets.

8. Since the 1960s, corporate liquidity has generally been: [p. 198]
   a. Falling.
   b. Rising.
   c. Unchanged.
   d. Sharply rising.
   c. Rising and falling.

9. A yield curve which depicts long -term interest rates to be lower than short-term interest rates is said to be: [p. 192]
   a. Inverted.
   b. Complex.
   c. Humped.
   d. Normal.
   e. Skewed.

10. Retail-oriented firms have been more successful in matching sales and orders in recent years as a result of: [p. 176]
   a. Hand-held calculators.
   b. Point-of-sales terminals.
   c. Level production.
   d. Reduction of liquidity.
   e. Using permanent current assets.

Multiple Choice Answer Key: Chapter 6

1.	e	2.	d	3.	a	4.	b	5.	c
6.	d	7.	c	8.	a	9.	a	10.	b

Chapter 6: Problems

6-1. Midnight Video requires $1 in current assets for each $4 of sales that it generates. If the firm has a net profit margin of 8% and the level of capital assets does not change, what amount of external financing will the company require if sales increase from $2,000,000 to $3,600,000 (assume all earnings are retained and disregard amortization)?

6-2. Holly Bofinger, owner of Bofinger Sporting Goods anticipates sales next year to be $780,000 if the economy is in recession as predicted by many analysts. Sales in the recently completed year were $975,000. Prior to the forecast of recession, Holly had hoped that sales would reach $1,100,000. Although it seems likely that the forecasted recession will occur, she feels that the probabilities of equaling last year's sales and reaching the $1,100,000 are 20% and 10%, respectively. What is the expected level of sales next year?

6-3. Broussard's U-Rent-It is rapidly expanding and needs to acquire several new items including two hydraulic log splitters, a ditching machine, two cement mixers, several lawn mowers of various sizes, five party tents, and three Santa Claus suits. Mr. Broussard needs $120,000 to acquire the new items and is contemplating two loan arrangements. National Bank will extend the $120,000 to be paid off over three years at the prime rate plus 2%. Provincial bank will extend the loan at a fixed rate of 12% per year. Mr. Broussard expects the prime rate to be 11%, 9%, and 8%, respectively over the next three years.

   (a)   Assuming that under each loan, Mr. Broussard will pay $40,000 on the principal at the end of the year, what is the total amount of interest on each loan?

   (b)   Which of the borrowing arrangements is the more risky to Mr. Broussard?

6-4. The Opti-Mist Sprinkler Company is analyzing two financing plans to support an anticipated increase in sales. Officials of the firm anticipate that the firm will be able to maintain its operating profit margin of 20% regardless of the level of sales.

   Using the probability estimates of the sales levels and associated financial characteristics, determine which financing plan will provide the highest expected net income. The firm is in the 40% tax bracket.

Plan A			
Conditions	Below Normal	Normal	Above Normal
Probability of occurrence	.3	.4	.3
Sales	$8,000,000	$10,000,000	$12,000,000
Interest on long-term debt	180,000	180,000	180,000
Interest on short-term debt	40,000	50,000	60,000

Plan B			
Conditions	Below Normal	Normal	Above Normal
Probability of occurrence	.3	.4	.3
Sales	$8,000,000	$10,000,000	$11,000,000*
Interest on long-term debt	100,000	100,000	100,000
Interest on short-term debt	60,000	100,000	130,000

*Sales are assumed to be less under above-normal conditions for Plan B than for Plan A due to lack of available short-term financing.

6-5.   Using the term structure of interest rates, determine the expected one-year interest rate on government bonds, one year from now and two years from now. Currently a one year government bond yields 12 percent, a two year bond yields 10 percent, and a three year bond yields 8.5 percent.

Chapter 6: Solutions

6-1.   **Midnight Video**

$1,600,000 ÷ 4 = $400,000 additional current assets required

$3,600,000
    .08
$ 288,000   profit

$ 400,000
  288,000
$112,000   external financing required

6-2.   **Bofinger Sporting Goods**

Expected sales   = $780,000 (.70) + $975,000 (.20) + $1,100,000 (.10)
                      = **$851,000**

6-3.   **Broussard's U-Rent-It**

(a)   National Bank
        Total interest = .13 ($120,000) + .11 ($80,000) + .10 ($40,000) = **$28,400**
        Provincial Bank
        Total interest = .12 ($120,000) + .12 ($80,000) + .12 ($40,000) = **$28,800**

(b)   Although the predicted total interest on the National Bank loan is less, the actual interest may be much more if interest rates rise. Of course, interest rates may be less than predicted. Mr. Broussard must weigh the expected savings against the potentially higher interest costs. (Timing, a very important consideration, is ignored in this analysis. The concept will be fully explored in chapter 9.)

6-4. **Opti-Mist Sprinkler Company**

Plan A

Sales	$8,000,000	$10,000,000	$12,000,000
EBIT (20%)	$1,600,000	$ 2,000,000	$ 2,400,000
Interest:			
Long-term debt	180,000	180,000	180,000
Short-term debt	40,000	50,000	60,000
Taxable income	$1,380,000	$ 1,770,000	$ 2,160,000
Taxes	552,000	708,000	864,000
Net income	$ 828,000	$ 1,062,000	$ 1,296,000

Expected net income from Plan A = $828,000(.3) + $1,062,000(.4) + $1,296,000(.3)
= $248,400 + $424,800 + $388,800
= **$1,062,000**

Plan B

Sales	$8,000,000	$10,000,000	$11,000,000
EBIT (20%)	$1,600,000	$ 2,000,000	$ 2,200,000
Interest:			
Long-term debt	100,000	100,000	100,000
Short-term debt	60,000	100,000	130,000
Taxable income	$1,440,000	$ 1,800,000	$ 1,970,000
Taxes	576,000	720,000	788,000
Net Income	$ 864,000	$ 1,080,000	$ 1,182,000

Expected net income from Plan B = $864,000(.3) + $1,080,000(.4) + $1,182,000(.3)
= $259,200 + $432,000 + $354,600
= **$1,045,800**

6-5. **Term structure of interest rates**

Expected interest rate one year from now:

$$10\% = \frac{12\% + (one\text{-}year\ rate, one\ year\ from\ now)}{2}$$

20% = 12% + (one-year rate, one year from now)
8% = one-year rate, one year from now

Expected interest rate two years from now:

$$8.5\% = \frac{12\% + 8\% + (one\text{-}year\ rate, two\ year\ from\ now)}{3}$$

25.5% = 12% + 8% (from above) + (1-year rate, 2 years from now)
25.5% − 12% − 8% = 1-year rate, 2 years from now
5.5% = 1-year rate, 2 years from now

Chapter 7

Summary: This chapter examines the characteristics of cash, marketable securities, accounts receivable, and inventory and the processes utilized in determining the appropriate level of cash.

I. **Cost - Benefit Analysis [p. 213]**

    A. Provides a framework to identify and evaluate all changes resulting from a decision.

    B. Considers explicit, implicit and opportunity costs.

II. **Cash Management [p. 213]**

    A. Cash is a necessary but low earning asset.

    B. Financial managers attempt to minimize cash balances, while maintaining sufficient amounts of cash to meet obligations in a timely manner. Tie in to cash flow cycle of chapter 6 and forecasting of chapter4.

    C. The three main reasons for holding cash are for:

        1. **Transactions balances** are needed for recurring expenses such as payrolls and taxes. The acquisition of long-term assets, though less frequent, also requires such balances.
        2. Banks are compensated for services by maintaining cash balances on deposit. Such amounts are called **compensating balances**.
        3. **Precautionary balances** are held as a hedge against non-projected negative cash flows.

    D. The level of cash balances in a firm is largely determined by the pattern of its cash inflows and outflows. A firm's cash flow pattern is affected by many factors including:

        1. Payment pattern of customers
        2. The mix of cash sales and credit sales
        3. Credit terms; 30 days, 60 days, etc
        4. Clearing time of disbursed checks
        5. Efficiency of the banking system
        6. The shelf life of inventory and/or production cycle of the firm

    E. Temporarily, excess cash balances are transferred into interest-earning marketable securities.

III. **Collections and Disbursements [p. 214]**

    A. The financial manager attempts to get maximum use of minimum balances by speeding up inflows and slowing outflows.

    B. Playing the **float**: Using the difference in the cash balances shown on the bank's records and those shown on the firm's records.

    C. Improving collections for increased efficiency.

        1. Decentralized collection centers speed collection of accounts receivable by reducing mailing time.
        2. **Electronic transfer of funds:** excess cash balances are transferred from collection points to a centralized location for use. This can be initiated by the corporate treasurer.
        3. **Lock-box system**: customers mail payment to a post office box serviced by a local bank in their geographical area. Cheques are cleared locally and balances transferred by wire to a central location.

D. Remote disbursement to take advantage of slower mailing of cheques.

E. The movement towards an **electronic funds transfer**, a system in which funds are moved between computer terminals without the use of a cheque. Additionally **electronic data interchange (EDI)** is growing rapidly as information and funds are bundled together for electronic transfer. The debit card has been well received.

F. Cash management analysis. Example on text **page 218**.

G. International Cash Management

   1. Multinational firms shift funds from country to country daily, maximizing returns and balancing foreign exchange risk.

   2. The same techniques of cash management used domestically are utilized in the expanding international money markets but with additional risks.

   3. Difference in time zones, banking systems, culture and other differences create a non uniform system in some cases.

   4. Over 6500 banks and numerous non-bank financial institutions, such as the International Stock Exchange in London, use SWIFT (see Finance in Action) for standardized interbank electronic funds transfer, around the clock.

IV. **Marketable Securities [p. 220]**

A. Because marketable securities normally represent temporary funds held in reserve, the maturity should be kept reasonably short to avoid interest rate risk.

B. Many factors influence the choice of marketable securities:
   1. Yield.
   2. Maturity (interest rate risk).
   3. Minimum investment required.
   4. Safety.
   5. Marketability

C. Money market or short-term investments are most often sold on a discount basis. Yield is calculated using formula:

$$\frac{100-P}{P} \times \frac{365}{d} = r \qquad \text{(7-1a; page 221)}$$

P = discounted price as % of maturity value
d = number of days to maturity
r = annualized yield

An annualized effective yield calculation considering compounding is expressed by the formula:

$$\left(1 + \frac{100-P}{P}\right)^{\frac{365}{d}} - 1 = r \qquad \text{(7-1b; page 222)}$$

D. There is a wide array of securities from which to choose.

Refer to Table 7-3, text page 222.

V. **Management of Accounts Receivable [p.226]**

A. Accounts receivable represent a substantial and growing investment in assets by a company. The primary reasons for the increases have been:

1. Increasing sales.
2. Inflation.
3. Extended credit terms during recessions.

B. Accounts receivable are an investment.

1. Investment in accounts receivable should generate a return equal to or in excess of the return available on alternative investments.

> Refer to Figure 7-3, text page 228.

C. There are three primary variables for credit policy administration.

1. Credit standards
   a. The firm screens credit applicants on the basis of prior record of payment, financial stability, current net worth, and other factors.
   b. The four C's of Credit are a useful framework: character (willingness to repay), capacity (ability to repay), capital, and conditions.
   c. Many sources of information serve as a basis for credit evaluation.
      i. Dun & Bradstreet's Reference and individualized reports
      ii. Industry credit reporting agencies, such as Equifax Canada
      iii. Local credit bureaus
      iv. Sales reports and visits to the potential customer's place of business
      v. Customer financial statements
      vi. Financial institutions
      vii. Other suppliers and industry contacts

2. Terms of trade
   a. Discounts
   b. Credit period

3. Collection policy: **[p. 230-231]** Some measures used to assess collection efficiency are:
   a. Average collection period
   b. Ratio of bad debts to sales
   c. Aging of accounts receivable

4. An actual credit decision, including the opportunity cost of the investment in accounts receivable.

> Refer to credit decisions, text pages 233-234.

VI. **Inventory Management [p. 234]**

A. Inventory is the least liquid of current assets.

B. A firm's level of inventory is largely determined by the cyclicality of sales and whether it follows a seasonal or level production schedule. The production decision is based on the trade-off of cost savings of level production versus the additional inventory carrying costs.

C. Rapid price movements complicate the inventory level decision. One way of protecting an inventory position is by hedging with a futures/commodities contract.

D. There are two basic costs associated with inventory:

    1. **Carrying costs**:
       a. Interest on funds tied up in inventory
       b. Warehouse space costs
       c. Insurance
       d. Material handling expenses
       e. Risk of obsolescence (implicit cost)

    2. **Ordering and processing costs**.

E. Carrying costs vary directly with average inventory levels.

F. Total carrying costs increase as the order size increases.

G. Total ordering costs decrease as the order size increases.

$$TC = \frac{SO}{Q} + \frac{CQ}{2}$$
                                                                    (7-3; page 238)

Where *TC*   = total costs
         S   = total sales in units
         O   = ordering cost for each order
         C   = carrying cost per unit in dollars
        EOQ = economic ordering quantity

H. The first step toward achieving minimum inventory costs is determination of the optimal order quantity. This quantity may be derived by use of the economic order quantity formula:

$$EOQ = \sqrt{\frac{2SO}{C}}$$
                                                                  (7-2; page 238)

> Refer to Figure 7-4, text page 237.

I. Assumptions of the basic EOQ model:

    1. Inventory usage is at a constant rate.
    2. Order costs per order are constant.
    3. Delivery time of orders is consistent and order arrives as inventory reaches zero.

J. Minimum total inventory costs will result if the assumptions of the model are applicable and the firm's order size equals the economic ordering quantity.

K. The EOQ model has also been applied to management of cash balances. The opportunity cost (lost interest on marketable securities) of having cash is analogous to the carrying costs of inventory. Likewise, the transactions cost of shifting in and out of marketable securities is very similar to inventory order costs.

L. Stock outs and safety stock

    1. A **stock out** occurs when a firm misses sales because it is out of an inventory item.
    2. A firm may hold **safety stock**, inventory beyond the level determined by the EOQ model, to reduce the risk of losing sales. Safety stock hedges against stock outs caused by delayed deliveries, production delays, equipment breakdown, unexpected surges in sales, etc.

3. Safety stock will increase a firm's average inventory and carrying costs.

Average inventory = EOQ/ 2 + safety stock

Carrying costs = average inventory units × carrying costs per unit

4. Ideally, the additional carrying costs from having safety stock is offset by eliminating lost profits on missed sales and/or maintenance of good customer relations.

M. Just-in-Time Inventory Management

1. **Just-in-time inventory management (JIT)** seeks to minimize the level of inventory within a highly effective quality control program.
2. Suppliers are located near manufactures that are able to make orders in small lot sizes because of short delivery time.
3. The JIT process has enabled firms to reduce their number of suppliers, reduce ordering complexity, and enhance quality control.
4. JIT has resulted in various cost savings.
    a. Lower carrying costs.
    b. Lower investment in space and, therefore, lower costs of construction, utilities, and manpower.
    c. Lower clerical costs (computerized tracking systems).
    d. Lower defects and waste-related costs.

VII. **Review of Formulas**

See text page 242 or insert card.

Chapter 7: Multiple Choice Questions

1. The primary purpose of a lock-box system is to: [p. 216]
    a. Increase float.
    b. Delay disbursement.
    c. Speed up inflows.
    d. Reduce excess cash balances.
    e. Reduce marketable securities.

2. Which of the following short-term securities is the least liquid? [p. 223-225]
    a. Treasury bills
    b. Eurodollar deposits
    c. Banker's acceptances
    d. Large certificates of deposit
    e. Commercial paper

3. If other costs remain the same, an increase in the ordering cost per order will: [p. 237]
    a. Decrease the EOQ.
    b. Have no impact on the EOQ.
    c. Increase the number of orders each period.
    d. Increase the EOQ.
    e. Increase the level of accounts receivable.

4. An organization that facilitates the transmission of international transactions and messages is called: [p. 218]
   a. SPEEDO.
   b. NASDAQ.
   c. SWIFT.
   d. ZIFFLE.
   e. CASHCO.

5. Maintaining safety stock will usually: [p. 240]
   a. Reduce the risk of stock outs.
   b. Increase a firm's carrying cost.
   c. Increase a firm's ordering cost.
   d. Decrease the EOQ.
   e. Both *a* and *b* are correct.

6. An increase in the average collection period will: [p. 226-227]
   a. Decrease the account receivable balances.
   b. Reduce the ratio of bad debts to sales.
   c. Reduce the average age of accounts receivable.
   d. Increase the accounts receivable balance.
   e. None of the above is correct.

7. If a firm's order quantity is the EOQ: [p. 238-239]
   a. Total carrying costs are minimized.
   b. Total ordering costs are minimized.
   c. Total inventory costs are minimized.
   d. The inventory level is minimized.
   e. All of the above are correct

8. Just-in-time inventory management, JIT, has: [p. 240-241]
   a. Lowered inventory levels.
   b. Reduced the number of a firm's suppliers.
   c. Reduced the amount of space a firm requires.
   d. Reduced overhead expenses for utilities and manpower.
   e. All of the above are correct.

9. The yields on short-term marketable securities in 2002 were _____ relative to the yields in 1990. [p. 222]
   a. Lower
   b. Higher
   c. Unchanged
   d. Some higher, some lower
   e. Much higher

10. Which of the following is an incorrect statement? [Chapter. 7]
    a. The management of marketable securities involves choosing between various short-term investments.
    b. Cash management focuses on controlling the receipt and payment of cash in order to maximize cash balances.
    c. The less liquid an asset, the higher the required rate of return.
    d. Total carrying costs vary directly with average inventory levels.
    e. Credit decisions are made within a risk-return framework.

Multiple Choice Answer Key: Chapter 7

| 1. | c | 2. | e | 3. | d | 4. | c | 5. | e |
| 6. | d | 7. | c | 8. | e | 9. | a | 10. | b |

Chapter 7: Problems

7-1.   The New Century Oil Company uses a continuous billing system that results in average daily receipts of $600,000. The company treasurer estimates that a proposed lock-box system could reduce its collection time by 2 days.

(a)   How much cash would the lock-box system free up for the company?

(b)   What is the maximum amount that Century would be willing to pay for the lock-box system if it can earn 6% on available short-term funds?

(c)   If the lock-box system could be arranged at an annual cost of $40,000, what would be the net gain from instituting the system?

7-2.   A money market instrument is sold on a discount basis. It is sold at 98.965 percent of par (maturity value). Maturity is in 60 days. Calculate its annualized yield.

7-3.   Delcoure Industries has annual credit sales of $3,062,350 and an average collection period of 45 days. The firm uses about 40,000 units of raw materials each year. The firm estimates its cost per order to be $500 and the carrying cost per unit to be $8.

(a)   What is the firm's average receivables balance?

(b)   What is the firm's EOQ?

7-4.   The owner of Delcoure Industries, Natalya Delcoure, is evaluating the current credit and inventory policies of the firm (7-3 above). As her assistant, she has requested that you bring the following information to his office--in 15 minutes.

(a)   What is the total inventory cost associated with the EOQ of the firm?

(b)   If the average collection period could be reduced to 30 days with no loss of sales, what would be the annual savings (before tax adjustment) to the firm assuming the freed-up balance could be invested to earn 12%?

7-5.   In an effort to lower its receivables balances, Apex Manufacturing is considering switching from its no-discount policy to a 2% discount for payment by the 15th day. It is estimated that 60% of Apex's customers would take the discount and the average collection period is expected to decline from 60 days to 45 days. Company officials project a 2,000-unit increase in sales to 22,000 units, at the existing price of $25 per unit. The variable cost per unit is $21 and the average cost per unit is $23. If the firm requires a 15% beforetax return on investment, should the discount be offered?

7-6.   The EOQ of QOE Plastics is 4,000 units. The firm's ordering cost per order is $200 and its carrying cost per unit is $2.

(a)   How many units does QOE purchase per year?

(b)   If QOE increases the annual purchase of units to 96,000, what will its new EOQ be?

(c)   How much will the firm's total inventory cost increase when its EOQ changes?

(d)   How much would the maintenance of a safety stock of 4,000 units add to total inventory costs?

7-7. The new credit manager of Kay's Department Store plans to liberalize the firm's credit policy. The firm currently generates credit sales of $575,000 annually. The more lenient credit policy is expected to produce credit sales of $750,000. The bad debt losses on additional sales are projected to be 5% despite an additional $15,000 collection expenditure. The new manager anticipates production and selling costs other than additional bad debt and collection expenses will remain at the 85% level.

(a) If the firm maintains its receivables turnover of 10 times, should the credit policy be changed if the firm's opportunity cost of funds is 14 percent?

(b) Assuming additional inventory of $35,000 is required to support the additional sales, should Kay's proceed with the more lenient credit policy?

7-8. The Hy-Voltage Electric Car Company purchases 20,000 units of a major component part each year. The firm's order costs are $200 per order, and the carrying cost per unit is $2 per year.

(a) Compute the total inventory costs associated with placing orders of 20,000; 10,000; 5,000; 2,000; and 1,000 units.

(b) Determine the EOQ for the component part. Is the answer consistent with calculations in (a)?

(c) Assuming the firm places orders of EOQ amount, how many orders will be required during the year?

(d) Assuming a 50-week year, how often will orders be placed?

7-9. Evergreen Company is considering switching from level production to seasonal production in order to lower very high inventory costs. Average inventory levels would decline by $300,000 but production costs would raise about $40,000 because of additional startups and other inefficiencies. The firm's cost of financing inventory balances is 15%.

(a) Should the firm switch to seasonal production? (Ignore tax effects.)

(b) At what interest rate would the cost of financing additional inventory under level production be equal to the added production costs of seasonal production? (Ignore tax effects.)

(c) Answer (a) and (b) if the applicable tax rate is 40%.

Chapter 7: Solutions

7-1. **New Century Oil Company**
    (a)   Cash freed up = 2 × $600,000
                    = **$1,200,000**

    (b)   Benefit   = .06 × $1,200,000
                    = **$72,000** = amount of savings

    (c)   Benefit $72,000
            Cost   40,000
            Net gain   **$32,000**

7-2. **Market quoted yield:**

$$r = \frac{100 - P}{P} \times \frac{365}{d} = \frac{100 - 98.965}{98,965} \times \frac{365}{60}$$

$$= 0.0636 = 6.36\%$$

Effective annual rate:

$$r = \left(1 + \frac{100 - P}{P}\right)^{\frac{365}{d}} - 1 = \left(1 + \frac{100 - 98.965}{98.965}\right)^{\frac{365}{60}} - 1$$

$$= 0.0653 = 6.53\%$$

7-3. **Delcoure Industries**

(a)

$$Average\ collection\ period = \frac{Accounts\ receivable}{Average\ daily\ credit\ sales}$$

$$45 = \frac{Accounts\ receivable}{\$3,062,350 / 365} = \frac{Accounts\ receivable}{\$8,390}$$

$$Accounts\ receivable \quad = 45 \times \$8,390$$
$$= \$377,550$$

(b)

$$EOQ = \sqrt{\frac{2SO}{C}} = \sqrt{\frac{2 \times 40,000 \times \$500}{\$8}} = \sqrt{\frac{\$40,000,000}{\$8}} = \sqrt{5,000,000} = 2,236$$

7-4. **Delcoure Industries (continued)**

(a)   Total inventory cost = total carrying cost + total ordering cost

$$TC = \frac{SO}{Q} + \frac{CQ}{2}$$

$$= \frac{40,000 \times \$500}{2,236} + \frac{\$8 \times 2,236}{2}$$

$$= \$8,945 + \$8,944$$

$$= \$17,889$$

Note: Total ordering cost differs slightly from total carrying cost because of the need to round up on the number of orders.

(b)

$$Average\ collection\ period = \frac{Accounts\ receivable}{Average\ daily\ credit\ sales}$$

$$30 = \frac{Accounts\ receivable}{\$3,062,350/365} = \frac{Accounts\ receivable}{\$8,390}$$

$$Accounts\ receivable = 30 \times \$8,390$$
$$= \mathbf{\$251,700}$$

Reduction in AR = $377,550 – $251,700 = $125,850
Annual savings = .12 × $125,850 =   **$15,102**

7-5.   Apex Manufacturing

$$Existing\ accounts\ receivable\ turnover = \frac{365}{60} = 6.08$$

$$Expected\ accounts\ receivable\ turnover = \frac{365}{45} = 8.11$$

Marginal revenue = 2,000 × ($25 – $21) = $8,000

$$Existing\ accounts\ receivable\ (investment) = \frac{20,000 \times \$25}{6.08} = \$82,236.84$$

$$Expected\ accounts\ receivable\ (investment) = \frac{22,000 \times \$25}{8.11} = \$67,817.51$$

Reduction in accounts receivable investment   = $82,236.84 – $67,817.51
    = $14,419.33

Benefit (savings) on reduction in investment   = 0.15 ($14,419.33)
    = $2,162.90

Cost/ benefits of offering discount:

Marginal revenue	$ 8,000.00
Discount cost = .02 (.60) 22,000 ($25)	6,600.00
Benefit of AR reduction	2,162.90
Net benefit	**$3,562.90**

Since the net benefit is $3,562.90, **the discount should be offered**.

7-6.   **QOE Plastics**

(a)

$$EOQ = \sqrt{\frac{2SO}{C}} = \sqrt{\frac{2 \times S \times \$200}{\$2}} = \sqrt{200\,S}$$

$$4000 = \sqrt{200\,S}$$

$$16,000,000 = 200\,S$$

$$S = \mathbf{80,000}$$

(b)

$$EOQ = \sqrt{\frac{2SO}{C}} = \sqrt{\frac{2 \times 96,000 \times \$200}{\$2}} = \sqrt{19,200,000} = \mathbf{4,382} \ (rounded)$$

(c)

$$TC\ (original) = \frac{SO}{Q} + \frac{CQ}{2} = \frac{80,000 \times \$200}{4,000} + \frac{\$2 \times 4,000}{2} = \$4,000 + \$4,000$$

$$= \mathbf{\$8,000}$$

$$TC\ (new) = \frac{SO}{Q} + \frac{CQ}{2} = \frac{96,000 \times \$200}{4,382} + \frac{\$2 \times 4,382}{2} = \$4,382 + \$4,382$$

$$= \mathbf{\$8,764}$$

Increase in TC = $8,764 – $8,000 = **$764**

(d)   Safety stock of 4,000 units would increase total inventory cost by 4,000 × the carrying cost per unit
= 4,000 x $2 = **$8,000**.

7-7.

(a)

Incremental sales ($750,000 - $575,000) =	$175,000	
Incremental contribution margin (1 - .85)		$26,250
(including selling expense)		
Incremental bad debts	5%	(8,750)
Incremental collection expense		(15,000)
Incremental accounts receivable	$175,000	
	10	
	= $17,500	
Incremental opportunity cost of investment in A/R at	14%	(2,450)
Total incremental change		$ 50

Proceed with change.

Additional inventory investment of $35,000 has an incremental opportunity cost of $35,000 ×
14% = $4,900 per year. Do not proceed with change.

7-8.

(a)

Quantity Ordered	Number of Orders	Order Costs	Average Inventory	Annual Carrying Costs	Total Costs
20,000	20K/20K = 1	$200(1) = $ 200	20K/2 = 10K	10,000($2) = $20,000	$20,200
10,000	20K/10K = 2	$200(2) = $ 400	10K/2 = 5K	5,000($2) = $10,000	$10,400
5,000	20K/5K = 4	$200(4) = $ 800	5K/2 = 2.5K	2,500($2) = $ 5,000	$ 5,800
2,000	20K/2K = 10	$200(10) = $2,000	2K/2 = 1K	1,000($2) = $ 2,000	$ 4,000 minimum
1,000	20K/1K = 20	$200(20) = $4,000	1K/2 = .5K	500($2) = $ 1,000	$ 5,000

(b)

$$EOQ = \sqrt{\frac{2SO}{C}} = \sqrt{\frac{2 \times 20,000 \times \$200}{\$2}} = \sqrt{4,000,000} = \textbf{2,000 } units$$

$S = 20,000$
$O = \$200$
$C = \$2$

(c) $$Orders\ per\ year = \frac{20,000}{2,000} = \textbf{10}$$

(d)

$$Number\ of\ weeks\ between\ orders = \frac{50}{10} = \textbf{5}$$

7-9.

(a) Reduction in inventory costs = 0.15 × ($300,000) = $45,000
Savings from seasonal production = $45,000 – $40,000 = $5,000

Based solely on the information given, **the switch should be made**.

(b) $40,000/ $300,000 = 13.33%
If the firm's financing costs were below 13.33%, it would be preferable to continue level production.

Example: Suppose the firm's financing cost was 12%.
Reduction in inventory cost = .12 × ($300,000) = $36,000
Additional production costs =   40,000
Net benefit   ($4,000)

At **13.33%**, additional production costs equal the reduction in inventory financing costs (0.1333 × $300,000 = $40,000).

(c) Reduction in aftertax inventory costs = (.15) ($300,000)(1 – .4) = $27,000
Additional production costs = ($40,000) (1 – .4) =   24,000
Savings from seasonal production = $ 3,000
The aftertax interest rate that would yield equal costs of financing and production costs would be:

$$\frac{(\$40,000)(1 - .4)}{\$300,000} = \frac{\$24,000}{\$300,000} = .08 = \textbf{8.0\%}$$

The before tax rate that would yield equivalent costs is .08/.6 = .1333 or 13.33% the same as when taxes were ignored.

Summary: The cost and availability of various sources of short-term funds are examined. Emphasis is given to trade credit, bank loans, corporate promissory notes, and loans against receivables and inventory. Hedging of interest rate risk is discussed briefly.

I.   **Trade Credit [p. 253]**

   A.   Usually the largest source of short-term financing.

   B.   A spontaneous source of financing that increases as sales expand or contract. For example, if the annual purchase of inventory items is $3,650,000, and present payables policy is 20 days, average accounts payable position is:

   $3,650,000 / 365 × 20 = $200,000

   However if the policy is changed to 30 days, the accounts payable position is increased to $300,000 representing an increase on an average daily basis in sources of funding of $100,000.

   C.   Credit period is set by terms of credit but firms may be able to "stretch" the payment period.

   D.   Cash discount policy

   1.   Suppliers may provide a **cash discount** for early payment. For example, a 3/15, net 60 policy would allow a buyer to deduct 3% from the billed charges if payment is made within 15 days. If not, the purchaser is expected to pay by the 60th day.

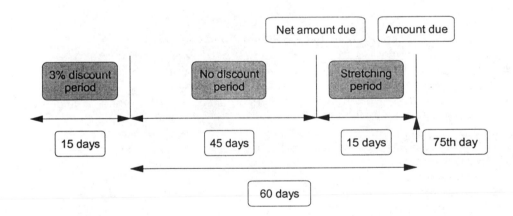

   2.   Forgoing discounts can be very expensive. The cost of failing to take a discount is computed as follows:

$$K_{DIS} = \frac{d\,\%}{100\% - d\,\%} \times \frac{365}{f\,(\text{date}) - d\,(\text{date})} \qquad \text{(8-1; page 254)}$$

   $d\,\% =$ discount percentage
   $f\,(\text{date}) =$ final payment period
   $d\,(\text{date}) =$ discount period

In the example above, the cost would be:
Cost of failing to take a discount =

$$K_{DIS} = \frac{3\%}{100\% - 3\%} \times \frac{365}{60 - 15} = \frac{3}{97} \times \frac{365}{45} = 25.1\%$$

The buyer obtains the use of the amount not paid (billed charges – discount) for 45 days and agrees to forgo the discount for such use. The cost, 25.1% on an annual basis, is rather expensive. If, however, the supplier "permits" stretching payment of the account by 15 days, the buyer gains use of the funds for 60 days and the cost of forgoing the discount is reduced.

Cost of failing to take a discount =

$$K_{DIS} = \frac{3\%}{100\% - 3\%} \times \frac{365}{75 - 15} = \frac{3}{97} \times \frac{365}{60} = 18.81\%$$

3.   Whether a firm should take a discount depends on the relative costs of alternative sources of financing.

E.   Net Credit Position **[p. 255]**

1.   The relationship between a firm's level of accounts receivable and its accounts payable determines its net credit position.
2.   If the firm's average receivables exceed average payables, it is a net provider of credit. If payables exceed receivables, the firm is a net user of trade credit.

II.   **Bank Credit [p. 256]**

A.   Banks prefer short-term, **self-liquidating loans**.

B.   Bank loan terms and concepts

1.   Prime rate: The interest rate charged the most credit-worthy borrowers
   a.   The **prime rate** serves as a base in determining the interest rate for various risk classes of borrowers.
   b.   The prime rate of banks receives much attention from government officials in managing the economy.
   c.   The prime rate has been more volatile in the last couple of decades than in previous decades.
   d.   The London Interbank Offer Rate (LIBOR) is being used worldwide as a base lending rate on dollar loans.

2.   Compensating Balances
   a.   As a loan condition, a borrower may be required to maintain an average minimum account balance in the bank equal to a percentage of loans outstanding or a percentage of future commitments and/or pay a fee for services.
   b.   **Compensating balances** raise the cost of a loan and compensate the bank for its services.
   c.   If a compensating balance is required, the borrower must borrow more than the amount needed.

   Amount borrowed = amount needed / (1 - C)
   Where C = compensating balance in percent

3.   Maturity provisions
   a.   Most bank loans are short-term and mature within a year.
   b.   In the last decade more banks have extended intermediate-term loans (one to seven years) that are paid in installments.

4. Costs of commercial bank financing
   a. The annual interest rate depends on the loan amount, interest paid, length of the loan, and method of repayment.
   b. Formula for various types of loans are as follows:

Annual rate on a loan

$$R_{ANNUAL} = \frac{I}{P} \times \frac{365}{d}$$ (8-2; page 259)

R_{ANNUAL} = annual rate
I = interest
P = principal
d = days loan is outstanding

Annual rate on discounted loan

$$R_{DIS} = \frac{I}{P-I} \times \frac{365}{d}$$ (8-3; page 260)

Annual rate with compensating balances

$$R_{COMP} = \frac{I}{(1-c)}$$ (8-4; page 260)

c is compensating balance requirement expressed as a decimal.

$$R_{COMP} = \frac{I}{P-B} \times \frac{365}{d}$$ (8-5: page260)

B = Compensating balance in $$

Annual rate on an installment loan

$$R_{INSTALL} = \frac{2 \times \text{Annual number of payments} \times I}{(\text{Total number of payments} + 1) \times P}$$ (8-6; page 262)

C. Bank credit availability tends to cycle

1. Credit crunches seem to appear periodically.
2. The pattern of the credit crunch has been as follows:
   a. The Bank of Canada tightens the money supply to fight inflation.
   b. Lendable funds shrink, interest rates rise.
   c. Business loan demand increases due to price-inflated inventories and receivables.
   d. Depositors withdraw savings from banks seeking higher return elsewhere, further reducing bank credit availability.
3. The Bank of Canada's policy of attempting to influence the level of the Canadian dollar closely ties Canadian interest rates to United States economic developments.

III. Commercial Paper [p. 263]

A. Short-term, unsecured promissory notes issued to the public in minimum units of $50,000.

B. Issuers

1. Finance companies such as General Motors Acceptance Corporation (GMAC) that issue paper directly. Such issues are referred to as **finance paper** or **direct paper**.
2. Industrial or utility firms that issue paper indirectly through dealers. This type of issue is called **dealer paper**.

C. There has been very rapid growth in the commercial paper market in the last few decades. There are over 200 major corporations in Canada that are issuers. Securitized paper has been increasingly significant.

D. Traditionally, commercial paper has been a paper certificate issued to the lender to signify the lender's claim to be repaid. There is a growing trend among companies that sell and buy commercial paper to handle the transaction electronically. Actual paper certificates are not created. Documentation of the transactions is provided by computerized book-entry transactions and transfers of money are accomplished by wiring cash between lenders and commercial paper issuers.

E. Advantages:

   1. Commercial paper may be issued at below the prime rate at chartered banks.
   2. No compensating balances are required, though lines of credit are necessary.
   3. Prestige

F. The primary limitation is the increased risk of the commercial paper market as demonstrated when Confederation Life or Olympia and York defaulted.

IV. **Bankers Acceptances [p. 266]**

A. Short term promissory notes to finance goods in transit, particularly foreign related trade with payment guaranteed by a bank.

V. **Foreign Borrowing [p. 267]**

A. The Eurocurrency market is an increasing source of funds for Canadian firms.

B. These loans are usually short to intermediate term in maturity.

C. Borrowing in foreign currencies subjects the borrower to foreign exchange risk.

VI. **The Use of Collateral in Short-Term Financing [p. 267]**

A. The lending institution may require collateral to be pledged when granting a loan.

B. Lenders lend on the basis of the cash-flow capacity of the borrower. Collateral is an additional but secondary consideration.

C. Accounts receivable financing.

   1. **Pledging accounts receivable** as collateral. **[p. 268]**
       a. Convenient means of financing. Receivable levels are rising as the need for financing is increasing.
       b. May be relatively expensive and preclude use of alternative financing sources.
       c. Lender screens accounts and loans a percentage (60% – 75%) of the acceptable amount.
       d. Lender has full recourse against borrower.
       e. The interest rate, which is usually in excess of the prime rate, is based on the frequently changing loan balance outstanding.

   2. **Factoring** receivables. **[p. 269]**
       a. Receivables are sold, usually without recourse, to a factoring firm.
       b. A factor provides a credit-screening function by accepting or rejecting accounts.
       c. Factoring costs.
           i.   Commission of 1% - 3% of factored invoices
           ii. Interest on advances

3. **Asset-backed public offerings [p. 270]**
   a. Public offerings of securities, backed by receivables as collateral, is a recently employed means of short-term financing. These have included mortgages, car loans and credit card receivables. Credit ratings often are better than the issuing firm. For example Sears.
   b. Several problems must be resolved:
      i.   Image: Historically, firms that sold receivables were considered to be in financial trouble.
      ii. Computer upgrading to service securities.
      iii. Probability of losses on default of underlying securities
   c. The creation of asset backed securities is referred to as **securitization of assets.**

VII.   **Inventory Financing [p. 271]**

A. The collateral value of inventory is based on several factors.

   1. Marketability
      a. Raw materials and finished goods are more marketable than goods-in-process inventories.
      b. Standardized products or widely traded commodities qualify for higher percentage loans.
   2. Price Stability
   3. Perishability
   4. Physical Control
      a. **Blanket inventory liens**: Lender has general claim against inventory of borrower. No physical control.
      b. **Trust receipts**: Also known as floor planning; the borrower holds specifically identified inventory and proceeds from sale in trust for the lender.
      c. Warehousing: Goods are physically identified, segregated, and stored under the director of an independent warehousing company. Inventory is released from warehouse openly upon presentation of warehouse receipt controlled by the lender.
         i. **Public warehouse**: facility on the premises of the warehousing firm.
         ii. **Field warehouse**: independently controlled facility on the premises of borrower.

B. Inventory financing and the associated control methods are standard procedures in many industries.

VIII. **Hedging to Reduce Borrowing Risk [p. 272]**

A. Firms that continually borrow to finance operations are exposed to the risk of interest rate changes.

B. **Hedging** activities in the financial futures market reduce the risk of interest rate changes.

IX.   **Review of Formulas**

   See text page 275 or insert card.

Chapter 8: Multiple Choice Questions

1. Many of the services of modern banks have been made possible by the development of the _____[p. 256]
   a. Bank Act.
   b. Investment Dealers Act.
   c. Schedule II.
   d. Bank of Canada.
   e. Citizen's Bank.

2. The interest rate charged to the most creditworthy customers of a bank is referred to as: [p. 268]
    a. Bank rate.
    b. Prime rate.
    c. Discount rate.
    d. Compensating rate.
    e. Asset-backed securities rate.

3. The difference between a firm's accounts receivable and its accounts payable is called its: [p. 257]
    a. Net working capital.
    b. Working capital.
    c. Trade credit.
    d. Net credit position.
    e. Compensating balance.

4. Which of the following is typically the largest source of short-term credit for a firm? [p. 253]
    a. Bank loans
    b. Commercial paper
    c. Factoring
    d. Asset-backed public offerings
    e. Trade credit

5. Trust receipt financing is also called: [p. 272]
    a. Warehousing.
    b. Pledging.
    c. Floor planning.
    d. Trade credit.
    e. Commercial paper.

6. Instead of issuing the traditional paper certificates when financing with commercial paper, there is a trend towards documenting the transaction by: [p. 264]
    a. Direct paper.
    b. Computerized book entry.
    c. Factoring.
    d. Securitization.
    e. Stretching.

7. Which of the following usually has the lowest interest rate? [Chapter. 8; p. 265]]
    a. Prime rate bank loans
    b. Inventory loans
    c. Directly-placed commercial paper
    d. Dealer-placed commercial paper
    e. Secured loans

8. A firm that buys on credit terms of 2/10 net 30: [p. 253]
    a. May take a 2% discount if the amount is paid by the 10th day.
    b. Will normally wait until the 30th day to pay if the discount is not taken.
    c. Will experience a cost of more than 36% if the discount is foregone.
    d. Should normally take the discount if the funds can be obtained at a cost of 14%.
    e. All of the above are correct.

9. A general claim against the inventory of a borrower is a: [p. 272]
    a. Trust receipt.
    b. Blanket lien.
    c. Pledge.
    d. Warehouse receipt.
    e. All of the above are correct

10. Which of the following inventory financing arrangements provides the lender with the greatest control of the inventory? [p. 272]
   a. Trade credit
   b. Blanket liens
   c. Floor planning
   d. Public warehousing
   e. Trust receipts

Multiple Choice Answer Key: Chapter 8

1.	a	2.	b	3.	d	4.	e	5.	c
6.	b	7.	c	8.	e	9.	b	10.	d

Chapter 8: Problems

8-1.   Friendly Bank will lend you $5,000 for a year for $600 in interest.

    (a)   What is the annual rate of interest?

    (b)   If you are required to repay the principal and interest in 12 monthly installments, what is the rate of interest?

8-2.   Katz Supply currently purchases on terms of 3/20 net 60.

    (a)   What is the cost to Katz if the discount is not taken?

    (b)   If Ms. Katz can stretch her payment to 75 days if the discount is not taken, what is the cost?

    (c)   Suppose that Katz purchases $1,000,000 annually on the 3/20 net 60 terms. Ignoring other financing costs, what is the impact on before tax profits of not taking the discount?

8-3.   Myopic Optical is seeking to borrow $75,000 from National Bank.

    (a)   If the bank requires a 20% minimum compensating balance, how much will Myopic Optical be able to effectively use?

    (b)   If the bank quotes a rate of 12%, what will the interest rate be after considering the compensating balance requirement?

    (c)   If Myopic must gain the use of $75,000, how much must be borrowed?

    (d)   If Myopic normally maintains a balance in National Bank of $20,000, would your answers to (a), (b), and (c) be the same?

8-4.   Your banker indicates that she will lend you $5,000 at 10% interest. What is the annual rate under each of the following conditions?

(a)   The principal and interest are to be repaid at the end of one year.

(b)   The loan is discounted and the principal is repaid at the end of the year.

(c)   The loan is to be repaid in 12 monthly installments.

8-5.   Pfc. Bisping is considering borrowing $100 from a loan company advertised in a service newspaper. The advertisement indicates that he may repay the principal plus "only $3.50 interest" at the end of the 30-day period. What rate of interest would he be paying?

8-6.   Hammer and Nail Hardware can buy equivalent materials from two distributors. Supplier A offers terms 1/10, net 30 whereas Supplier B provides terms of 2/15, net 60.

(a)   If Hammer and Nail foregoes the discount, from which of the two suppliers should it purchase if supply prices are comparable.

(b)   If Hammer and Nail can borrow from Lendzit Bank at a 16% rate, should it forego the discount?

(c)   If in (b) above the bank requires a 20% compensating balance for the loan, should the firm forgo the discount?

8-7.   The High Fashion Dress Shop can borrow from a local bank at 12% interest if it maintains a 20% compensating balance. Alternatively, it may finance its operations by factoring its accounts receivable. The factor charges a commission of 1% of the monthly accounts factored and 1% per month for advances. Which of the two sources of financing is the least expensive?

8-8.   Meyer Appliance needs $100,000 to take advantage of a trade discount based on terms of 3/10, net 60. South Bank has agreed to lend the money at a 12% rate with a 15% compensating balance requirement. North Bank will lend at a 13% interest rate on a discounted loan for three months.

(a)   What is the annual rate of interest charged by each bank?

(b)   What is the cost of forgoing the discount?

(c)   How much would Meyer have to borrow from each bank in order to take the discount?

(d)   Suppose that Meyer normally banks with South Bank and maintains deposit balances of $15,000, what amount would have to be borrowed, and what would the annual interest rate be?

8-9.   Estate Enterprises is holding as an investment, a bankers 'acceptance, payable 91 days from today at a face value of $250,000. Wiley Corporation is prepared to pay Estate Enterprises $241,500 from their excess cash balances if Estate Enterprises endorses over the acceptance to Wiley.

Calculate the annual return to Wiley of this transaction.

8-10. Peyto Lake Colours' present accounts payable policy is to stretch all payables to 50 days although 70 percent of its suppliers offer terms of 2/10 net 30 and the other 30 percent are net 30. Apparently there have been no penalties or price adjustments to reflect Peyto's tardy payment policy. Annual credit purchases are $7.8 million and Peyto's current borrowing rate is 15.25 percent. Peyto's banker has suggested that the bank will lower Peyto's borrowing rate to 14.25 percent if Peyto meets the credit terms offered by its suppliers.

Should Peyto change its payable policy?

Chapter 8: Solutions

8-1. **Friendly Bank**
  (a)

$$R_{ANNUAL} = \frac{I}{P} \times \frac{365}{d} = \frac{\$600}{\$5,000} \times \frac{365}{365} = 0.12 = \textbf{12\%}$$

  (b)

$$R_{INSTALL} = \frac{2 \times \text{Annual number of payments} \times I}{(\text{Total number of payments} + 1) \times P} = \frac{2 \times 12 \times \$600}{(12+1) \times \$5,000} = \frac{\$14,400}{\$65,000} = 0.2215 = \textbf{22.15\%}$$

8-2. Katz Supply
  (a)   *Cost of failing to take discount =*

$$K_{DIS} = \frac{d\%}{100\% - d\%} \times \frac{365}{f(\text{date}) - d(\text{date})} = \frac{3\%}{100\% - 3\%} \times \frac{365}{60 - 20} = 0.2822 = \textbf{28.22\%}$$

  (b)   *Cost of failing to take discount =*

$$K_{DIS} = \frac{d\%}{100\% - d\%} \times \frac{365}{f(\text{date}) - d(\text{date})} = \frac{3\%}{100\% - 3\%} \times \frac{365}{75 - 20} = 0.2052 = \textbf{20.52\%}$$

  (c)   *Cost of failing to take the discount (in dollars)*
         = $1,000,000 × .03 = **$30,000**

8-3. **Myopic Optical**
  (a)   *Amount that can be effectively used* = (1 − .20) ($75,000) = **$60,000**

  (b)

$$R_{COMP} = \frac{I}{(1-c)} = \frac{.12}{1-.2} = 0.15 = \textbf{15\%}$$

  (c)

$$\text{Amount of funds borrowed} = \frac{\text{Amount needed}}{1-c} = \frac{\$75,000}{1-.2} = \textbf{\$93,750}$$

  (d)   If Myopic maintains a balance of $20,000 in National Bank, the compensating balance requirement will not impact the loan. The answers for (a), (b), and (c) would be **$75,000**; **.12**; and **$75,000**; respectively.

8-4.

(a)

$$R_{ANNUAL} = \frac{I}{P} \times \frac{365}{d} = \frac{\$5,000 \times 0.10}{\$5,000} \times \frac{365}{365} = \frac{\$500}{\$5,000} \times \frac{365}{365} = 0.10 = \textbf{10\%}$$

(b)

$$R_{DIS} = \frac{I}{P - I} \times \frac{365}{d} = \frac{\$500}{\$5,000 - \$500} \times \frac{365}{365} = \frac{\$500}{\$4,500} \times 1 = .1111 = \textbf{11.1\%}$$

(c)

$$R_{INSTALL} = \frac{2 \times \text{Annual number of payments} \times I}{(\text{Total number of payments} + 1) \times P} = \frac{2 \times 12 \times \$500}{(12 + 1) \times \$5,000} = \frac{\$12,000}{\$65,000} = 0.1846 = \textbf{18.46\%}$$

8-5.   Pfc. Bisping

$$R_{ANNUAL} = \frac{I}{P} \times \frac{365}{d} = \frac{\$3.50}{\$100} \times \frac{365}{30} = 0.4258 = \textbf{42.58\%}$$

8-6.   Hammer and Nail Hardware

(a)   *Cost of failing to take a cash discount =*

$$K_{DIS}(Supplier\ A) = \frac{d\,\%}{100\% - d\,\%} \times \frac{365}{f\,(\text{date}) - d\,(\text{date})} = \frac{1\%}{100\% - 1\%} \times \frac{365}{30 - 10} = 0.1843 = \textbf{18.43\%}$$

$$K_{DIS}(Supplier\ B) = \frac{d\,\%}{100\% - d\,\%} \times \frac{365}{f\,(\text{date}) - d\,(\text{date})} = \frac{2\%}{100\% - 2\%} \times \frac{365}{60 - 15} = 0.1655 = \textbf{16.55\%}$$

(b)   No, H&N should borrow from the bank at 16% and take the discount.

(c)

$$R_{COMP} = \frac{I}{(1 - c)} = \frac{.16}{1 - .2} = 0.20 = \textbf{20\%}$$

H&N should forgo the discount rather than borrow from the bank since the bank loan would cost 20% and the cost of forgoing the discount would be less.

8-7.   High Fashion Dress Shop

$$R_{COMP} = \frac{I}{(1 - c)} = \frac{.12}{1 - .2} = 0.15 = \textbf{15\%}$$

Cost of factoring: 1%   Commission
                        1%   Interest/ month for advances
                        2%
                        × 12
                        24%   Annual rate

Bank borrowing is the least expensive alternative.

8-8.   **Meyer Appliance**

(a)   Cost of borrowing from South Bank

$$R_{COMP} = \frac{I}{(1-c)} = \frac{.12}{1-.15} = 0.1412 = \textbf{14.12\%}$$

Cost of borrowing from North Bank:
Interest = (.13) ($100,000) (90/365) = $3,205

$$R_{DIS} = \frac{I}{P-I} \times \frac{365}{d} = \frac{\$3,205}{\$100,000 - \$3,205} \times \frac{365}{90} = .1343 = \textbf{13.43\%}$$

(b)

$$K_{DIS} = \frac{d\%}{100\% - d\%} \times \frac{365}{f(date) - d(date)} = \frac{3\%}{100\% - 3\%} \times \frac{365}{60 - 10} = 0.2258 = \textbf{22.58\%}$$

(c)   Meyer needs $100,000 in order to take the discount. The amount to be borrowed from:

$$\textit{Amount of funds borrowed (South Bank)} = \frac{\textit{Amount needed}}{1-c} = \frac{\$100,000}{1-.15} = \textbf{\$117,647.06}$$

$$\textit{Amount of funds borrowed (North Bank)} = \frac{\textit{Amount needed}}{1-c} = \frac{\$100,000}{1-\dfrac{.13}{4}} = \frac{\$100,000}{.9675} \textbf{\$103,359.17}$$

(d)   The compensating balance would not impact the loan since Meyer's normal balances would satisfy the compensating balance requirement. Meyer would need to borrow $100,000; and the annual rate of interest would be 12%.

8-9.   Return (yield) to Wiley Corporation from purchasing bankers' acceptance (B.A.).

Market quoted yield:

$$r = \frac{100 - P}{P} \times \frac{365}{d} = \frac{\$250,000 - \$241,500}{\$241,500} \times \frac{365}{91} = 0.1411 = \textbf{14.11\%}$$

Annual effective yield:

$$r = \left(1 + \frac{100 - P}{P}\right)^{\frac{365}{d}} - 1 = \left(1 + \frac{\$250,000 - \$241,500}{\$241,500}\right)^{\frac{365}{91}} - 1 = 0.1488 = \textbf{14.88\%}$$

8-10. **Peyto Colours**
Present accounts payable
    = Annual purchases/ 365 × Average payment period
    = $7,800,000/ 365 × 50
    = $1,068,493

Accounts payable if terms met
    = Annual purchases/ 365 × Average payment period
    = $7,800,000/ 365 × 16
    = $341,918

Average payment period	=	70% × 10 days + 30% × 30 days
	=	16 days
Bank financing required	=	$1,068,493 − $341,918 = **$726,575**
Cost of bank financing	=	$726,575 × 14.25%
	=	$103,537
Cost of forgoing the discount	=	2% × 70% × $7,800,000 = **$109,200**
As a percent	=	$109,200/ $726,575 = **.1502 or 15.02%**

Bank financing will save Peyto Colours ($109,200 − $103,537) = $5,663 a year. Peyto should accept the bank's offer.

****

There is another alternative, as follows. Continue to stretch payables to 50 days where no discount is offered and take the discount where offered replacing the financing with the bank financing at 15.25%.

Accounts payable
    = Annual purchases/ 365 × Average payment period
    = $7,800,000/ 365 × 22
    = $470,137

Average payment period	=	70% × 10 days + 30% × 50 days
	=	22 days
Bank financing required	=	$1,068,493 − $470,137
	=	$598,356
Cost of bank financing	=	$598,356 × 15.25%
	=	$91,249
Cost of forgoing the discount	=	2% × 70% × $7,800,000
	=	$109,200
As a percent	=	$109,200/ $598,356
	=	.1825 or 18.25%

This would be Peyto Colours' best alternative.

Chapter 9

The Time Value of Money

Summary: Money has time value because it can be put to work to earn a return. The sooner dollars are received the sooner they can begin working. This **time value of money** concept is an integral part of business decisions because cash inflows and outflows often take place at different points in time. To make appropriate business decisions, the cash inflows and outflows must be expressed in value units at the same point in time. In this chapter, the mathematical tools of the time value of money concept are developed and related to capital allocation decisions.

I. **Money has a time value associated with it. [p. 287]**

    A. The investor/lender demands that financial rent be paid on his or her funds.

    B. Understanding the effective rate on a business loan, the return on an investment, etc., is dependent on using the time value of money.

    C. Calculator

        1. Study the time value keys on a business calculator.
        2. Shown on the time line the calculator keys should be similar to those below:

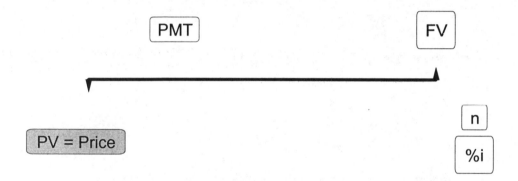

        PV =   single value at the start of a period
        FV =   single value at the end of a period
        PMT =   series of equal payments over the period
        N =   number of interest compounding periods
        %i =   interest rate per compounding period

        3. The compute key assumes payments (PMT) are at the end of each period (n). The begin (BGN) or due key assumes payments (PMT) are at the start of each period (n).
        4. Input known values and solve for the unknown value.

    D. The interest rate is also referred to as a discount rate, rate of return, or yield.

II. **Future Value: Single Amount [p. 287]**

    A. In determining **future value**, we measure the value of an amount that is allowed to grow at a given interest rate over a period of time.

Suppose an individual deposits $1,000 in a savings account paying 6% annual interest. At the end of one year, the account balance will be $1,060 = [$1,000 the original amount + the interest earned ($1,000 × .06)]. If the new amount is left on deposit during year two, interest will be paid on $1,060. The amount at the end of each of the following two years will be:

Year	Beginning Amount	Interest	Future Value
2nd year	$1,060.00	[($1,060) (.06) = $63.60] =	$1,123.60
3rd year	$1,123.60	[($1,123.60) (.06) = $67.42] =	$1,191.02
4th year	$1,191.02	[$1,191.02) (.06) = $71.46] =	$1,262.48

B. The relationship may be expressed by the following formula:

$$FV = PV(1+i)^n \qquad \text{(9-1; page 288)}$$

Applying the formula to the example above:

$FV = \$1{,}000\,(1.06)^4$
$FV = PV\,(1.26248)$
$FV = \$1{,}262.48$

C. **(Optional)** The formula may be restated as:

$$FV = PV \times FV_{IF}$$

The FV_{IF} term is found in appendix A. The factor term FV_{IF} is equal to $(1+i)^n$ from above.

D. Calculator

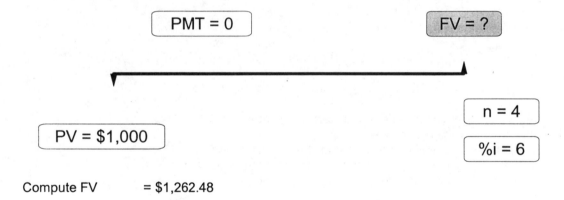

Compute FV   = $1,262.48

E. To get the interest factor with the calculator input 1 for the present value.

III.   **Effective or Nominal Interest Rate [p. 289]**

A. The effective interest rate includes any compounding effects over the relevant time period. By formula:

$$(1+i)^n - 1 = \text{effective annual interest rate} \qquad \text{(page 289)}$$

Where i = interest rate per compounding period

IV.   **Present Value: Single Amount[p.290]**

   A. The present value of a future sum is the amount invested today, at a given interest rate that will equal the future sum at a specified point in time.

   B. The relationship may be expressed in the following formula:

$$PV = FV\left[\frac{1}{(1+i)^n}\right]$$ (9-3; page 291)

   C. **(Optional)** The formula may be restated as:

$$PV = FV \times PV_{IF}$$

   The PV_{IF} term is found in appendix B.

   D. Calculator

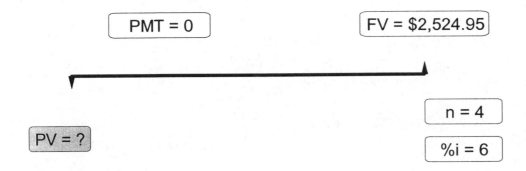

   PMT = 0   FV = \$2,524.95

   PV = ?

   n = 4

   %i = 6

   Compute PV = \$2,000.

V.   **Future Value: Annuity [p. 292]**

   A. An annuity represents consecutive payments or receipts of equal amount.

   B. The annuity value is normally assumed to take place at the end of the period.

   C. The future value of an annuity represents the sum of the future value of the individual flows.

   Refer to Figure 9-2; text page 293.

   D. The formula for the future value for an annuity is:

$$FV_A = A\left[\frac{(1+i)^n - 1}{i}\right]$$ (9-4a; page 293)

   E. **(Optional)** The formula may be restated as:

$$FV_A = A \times FV_{IFA}$$

   The FV_{IFA} term is found in appendix C.

F. Calculator

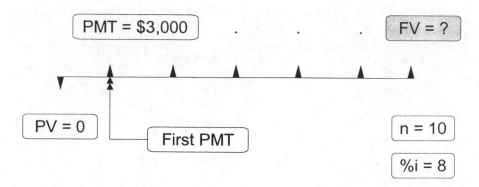

Compute FV = $43,459.69

Notice that the first payment earns interest for one less period than the total annuity periods and the last payment does not earn any interest. This is a result of receiving payments at the end of the period.

G.

    1. Future Value: Annuity in Advance **[p.294]**

$$FV_A = A_{BGN}\left[\frac{(1+i)^{n+1} - (1+i)}{i}\right]$$

(9-4b; page 294)

    Also: FV_A (BGN) $= FV_A \times (1 + i)$

    2. Calculator

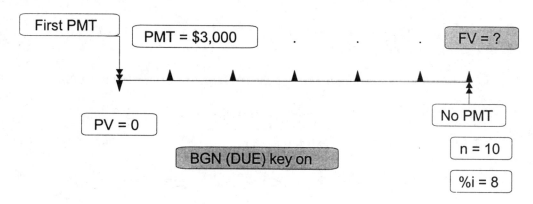

Compute FV = $46,936.46

VI.   **Present Value: Annuity [p. 294]**

A. The present value of an annuity represents the sum of the present value of the individual flows.

B. The formula for the present value of an annuity is:

$$PV_A = A\left[\frac{1 - \dfrac{1}{(1+i)^n}}{i}\right]$$

(9-5a; page 295)

C. **(Optional)** The formula may be restated as:

$$PV_A = A \times PV_{IFA}$$

The PV_{IFA} term is found in appendix D.

D. Calculator

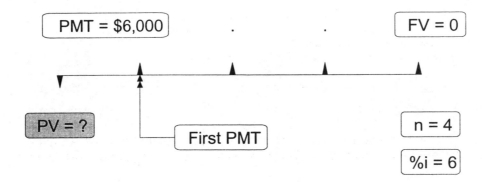

Compute FV = $20,790.63

E.

    1. Present Value: Annuity in Advance **[p. 295]**

$$PV_A = A_{BGN} \left[\frac{(1+i) - \dfrac{1}{(1+i)^{n-1}}}{i} \right]$$

(9-5b; page 295)

    Also: $PV_A \, (BGN) = PV_A \times (1 + i)$

    2. Calculator

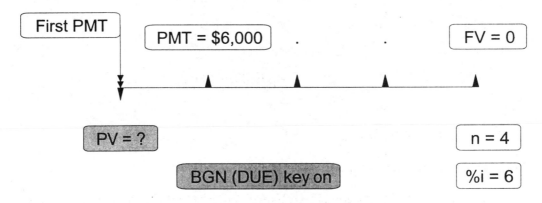

Compute FV = $22,038.07

VII. **Annuity Equalling a Future Value [p. 296]**

    A. The process can be reversed to find an annuity value that will grow to equal a future sum.

    B. The formula for an annuity equal to a future value is:

$$A = FV_A \left[\frac{i}{(1+i)^n - 1} \right]$$

(9-6a; page 296)

C. The formula may be restated as:

$$FV_A = A \times FV_{IFA}$$

$$A = \frac{FV_A}{FV_{IFA}}$$

The FV_{IFA} term is found in Appendix C.

D. Calculator

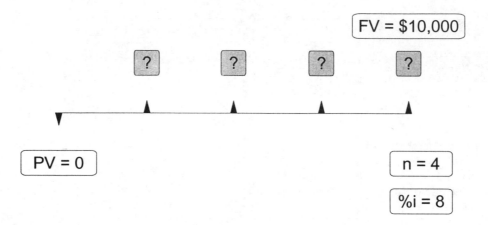

FV = $10,000

?   ?   ?   ?

PV = 0

n = 4

%i = 8

Compute PMT = $2,219.21

E. Annuity equalling a future value: Annuity in advance

$$A_{BGN} = FV_A \left[\frac{i}{(1+i)^{n+1} - (1+i)} \right]$$
(9-6b; page 297)

VIII. **Annuity Equalling a Present Value [p. 297]**

A. The formula for the present value of an annuity is:

$$A = PV_A \left[\frac{i}{1 - \frac{1}{(1+i)^n}} \right]$$
(9-7a; page 297)

B. The formula may be restated as:

$$PV_A = A \times PV_{IFA}$$

$$A = \frac{PV_A}{PV_{IFA}}$$ The PV_{IFA} term is found in Appendix D.

C. The annuity value equal to a present value is often associated with withdrawal of funds from an initial deposit or the repayment of a loan.

D. Annuity equalling a present value: Annuity in advance **[p 298]**

$$A_{BGN} = PV_A \left[\frac{i}{(1+i) - \dfrac{1}{(1+i)^{n-1}}} \right]$$

(9-7b; page 298)

IX. **Determining the Yield on an Investment [p. 299]**

A. The formula for the yield on an investment is:

$$i = \left(\frac{FV}{PV} \right)^{\frac{1}{n}} - 1$$

(9-8; page 300)

B. **(Optional)** The unknown value is now assumed to be the yield.
   1. Yield: Present value of a single amount (page 300)
      a. The rate equating FV to PV must be found.

$$PV_{IF} = \frac{PV}{FV}$$

      b. The first step is to determine PV_{IF}.
      c. The next step is to find this value in Appendix B to identify the yield.
      d. Interpolation may be used to find a more exacting answer.

   2. Yield: Present value of an annuity (page 302) (no formula).
      a. The rate equating A to PV must be found.

$$PV_{IFA} = \frac{PV_A}{A}$$

      b. The first step is to determine PV_{IFA}.
      c. The next step is to find this value in Appendix D to identify the yield.
      d. Interpolation may be used to find a more exacting answer.

C. Calculator

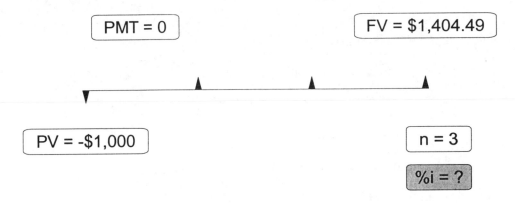

PMT = 0   FV = $1,404.49

PV = -$1,000   n = 3

%i = ?

Compute %i = 11.99%

101

X.   **Special Considerations in Time Value Analysis [p. 302]**

  A. More frequent than annual compounding. (Semi-annual, quarterly, monthly, etc compounding).

    1. Multiply the number of years by the number of compounding periods during the year.
    2. Divide the stated interest rate by the number of compounding periods during the year. The future value of $10,000 after three years at 8% annual interest, compounded quarterly would be:

$$FV = 10,000\left(1 + \frac{.08}{4}\right)^{(3)(4)} = 10,000(1 + .02)^{12} = 10,000(1.268)$$

$$FV = 12,680$$

  B. Present value of series of unequal payments.

    1. Many business transactions generate differing cash flows each year. In such cases, the present value of each payment must be computed individually and summed.

       Assume a 10% discount rate:

n = 1	FV = 8,000	PV =	$ 7,273
n = 2	FV = 6,000	PV =	4,958
n = 3	FV = 3,000	PV =	2,254
			$14,485

    2. Some series of payments may combine an annuity with unequal payments. The present value of the annuity may be determined and added to the present value of the other payments.

       Assume a 12% discount rate:

n = 1	FV = 8,000		PV = $ 7,143
n = 2	FV = 6,000		
n = 3	FV = 6,000	PV = 14,411 (n = 1)	PV = 12,867
n = 4	FV = 6,000		
n = 5	FV = 3,000		PV = 1,702
			$21,712

  C. Present value of deferred annuity.

    1. Two step solution process
    2. Single step solution

       PV_{IFA} for total period
       $- PV_{IFA}$ for initial period

       PV_{IFA} for deferred period × annuity

XI.   **Canadian Mortgages [p. 306]**

  A. Monthly payments and semiannual interest compounding require a monthly effective interest rate by formula:

$$i = \left(1 + \frac{r}{2}\right)^{\frac{1}{6}} - 1$$

     r = nominal annual rate

B. If $95,999 is borrowed over 20 years at 8%.

Calculator

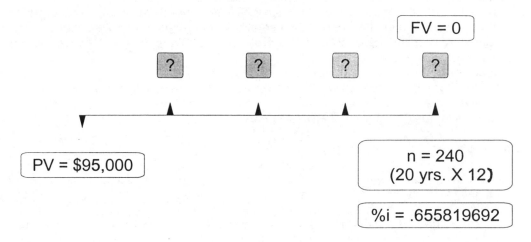

Compute PMT = $786.94

XII. Review of Formulas

See text pages 308-310 or insert card.

XIII. Study Hints for Time Value of Money

A. Tables

1. The key to using future value and present value tables efficiently is to be thoroughly familiar with their characteristics. Study them closely.
    a. Each table has three dimensions: interest rate, number of periods, and an internal value called the interest factor.
    b. Whenever two of the three dimensions of a table are known, the third is also determined. The process is similar to determining the mileage between two cities on a roadmap mileage chart.

2. Knowing the relationship between the present-value tables is particularly important in solving present value problems that combine annuity streams with uneven payments. An interest factor in the present value of an annuity table is the summation of the interest factors in the corresponding column of the present value of $1 table.

Present value of $1 10%				Present value of Annuity of $1 10%	
1	.909			1	.909
2	.826	1.736		2	1.736
3	.751		2.487	3	2.487

3. Notice that the present-value interest factor for any particular year may be determined from the present value of an annuity table.

   IF (n = 3, i = 10%) = 2.487 − 1.736 = 0.751

B. Calculators

1. A time line, especially for more complex problems indicating cash inflows and cash outflows, is of great assistance in handling and conceptualizing a time line problem.
2. Today, most students use calculators extensively to make time value of money related calculations. In fact, many professors require the use of calculators and sometimes preclude the use of future-value and present-value tables. Other professors require students to do the calculations the "hard" way - with paper and pencil.
While efficiency argues for the use of calculators, it is very important for the student to understand the mathematics involved; in other words, avoid the "black box" syndrome. Study the equations so that you may have insight as to the range of a reasonable answer. Such study will help you recognize hastily made, embarrassing errors.

C. Overall

1. A real world experience will further indicate the need to understand the mathematics of your calculator generated answer. The author once received a phone call from the senior loan officer of a billion dollar lending institution asking for help in the calculation of an interest rate on a loan. A customer had demanded to see the interest rate calculated by hand--paper and pencil, not by the calculator. The loan officer had used the calculator and/or computer for so long, he could not calculate the interest rate by hand. Needless to say, he was embarrassed.
2. If you are required or choose to use a calculator for your calculations, you should become thoroughly familiar with the instrument prior to an exam. Purchasing a calculator that will handle uneven cash flows the day before the exam is risky business. Block, Hirt and Short provide basic instructions for using three commonly-used calculators in Appendix E of the text.

Chapter 9: Multiple Choice Questions

1. The formula for computing the present value of a single amount is: [p. 291]

   a. $PV = FV\left[\dfrac{1}{(1+i)^n}\right]$

   b. $FV = PV(1+i)^n$

   c. $FV_A = A\left[\dfrac{(1+i)^n - 1}{i}\right]$

   d. $PV_A = A\left[\dfrac{1 - \dfrac{1}{(1+i)^n}}{i}\right]$

   e. None of the above are correct

2. To determine the future value of an amount that will earn 8% interest paid quarterly for five years, the number of periods and discount rate will be: [p. 303]
   a. 8%, 5.
   b. 2%, 5.
   c. 32%, 20.
   d. 8%, 20.
   e. 2%, 20.

3. The owner of a building that costs $100,000 who wishes to determine the annual rent necessary to earn a 10% return on the investment in 10 years should use the: [p. 297]
   a. Annuity equaling a future value.
   b. Annuity equaling a present value.
   c. Future value of annuity formula.
   d. Future value formula.
   e. Any of the above are correct

4. The time value of money must be considered in capital outlay decisions because: [Chapter. 9]
   a. Accounting rules require it.
   b. Cash flows are not known with certainty.
   c. Cash inflows and cash outflows occur at different points in time.
   d. Inflation greatly reduces the outflows.
   e. A dollar received in the future is more valuable than a dollar received today.

5. One seeking to find the amount that must be deposited each year at 12% interest in order to accumulate $500,000 by retirement in 30 years should use which of the following formulas? [p. 293]

   a. $PV = FV\left[\dfrac{1}{(1+i)^n}\right]$

   b. $FV = PV(1+i)^n$

   c. $FV_A = A\left[\dfrac{(1+i)^n - 1}{i}\right]$

   d. $PV_A = A\left[\dfrac{1 - \dfrac{1}{(1+i)^n}}{i}\right]$

   e. Either b or d may be used.

6. The interest rate used to determine the present value of future cash flows is known as the: [p. 287]
   a. Annuity.
   b. Interest factor.
   c. Internal value.
   d. Discount rate.
   e. Interpolation.

7. A series of consecutive end-of-period payments or receipts of equal amount is called a(n): [p. 292]
   a. Annuity.
   b. Future value.
   c. Present value.
   d. Uneven series.
   e. Annuity due.

8. The values found in the present value and compound value tables are called: [p. 288]
   a. Interest rates.
   b. Interest factors.
   c. Discount rates.
   d. Annuities.
   e. Present values.

9. As long as an individual or business can employ dollars to earn a positive return, money will have: [p. 287]
   a. Time value.
   b. Present value greater than future value.
   c. Future value less than beginning value.
   d. Present value greater than beginning value.
   e. All of the above are correct

10. The present value of a 10-year annuity is $100,000. The future value of the annuity is $500,000. If the appropriate interest rate is 8%, which formula would be appropriate to compute annual annuity payment (or receipt)? [p. 296-299]
   a. Annuity equaling a future value.
   b. Annuity equaling a present value.
   c. Future value of annuity formula.
   d. Future value formula.
   e. Either annuity equaling a present value or future value may be used.

Multiple Choice Answer Key: Chapter 9

1.	a	2.	e	3.	b	4.	c	5.	c
6.	d	7.	a	8.	b	9.	a	10.	e

Chapter 9: Problems

9-1.   Mark Anderson deposits $5,000 in a savings account earning 8% interest annually.

   (a)   How much will be in the account at the end of the twelfth year?

   (b)   How many years would be required to accumulate $20,000 under the same assumptions?

9-2.   Shorty Stop, a professional baseball rookie, has just signed a five-year contract for $200,000 per year.

   (a)   Assuming an opportunity rate of 12%, what is the present value of Mr. Stop's contract?

   (b)   Suppose that Mr. Stop's contract requires a salary of $200,000 in each of the first three years and $400,000 in the latter two years, what is the present value of the contract?

9-3.   Mr. Paul Bearer may elect to take a lump-sum payment of $25,000 from his insurance policy or an annuity of $3,200 annually as long as he lives. How long must Mr. Bearer anticipate living for the annuity to be preferable to the lump sum if his opportunity rate is 8%?

9-4.   Ms. Erica Barham wishes to retire on the accumulation of $1,000,000.

   (a)   How many years must she work if she is able to save and invest $6,080 at 10% interest compounded annually?

   (b)   Suppose Ms. Barham wishes to retire in 40 years; how much must she save annually if the amount can be employed to earn 12%?

9-5.   The B&H Company recently issued $5,000,000 of 20-year bonds. The bond contract requires that a sinking fund be established that will enable the firm to pay off the bonds upon maturity.

   (a)   If the firm can earn 6% on the sinking fund payments, what annual payment will be required?

   (b)   Suppose the firm is not required to make the first sinking fund payment until the end of the sixth year. What annual payment would be required?

9-6.   Ms. Kristy Doler purchased 100 acres of land in 1990 for $100,000. If she sells the land for $5,000 per acre in 2010, what rate of return will she have earned on her investment? (Disregard property and income taxes.)

9-7.   Roy and Dale saved $5,000 per year for the first five years of their marriage. After the arrival of twin boys, Dale took a sabbatical from her job until the boys were six years old. Because of the decline in family income, saving was not possible, and withdrawals of $3,000 per year for six years were necessary. After Dale returned to a "paying" job, Roy and Dale were able to save $8,000 each year for the next 19 years before retiring.

   (a)   Using 10% as the appropriate interest rate, how much will Roy and Dale have accumulated at retirement?

   (b)   Assuming investment of their accumulated savings at 12%, how much can be withdrawn each year for 20 years? (Assume all contributions and withdrawals at the end of the year and disregard taxes.)

9-8.   Alicia Price just won the Publishers' Sweepstakes. She must decide whether to take a lump sum payment of $5,000,000 now or $1,000,000 at the end of each year for 25 years.

   (a)   If Alicia uses a discount rate of 14%, which payment plan should she choose? (Ignore tax effects--in the real world, however, taxes may be a major factor in the decision.)

   (b)   If Alicia assumes a discount rate of 20%, does your advice remain the same?

   (c)   If taxes at a rate of 30% must be paid on the lump sum or stream of receipts, will your choice in (a) above change?

9-9.   Jared Beville recently sold his baseball card collection for $10,000.

   (a)   If he reinvests the money in a mutual fund and earns 12% per year until he retires 40 years later, what is the value of his account? (Ignore taxes.)

   (b)   At retirement Jared will roll his investment into a fixed return account paying 8% per year. How much will he be able to withdraw each year over his projected 30-year retirement?

9-10.   Brandon Blow recently graduated with a B.S. in Finance. He is suffering from a malady common to new graduates--Car Fever. Brandon is trying to decide between two automobiles--a $20,000 ZZZ or a $15,000 XXX. Brandon must finance his purchase over a three-year period regardless of his choice of cars.

   (a)   Assuming an interest rate of 12%, what will Zachary's annual payment be on each car? (You may wish to calculate monthly payments to be more realistic.)

   (b)   Zachary plans to buy a new car every three years. If the difference in the price of cars is maintained through Zachary's 40-year career, how much could he accumulate if he always bought the cheaper car and earned 8% on the difference in annual payments? (Ignore resale values.)

9-11.   Smokey Stack smokes a pack of cigarettes a day. Each pack of cigarettes costs $1.80. Smokey is wondering how much money he could accumulate if he quit smoking and invested the money.

(a)   Assuming the saved amount is invested at the end of the year at a 6% rate of return, how much could he accumulate during the next 40 years. (Assume 365-day year; ignore taxes.)

(b)   How much could Smokey accumulate if he was able to earn 10%?

(c)   If Smokey earns 6% on the accumulated amount from (b) above, how much can he withdraw each year for the next 20 years before depleting his accumulation? (Ignore taxes.)

9-12.   Gretchen Cooper is considering opening a savings account as a precaution against unexpected expenses. Busy Bank promises to pay 8% compounded quarterly on amounts deposited for one year. Gretchen can earn 8% paid annually on deposits in her credit union without the one-year restriction on withdrawals.

(a)   In which of the institutions will Gretchen earn the most interest on a $2,000 deposit?

(b)   In which institution should Gretchen deposit her money?

9-13.   Dana Gulley is considering purchasing a house. Dana does not want to pay more than 25% of his income in annual house payments (principal and interest). Dana has determined that he can obtain a 30-year mortgage at a 10% interest rate. Use monthly payments, with semiannual compounding.

(a)   If Dana's annual income for the foreseeable future is $50,000, can he purchase a $140,000 home and remain within his limit?

(b)   What is the maximum price that Dana can pay for a house without exceeding his limit?

9-14.   Stacey Katz wishes to retire in 40 years. She is trying to determine what amount must be accumulated to provide $60,000 annually in **today's** dollars. (Ignore taxes.)

(a)   If Stacey assumes a 5% inflation rate, what annual income will be required to provide an amount equivalent in purchasing power to $60,000 today?

(b)   Stacey wishes to withdraw the amount calculated in (a) each year over his expected 30-year life span after retirement. If he expects to earn 8% interest on his portfolio during retirement, how much must he have accumulated at retirement?

(c)   The amount that Stacey calculated in (b) above is certainly eye-opening (scary even!). Can he possibly accumulate such a large sum? If he can earn 12% on his savings (investments), how much would he have to save each year to achieve his goal?

Chapter 9: Solutions

9-1.   **Mark Anderson**

(a) $FV = PV (1 + i)^n$
$FV = \$5,000 (1 + .08)^{12}$
$FV = \$5,000 (2.518)$
$FV = \textbf{\$12,590}$

Calculator:	$FV = ?$	$PV = \$5,000$	$PMT = 0$	$N = 12$	$\%i = 8.00\%$
Compute:	$FV = \textbf{\$12,590.85}$				

(b) $\$20{,}000 = \$5{,}000(1 + .08)^n$

$\dfrac{\$20{,}000}{\$5{,}000} = (1 + .08)^n$

$4 = (1.08)^n$

Read down the 8% column of the future value table until the value 4 is found. The value 4 is not found exactly, but it can be determined that N is approximately **18 years**.

Calculator:	$FV = \$20{,}000$	$PV = \$5{,}000$	$PMT = 0$	$N =?$	$\%i = 8.00\%$
Compute:	$N = 18.01$				

9-2. **Shorty Stop**
(a) *PV of an annuity*
$PV_A = A \times PV_{IFA}\ (n = 5,\ \%i = 12\%)$
$PV_A = \$200{,}000 \times 3.605$
$PV_A = \mathbf{\$721{,}000}$

Calculator:	$FV = 0$	$PV =?$	$PMT = \$200{,}000$	$N = 5$	$\%i = 12.00\%$
Compute:	$PV = \$720{,}955$				

(b) Present value of salary contract

Year	Salary	PV Factor 12%	Present Value
1	$200,000	.893	$178,600
2	200,000	.797	159,400
3	200,000	.712	142,400
4	400,000	.636	254,400
5	400,000	.567	226,800
			$961,600

An alternative way of computing the present value of the salary contract (b) is:
PV of contract $= \$200{,}000 \times 2.402 + 400{,}000\ (3.605 - 2.402)$
$= \$480{,}400 + \$481{,}200$
$= \mathbf{\$961{,}600}$

Calculator:	$FV = 0$	$PV =?$	$PMT = \$200{,}000$	$N = 3$	$\%i = 12.00\%$
Compute:	$PV = \$480{,}366$				

Calculator:	$FV = 0$	$PV =?$	$PMT = \$400{,}000$	$N = 2$	$\%i = 12.00\%$
Compute:	$PV = \$676{,}020$				
Then:	$FV = 0$	$PV =?$	$PMT = 0$	$N = 3$	$\%i = 12.00\%$
Compute:	$PV = \$481{,}178$				

$$\begin{array}{r} \$480{,}366 \\ \underline{481{,}178} \\ \textbf{Total: } PV = \quad \mathbf{\$961{,}544} \end{array}$$

9-3.   **Paul Bearer**

$$PV_A = A \times PV_{IFA}(n = ?, \%i = 8\%)$$
$$\$25,000 = \$3,200\ (PV_{IFA})$$
$$\frac{\$25,000}{\$3,200} = PV_{IFA}$$
$$PV_{IFA} = 7.81$$

N = approximately 13 years. Mr. Bearer must expect to live more than 13 years for the annuity to be preferable.

Calculator:	FV = $25,000	PV = 0	PMT = $3,000	N =?	%i = 8.00%
Compute:	**N = 12.74**				

9-4.   **Erica Barham**

(a)   *Future value of an annuity*

$$FV_A = A \times FV_{IFA}$$
$$\$1,000,000 = \$6,080 \times FV_{IFA}(n = ?, \%i = 10\%)$$
$$\frac{\$1,000,000}{\$6,080} = FV_{IFA}$$
$$164.474 = FV_{IFA}$$

N = **approximately 30 years**

Calculator:	FV = $1,000,000	PV = 0	PMT = $6,080	N =?	%i = 10.00%
Compute:	**N = 30**				

(b) $$\$1,000,000 = A \times FV_{IFA}(n = 40, \%i = 12\%)$$
$$\$1,000,000 = A \times 767.09$$
$$\frac{\$1,000,000}{767.09} = A = \$1,303.63$$

Calculator:	FV = $1,000,000	PV = 0	PMT =?	N = 40	%i = 12.00%
Compute:	**PMT = $1,303.63**				

9-5.   **B&H Company**

(a)   *Future value annuity*

$$FV_A = A \times FV_{IFA}$$
$$\$5,000,000 = A \times 36.786$$
$$\frac{\$5,000,000}{36.786} = A = \$135,921.27$$

Calculator:	FV = $5,000,000	PV = 0	PMT =?	N = 20	%i = 6.00%
Compute:	**PMT = $135,922.78**				

(b) $$FV_A = A \times FV_{IFA}(n = 15, i = 6\%)$$
$$\$5,000,000 = A \times 23.276$$
$$\frac{\$5,000,000}{23.276} = A = \$214,813.54$$ The first payment would not be made until the end of the sixth year.

Calculator:	FV = $5,000,000	PV = 0	PMT =?	N = 15	%i = 6.00%
Compute:	**PMT = $214,814.82**				

9-6. **Kristy Doler**

Selling price of land = $5,000 × 100 = $500,000
Future value
$$FV = PV (1 + i)^{20}$$
$$\frac{\$500,000}{\$100,000} = (1 + i)^{20}$$
$$5 = (1 + i)^{20}$$

Read across the twentieth row of the future value tables. The factor lies approximately halfway between the interest factors for 8% and 9%. Approximate rate of return = **8.5%**.
The rate of return can be determined more accurately by interpolation.

$$
\begin{array}{ll}
8\% & 4.661 \\
 & \left.\begin{array}{l} \\ 5.000 \end{array}\right\} .339 \\
9\% & 5.604
\end{array}\right\} .943
$$

$$Rate\ of\ return = 8\% + \frac{.339}{.943}(1\%) = 8\% + .359(1\%) = \textbf{8.36\%}$$

Calculator:	FV = $500,000	PV = $100,000	PMT = 0	N = 20	%i =?
Compute:	%i = **8.36%**				

9-7. **Roy and Dale**

(a)   *Accumulation at retirement*
FV_A *(Future value of an annuity)* = $A \times FV_{IFA}$ *(n = 5, %i = 10%)*
FV_A = $5,000 × 6.105 = $30,525

There are several ways to "handle" the next step of this problem. You may prefer a different procedure than the one shown.

PV_A *(Present value of an annuity)* = $A \times PV_{IFA}$ *(n = 6, %i = 10%)*
PV_A = $3,000 × 4.355 = $13,065

$30,525 – $13,065 = $17,460

FV *(Future value)* = $PV \times FV_{IF}$ *(n = 25, %i = 10%)*
FV = $17,460 × 10.835 = **$189,179.10**

An alternative approach to these steps follows.

Year	Beginning Amount	Interest Factor	Compound Amount	Withdrawal	Ending Amount
1*	$30,525.00	1.1	$33,577.50	$3,000	$30,577.50
2	$30,577.50	1.1	$33,635.25	$3,000	$30,635.25
3	$30,635.25	1.1	$33,698.78	$3,000	$30,698.78
4	$30,698.78	1.1	$33,768.66	$3,000	$30,768.66
5	$30,768.66	1.1	$33,845.53	$3,000	$30,845.53
6	$30,845.53	1.1	$33,930.08	$3,000	$30,930.08

*Year 1 (Year 6 – first year after twins are born).

$FV = PV \times FV_{IF}$ (n = 19, %i = 10%)
FV = $30,930.08 × 6.116 = **$189,168.37**

111

The $10.73 difference from the original calculation is due to rounding differences in the tables. Although both approaches yield the "same" result, the ease of the first approach should be obvious to the student.

To conclude the problem, the future value of the savings after Dale returns to the work force must be computed.

$FV_A = A \times FV_{IFA} (n = 19, i = 10\%)$
$FV_A = \$8,000 \times 51.159 = \textbf{\$409,272}$

Accumulation at retirement = $189,179.10 + $409,272 = **$598,451.10**

Calculator:	FV =?	PV = 0	PMT = $5,000	N = 5	%i = 10%
Compute	FV = **$30,525.50**				

Calculator:	FV =?	PV = $30,525.50	PMT = – $3,000	N = 6	%i = 10%
Compute	FV = **$30,930.96**				

Calculator:	FV =?	PV = $30,930.96	PMT = $8,000	N = 19	%i = 10%
Compute	FV = **$598,443.63**				

(b) Withdrawal each year for 20 years after retirement
Present value of an annuity
$PV_A = A \times PV_{IFA} (n = 20, \%i = 12\%)$
$\$598,451.10 = A \times 7.469$
$$\frac{\$598,451.10}{7.469} = A = \textbf{\$80,124.66}$$

Author's Note: This problem is not intended to be sexually discriminatory. If you are concerned with Dale's staying home to take care of the twins, simply change the names and let Roy remain at home or recompute the answer assuming that Dale returns to the work force immediately and savings contributions continue.

Calculator:	FV = 0	PV = $598,443.63	PMT =?	N = 20	%i = 12%
Compute	PMT = **$80,118.90**				

9-8. **Alicia Price**
(a) **Choose the annuity stream**
$PV_A = \$1,000,000 \times 6.873 = \textbf{\$6,873,000}$

Calculator:	FV = 0	PV =?	PMT = $1,000,000	N = 25	%i = 14%
Compute	PV = **$6,872,927**				

Although the 25, $1,000,000 payments may seem much greater than the lump-sum, once they are time-adjusted, the difference is much less.

(b) $PV_A = \$1,000,000 \times 4.948 = \textbf{\$4,948,000}$

Calculator:	FV = 0	PV =?	PMT = $1,000,000	N = 25	%i = 20%
Compute	PV = **$4,947,587**				

At the higher discount rate of 20%, the lump sum has a higher present value. **Choose the lump sum**.

(c) *Taxes on lump sum* = $\$5,000,000 \times .30 = \$1,500,000$
Net receipt = **$\$3,500,000$**

Taxes on annual receipt = $\$1,000,000 \times .30 = \$300,000$
Net annual receipt = $\$700,000$

$PV_A = \$700,000 \times 6.873 = \textbf{\$4,811,100}$

Calculator:	$FV = 0$	$PV =?$	$PMT = \$700,000$	$N = 25$	$\%i = 14\%$
Compute	$PV = \textbf{\$4,811,049}$				

The difference in the present values = $\$4,811,049 - \$3,500,000 = \$1,311,049$. This difference equals $(1 - \text{tax rate}) \times$ the difference when taxes were ignored: $(\$6,872,927 - \$5,000,000) \times (1 - .3)$ = $\$1,311,049$.

9-9. **Jared Beville**
(a) $FV = PV \times FV_{IF}$
$FV = \$10,000 \times 93.051 = \textbf{\$930,510}$

Calculator:	$FV =?$	$PV =10,000$	$PMT = 0$	$N = 40$	$\%i = 12\%$
Compute	$FV = \textbf{\$930,510}$				

(b) $PV_A = A \times PV_{IFA}$, solve for A
$\$930,510 = A \times 11.258$
$A = \textbf{\$82,653.22}$

Calculator:	$FV = 0$	$PV = \$930,510$	$PMT =?$	$N = 30$	$\%i = 8\%$
Compute	$PMT = \textbf{\$82,654.79}$				

9-10. **Brandon Blow**
(a) $PV_A = A \times PV_{IFA}$
$\$20,000 = A \times 2.402$
$A = \textbf{\$8,326.39}$ = annual payment on ZZZ

Calculator:	$FV = 0$	$PV = \$20,000$	$PMT =?$	$N = 3$	$\%i = 12\%$
Compute	$PMT = \textbf{\$8,326.98}$				

Calculator:	FV	$=$	0	Compute:	$PMT = \textbf{\$8,326.98}$
	PV	$=$	$\$20,000$		
	PMT	$=$	$?$		
	n	$=$	3		
	$i\%$	$=$	12%		

$\$15,000 = A \times 2.402$
$A = \textbf{\$6,244.80}$ annual payment on XXX

Calculator:	$FV = 0$	$PV = \$15,000$	$PMT =?$	$N = 3$	$\%i = 12\%$
Compute	$PMT = \textbf{\$6,245.23}$				

(b)   *Difference in annual payments* = $8,326.39 – $6,244.80 = $2,081.59 **(Calculator $2,081.75)**
$$FV_A = A \times FV_{IFA}$$
$$FV_A = \$2,081.59 \times 259.06 = \mathbf{\$539,256.71}$$

Calculator:	FV =?	PV = 0	PMT = $2,081.75	N = 40	%i = 8%
Compute	**FV = $539,289.69**				

That's a lot of money. Brandon had better really enjoy driving the more expensive car. Note that the price of the cars is not relevant to the calculation. As long as a $5,000 difference exists, the difference in financing costs will be the same.

9-11.   Smokey Stack
(a)   *Annual cost of cigarettes* = $1.80 × 365 = $657
$$FV_A = A \times FV_{IFA}$$
$$FV_A = \$657 \times 154.76 = \mathbf{\$101,677.32}$$

Calculator:	FV =?	PV = 0	PMT = $657	N = 40	%i = 6%
Compute	**FV = $101,678.61**				

(b) FV_A = $657 x 442.59 = **$290,781.63**

Calculator:	FV =?	PV = 0	PMT = $657	N = 40	%i = 10%
Compute	**FV = $290,783.31**				

(c) $$PV_A = A \times PV_{IFA}$$
$$\$290,781.63 = A \times 11.47$$
$$\frac{\$290,781.63}{11.47} = A = \mathbf{\$25,351.49}$$

Calculator:	FV = 0	PV = $290,783.31	PMT =?	N = 20	%i = 6%
Compute	**PMT = $25,351.81**				

Of course, Smokey may need to plan for a longer life span if he stops smoking.

9-12.   Gretchen Cooper
(a)   Credit Union:
Interest = .08 × $2,000 = **$160**

Busy Bank:

$$FV = \$2,000 \times \left(1 + \frac{.08}{4}\right)^4 = \$2,000 \times 1.08243 = \mathbf{\$2,164.86}$$

Interest = **$165**

Calculator:	FV =?	PV = $2,000	PMT = 0	N = 4	%i = 2%
Compute	**FV = $2,164.86**				

(b)   Although Gretchen will earn $4 more (actually more if calculated without using tables) because of quarterly compounding, she must consider the need to access the money quickly. In this situation, the lower interest may be the better choice.

9-13. **Dana Gulley**
    (a)   *Annual limit* = .25 × 50,000 = $12,500
         First: Calculate the monthly effective interest rate.
         $r = (1 + .10/ 2)^{1/6} - 1$

Calculator:	$FV = 1.05$	$PV = -1.00$	$PMT = 0$	$N = 6$	$\%i = ?$
Compute	$\%i = 0.816484604\%$				

Then calculate the monthly payment.

Calculator:	$FV = 0$	$PV = \$140,000$	$PMT = ?$	$N = 360\ (12 \times 30)$	$\%i = 0.816484604\%$
Compute	$PMT = \$1,207.74$				

Yearly payments = $1,207.74 × 12 = **$14,492.82**

No, he could not purchase a $140,000 home under the specified terms without exceeding his self-imposed limit.

    (b)   Maximum monthly payment = $12,500/ 12 = $1,041.67

Calculator:	$FV = 0$	$PV = ?$	$PMT = \$1,041.67$	$N = 360\ (12 \times 30)$	$\%i = 0.816484604\%$
Compute	$PV = \$120,749.43$				

9-14. **Stacey Katz**
    (a) $FV = PV \times FV_{IF} = \$60,000 \times 7.040 = \textbf{\$422,400}$

Calculator:	$FV = ?$	$PV = \$60,000$	$PMT = 0$	$N = 40$	$\%i = 5\%$
Compute	$FV = \$422,399.32$				

At an annual inflation rate of 5%, it will take $422,400, forty years from now to maintain $60,000 purchasing power in today's dollars.

    (b) $PV_A = A \times PV_{IFA} = \$422,400 \times 11.258 = \textbf{\$4,755,379.20}$

Calculator:	$FV = ?$	$PV = 0$	$PMT = \$422.399.32$	$N = 30$	$\%i = 8\%$
Compute	$FV = \$4,755,280.06$				

Note: This calculation ignores any inflation during the retirement period. With inflation (which is probable), a larger amount would be necessary to maintain purchasing power.

    (c) $FV_A = A \times FV_{IFA}$
         $\$4,755,379.20 = A \times 767.09$

$$\frac{\$4,755,379.20}{767.09} = A = \textbf{\$6,199.25}$$

Calculator:	$FV = \$4,755,280.06$	$PV = 0$	$PMT = ?$	$N = 40$	$\%i = 12\%$
Compute	$PMT = \$6,199.10$				

The amount, though significant, is not nearly as large as one might initially think. Of course, Stacey might not be able to save much in the early years of her career, but may be able to save much more in the latter years. The problem also ignores several important components of retirement income, such as employer retirement plans and CPP.

Study Note: To avoid additional complexity, most of these problems explicitly or implicitly ignore taxes. In the "real world," this should never be done.

Summary: Valuation is the key concept of finance. This chapter focuses on how financial assets are valued and how investors establish the rate of return they demand.

I. **Valuation Concepts [p. 322]**

   A. The value of an asset is the present value of the expected cash flows associated with the asset. In order to compute the present value of an asset, an investor must know or estimate the amount of expected cash flows, the timing of expected cash flows and the risk characteristics of the expected flows (to assist in establishing the discount rate to be used as the required rate of return).

   B. Actually, the price (present value) of an asset will be based on the collective assessment of the asset's cash flow characteristics by the many capital market participants.

II. **Valuation of Bonds [p. 322]**

   A. The value of a bond is derived from cash flows composed of periodic interest payments and a principal payment at maturity.

   B. The present value (price) of a bond can be expressed as follows:

$$P_b = \sum_{t=1}^{n} \frac{I_t}{(1+Y)^t} + \frac{P_n}{(1+Y)^n}$$

(10-1; page 323)

Where:
$$
\begin{aligned}
P_b &= \text{the market price of the bond} \\
I_t &= \text{the periodic interest payments } \textbf{(Fixed by contract)} \\
P_n &= \text{the principal payment at maturity } \textbf{(Fixed by contract)} \\
t &= \text{the period from 1 to n} \\
n &= \text{the total number of periods} \\
Y &= \text{the yield to maturity (required rate of return)}
\end{aligned}
$$

or graphical as:

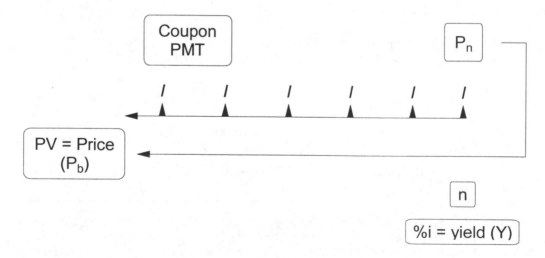

C. (Optional) The present value tables may be used to compute the price of a bond. The stream of periodic interest payments constitutes an annuity. The present value of the stream of interest payments may be computed by multiplying the periodic interest payment by the present value of an annuity interest factor.

$$PV_A = A \times PV_{IFA} \ (n, \ i)$$

Where: PV_A = present value of a stream of n interest payments
A = periodic interest payment (same as I_t above)
I = the market required rate of return

The present value of the principal payment may be computed by applying the present value of a $1 formula.

$$PV = FV \times PV_{IF} \ (n, \ i)$$

Where: PV = present value of principal payment
FV = the principal payment at the end of the nth period
I = the market required rate of return (yield to maturity)

The present value (price) of the bond will be the sum of the present value of the interest payments plus the present value of the principal.

Example: Compute the present value (price) of a bond that is paying $100 annually (assume a $1,000 par value bond and a 10% coupon rate) in interest if the bond will mature in eight years and the market determined required rate of return (yield to maturity) is 12%.

$P_b = \$100 \times PV_{IFA} \ (n = 8, \ i = 12\%) + \$1,000 \times PV_{IF} \ (n = 8th, \ i = 12\%)$
$P_b = \$100 \ (4.968) + \$1,000 \ (0.404)$
$P_b = \$496.80 + \$404 = \$900.80$

D. Calculator (using graphical illustration):

P_n	=	FV	=	$1,000
I	=	PMT	=	$100
N	=	N	=	8
Y	=	i	=	12%
Compute PV	=	P_b	=	$900.65

E. An understanding of the relationship between the required rate of return **(yield to maturity)** and the coupon rate (the annual interest payment divided by the par value) will allow one to "anticipate" the value of a bond prior to calculation.

If the market rate is > the coupon rate, the bond will sell at a discount (below par value)
If the market rate is = the coupon rate, the bond will sell at par value
If the market rate is < the coupon rate, the bond will sell at a premium (above par value)

F. Yield to maturity **[p. 325]**

1. Three factors influence an investor's required rate of return on a bond.
   a. The required real rate of return-the rate of return demanded for giving up current use of funds on a non-inflation adjusted basis.
   b. An inflation premium-a premium to compensate the investor for the effect of inflation on the value of the dollar.
   c. Risk premium-all financial decisions are made within a risk-return framework. An astute investor will require compensation for risk exposure. There are two types of risk of primary interest in determining the required rate of return (yield to maturity) on a bond:
      i. Business risk-the possibility of a firm not being able to sustain its competitive position and growth in earnings.
      ii. Financial risk-the possibility that a firm will be unable to meet its debt obligations as they come due.

2. Bond prices are inversely related to required rates of return. A change in the required rate of return will cause a change in the bond price in the opposite direction. The impact of the change in required rate of return on the bond price is dependent upon the remaining time to maturity. The impact will be greater the longer the time to maturity.

G. Determining yield to maturity **[p. 330]**

1. If the bond price, coupon rate, and number of years to maturity are known, the yield to maturity (market determined required rate of return) can be computed.
   a. Trial and error process. This process requires one to "guess" various yields until the yield to maturity that will cause the present value of the stream of interest payments plus the present value of principal payment to equal the bond price is determined. The initial "guess" is not completely blind, however, since the relationship between the coupon rate, yield to maturity (market rate), and the bond price is known.

   For example, if a $1,000 par value bond maturing in 20 years with a coupon rate of 10% was priced in the market at $800, we would know that the yield to maturity was greater than 10%. As an initial guess, try 14%.

   $800 \neq $100 ($PV_{IFA}$, $n = 20$, $i = 14\%$) + $1,000 ($PV_{IF}$, $n = 20$, $i = 14\%$)
   $800 = $100 (6.623) + $1,000 (0.073)

   $800 \neq $662.30 + $73 = $735.30

   The initial estimate of 14% is too high. A lower rate must be "tried." Try 12%.

   $800 \neq $100(7.469) + $1,000(.104) = $850.90

   Now we know that the yield to maturity is less than 14% but more than 12%. Try 13%.

   $800 \neq $100(7.025) + $1,000(.087) = $702.50 + $87 = $789.50

   Again, 13% does not exactly equal the yield to maturity. The actual yield to maturity is slightly less than 13%. Interpolation will allow a more exact calculation.

   b. (Optional) Often, a less exact calculation of the yield to maturity is sufficient. Using the **approximate yield to maturity** approach:

   $$Y^I = \frac{Annual\ interest\ payment + \dfrac{Principal\ payment - Price\ of\ the\ bond}{Number\ of\ years\ to\ maturity}}{0.6\left(Price\ of\ the\ bond\right) + 0.4\left(Principal\ payment\right)}$$ (Footnote p. 332)

   Using the previous bond example, to illustrate:

   $$Y^I = \frac{\$100 + \dfrac{\$1,000 - \$800}{20}}{0.6\left(\$800\right) + 0.4\left(\$1,000\right)} = \frac{\$100 + \$10}{\$480 + \$400} = 0.1250 = 12.50\%$$

   c. An exact calculation of the yield to maturity can be made using a good calculator or computer software.

Calculator:	P_n	=	FV	=	$1,000
	I	=	PMT	=	$100
	N	=	N	=	20
	PV	=	P_b	=	$800
Compute:	Y	=	$i\%$	=	**12.82%**

118

H. Often interest payments are made more frequently than once a year. Semiannual interest payments are common. To compute the price of such a bond, we divide the annual amount of interest and yield to maturity by two and multiply the number of years to maturity by two.

A $1,000 bond with a 10% coupon rate would pay $100 per year. The bondholder would receive, however, $50 at the end of the first six months and the remaining $50 at the end of the year. Stated differently, the bondholder would receive a 5% payment each six months. In **II.D.**, a $1,000 bond with a 10% coupon rate and eight years to maturity was found to have a present value of $900.65 when the market required rate of return was 12%. Assuming that the bond has the same characteristics but pays $50 semiannually and the market rate of return is 12% compounded semiannually, the price of the bond would be: [p.333]

Calculator:	P_n	=	FV	=	$1,000	
	I	=	PMT	=	$50	($100/ 2)
	N	=	N	=	16	(8 × 2)
	Y	=	i	=	6%	(12%/ 2)
Compute PV	=		P_b	=	**$898.94**	

III. **Valuation of Preferred Stock [p. 334]**

A. Preferred stock is usually valued as a perpetual stream of fixed dividend payments.

$$P_p = \frac{D_p}{\left(1+K_p\right)^1} + \frac{D_p}{\left(1+K_p\right)^2} + \frac{D_p}{\left(1+K_p\right)^3} + \frac{D_p}{\left(1+K_p\right)^4} + \dots + \frac{D_p}{\left(1+K_p\right)^\infty} \qquad \text{(10-2; page 334)}$$

Where: P_p = the price of preferred stock.
D_p = the annual dividend for preferred stock.
K_p = the required rate of return (discount rate) applied to preferred stock dividends.

B. Since the dividend stream is a **perpetuity**, the preferred stock valuation formula can be reduced to a more usable form.

$$P_p = \frac{D_p}{K_p} \qquad \text{(10-3; page 335)}$$

An investor who required an 8% rate of return would value a share of preferred stock paying $5 in dividends per year as follows:

$$P_p = \frac{\$5}{.08} = \$62.50$$

If the investor's required rate of return increased to 12%, he would be willing to pay only $41.67 for a share of the stock.

C. If K_p changes after preferred stock is issued, P_p will change in an inverse fashion.

1. Since preferred stock theoretically has a perpetual life, it is highly sensitive to changes in the required rate of return (K_p).

D. If the market price of preferred stock and the annual dividend are known, the market determined required rate of return may be computed by using the valuation equation (10-3) and solving for K_p.

$$K_p = \frac{D_p}{P_p} \qquad \text{(10-4; page 336)}$$

IV. **Valuation of Common Stock [p. 336]**

A. The value of a share of common stock is the present value of an expected stream of dividends.

$$P_0 = \frac{D_1}{(1+K_e)^1} + \frac{D_2}{(1+K_e)^2} + \frac{D_3}{(1+K_e)^3} + \ldots + \frac{D_\infty}{(1+K_e)^\infty}$$ (10-5; page 336)

Where: P_o = price of the stock at time zero (today)
D = dividend for each year
K_e = the required rate of return for common stock

B. Unlike dividends on most preferred stock, common stock dividends may vary. The valuation formula may be applied, with modification, to three different circumstances: **no growth in dividends, constant growth in dividends, and variable growth in dividends.**

1. No growth in dividends: Common stock with constant (no growth) dividends is valued in the same manner as preferred stock.

$$P_0 = \frac{D_0}{K_e}$$ (10-6; page 337)

Where: P_o = price of common stock.
D_o = current annual dividend (common) = D_1 (expected to remain the same in the future).
K_e = required rate of return for common stock.

2. Constant growth in dividends: The price of common stock with constant growth in dividends is the present value of an infinite stream of growing dividends. Fortunately, in this circumstance the basic valuation equation can be reduced to the more usable form below if the discount rate (K_e) is assumed to be greater than the growth rate.

$$P_0 = \frac{D_1}{K_e - g}$$ (10-8; page 338)

Where: D_1 = dividend expected at the end of the first year = $D_o (1+g)$
g = constant growth rate in dividends
P_o, K_e = same as previously defined

a. The above formula, which is labeled 10-8 in the text, can also be thought to represent the present value of dividends for a period of time (such as n = 3) plus the present value of the stock price after a period of time (such as P_3). Since P_3 represents the present value of dividends from D_4 through D_∞, P_o will still represent the present value of all future dividends.
b. The value of P_o is quite sensitive to any change in K_e (required rate of return) and g (the growth rate).
c. Rearrangement of the constant growth equation allows the calculation of the required rate of return, K_e, when P_o, D_1, and g are given. The first term represents the dividend yield that the shareholder expects to receive and the second term represents the anticipated growth in dividends, earnings and stock price.

$$K_e = \frac{D_1}{P_0} + g$$ (10-9; page 341)

3. Variable growth in dividends: The present value of any pattern of dividends can be computed. Some variable patterns, however, are assumed to occur more often than others. Supernormal growth and the "no dividend" approach are the patterns most often assumed.

Refer to page 358 of text for a time line.

a. **Supernormal growth**--an exceptional rate of dividend growth is initially expected followed by a constant rate thereafter. Suppose a firm's current dividend of $2 is expected to increase by 14% each year for the next five years before settling down to a 5% rate of growth thereafter.

$$P_0 = \frac{\$2.00(1.14)^1}{(1+K_e)^1} + \frac{\$2.00(1.14)^2}{(1+K_e)^2} + \frac{\$2.00(1.14)^3}{(1+K_e)^3} + \frac{\$2.00(1.14)^4}{(1+K_e)^4} + \frac{\$2.00(1.14)^5}{(1+K_e)^5}$$

$$+ \frac{\$2.00(1.14)^5(1+.05)}{(1+K_e)^6} + ... + \frac{\$2.00(1.14)^5(1+.05)^\infty}{(1+K_e)^\infty}$$

Assuming a required rate of return of 12%, the price of a share of the firm's stock can be computed as follows:

P_0 = $2.28 (.893) + $2.60 (.797) + $2.96 (.712) + $3.37 (.636) + $3.84 (.567)

$$+ \frac{D_6}{(1+K_e)^6} + ... + \frac{D_\infty}{(1+K_e)^\infty}$$

Beginning with the sixth year, the dividend is assumed to grow at a constant rate.

$D_6 = D_5 (1.05)$
$D_6 = \$3.84(1.05) = \$4.03$

Using the constant growth formula previously discussed, the price of the firm's stock at the end of the fifth year can be computed. The price at the end of the fifth year, of course, is the present value (at the end of year 5) of dividends D_6 through D_∞ , as follows:

$$P_5 = \frac{D_6}{(1+K_e)^6} + ... + \frac{D_\infty}{(1+K_e)^\infty}$$

$$= \frac{D_6}{(K_e - g)} = \frac{\$4.03}{(.12 - .05)} = \mathbf{\$57.57}$$

P_5, $57.57, must be discounted (present valued), however, to determine the value at time zero.

P_0 = $2.28 (.893) + $2.60 (.797) + $2.96 (.712) + $3.37 (.636) + $3.84 (.567) + $57.57 (.567)
P_0 = $2.03 + $2.07 + $2.11 + $2.14 + $2.18 + $32.64
P_0 = $43.17

b. Another type of variable growth is where the firm is assumed to pay **no dividends** for a period of time and then begins paying dividends. In this case, the present value of deferred dividends can be computed as a representation of value.

  i. Suppose a firm will not pay a dividend during the next ten years but beginning in year eleven the firm will pay a $10 dividend each year. This is a "no-dividend-no-growth" situation.

$$P_0 = \frac{P_{10}}{(1+K_e)^{10}}, \qquad with \quad P_{10} = \frac{\$10}{K_e}$$

If an investor's required rate of return is 15%, P_{10} would be P_{10} = $10/ 0.15 = $66.67. The present value of this delayed dividend stream would be found as follows:

$$P_0 = \frac{D_{10}}{(1+K)^{10}} = \frac{\$66.67}{(1+.15)^{10}} = \frac{\$66.67}{4.04556} = \mathbf{\$16.48}$$

ii. Instead of a fixed dividend following a no-dividend period, a firm's dividend may grow at a constant rate. Replacing the assumption of a constant dividend in (1) above with an expectation of a 5% constant dividend growth rate, the present value (price of stock) of the expected dividends is:

$$P_0 = \frac{P_{10}}{(1 + K_e)^{10}}$$

P_{10}, however, in this situation is:

$$P_{10} = \frac{D_{11}}{(K_e - g)} = \frac{\$10}{(.15 - .05)} = \frac{\$10}{.10} = \$100$$

$$P_0 = \frac{P_{10}}{(1 + K_e)^{10}} = \frac{\$100}{1.15^{10}} = \frac{\$100}{4.04556} = \mathbf{\$24.72}$$

4. Stock valuation may also be linked to the concept of price-earnings ratios discussed in Chapter 2. Although this is a less theoretical, more pragmatic approach than the dividend valuation models, the end results may be similar because of the common emphasis on risk and growth under either approach.

V. **Review of Formulas**

See text pages 345 - 347 or insert card.

Chapter 10: Multiple Choice Questions

1. Which of the following is considered to be a hybrid security? [p. 334]
   a. Corporate bond
   b. Common stock
   c. Preferred stock
   d. Treasury bond
   e. None of the above are correct

2. Which of the following describes the relationship between bond prices and interest rates? [p. 327-329]
   a. Bond prices move in the same direction as interest rates.
   b. Bond prices may go up or down when interest rates rise (all other factors held constant).
   c. Bond prices move inversely with interest rates.
   d. Bond prices are independent of interest rates.
   e. All of the above are correct

3. A $1,000 30-year corporate bond that pays $80 annually in interest is current selling for $892. Which of the following relationships is correct? [p. 327-329]
   a. Market rate > coupon rate.
   b. Market rate = coupon rate.
   c. Market rate < coupon rate.
   d. Market rate may be more or less than the coupon rate.
   e. Market rate plus inflation premium = coupon rate.

4. The required rate of return on a corporate bond is often called the: [p. 323]
   a. Risk premium.
   b. Yield to maturity.
   c. Real rate of return.
   d. Approximate yield to maturity.
   e. Present value.

5. Which of the following is the valuation equation for common stock expected to have constantly growing dividends? [p. 338]
   a. $P_o = D_o / K_e$
   b. $P_o = D_1 / g$
   c. $P_o = D_1 / K_e$
   d. $P_o = D_1 / (K_e - g)$
   e. $P_o = D_o / (K_e - g)$

6. The primary determinant of the value of a share of stock is the: [p. 336]
   a. P/E ratio.
   b. EPS.
   c. Discount rate.
   d. Present value of an expected stream of future dividends.
   e. Risk premium.

7. The key concept of finance is: [p. 322]
   a. Profit.
   b. Rate of return.
   c. Revenues.
   d. Risk.
   e. Valuation.

8. Because of its normally fixed dividend and lack of maturity, preferred stock is often called a(n): [p. 334]
   a. Perpetuity.
   b. Bond.
   c. No-growth common stock.
   d. Money market security.
   e. Interpolation.

9. The possibility that a firm will be unable to meet its debt obligations is: [p. 326]
   a. Business risk.
   b. Financial risk.
   c. Purchasing power risk.
   d. Interest rate risk.
   e. Inflation risk.

10. The DCA Corporation issued bonds (20-year bonds, five years ago) with a coupon rate of 12%. The market-required rate of return on the bonds is currently 9%. The bonds will be priced: [pp. 327-329]
    a. At par.
    b. Below par.
    c. Above par.
    d. Above and below par.
    e. As a perpetuity.

Multiple Choice Answer Key: Chapter 10

1.	c	2.	c	3.	a	4.	b	5.	d
6.	d	7.	e	8.	a	9.	b	10.	c

Chapter 10: Problems

10-1.   The BJS Company is issuing preferred shares that will pay an annual dividend of $5.

   (a)   If you require a 12% return on the shares, what is the most you would be willing to pay for a share?

   (b)   If rates of return available in the market decline and you now require only a 10% rate of return, what would you be willing to pay for a share?

   (c)   Suppose that BJS experiences a severe financial decline, and you require a 20% return on the share. What is the most you would pay for the share?

10-2.   Doldrum Plastics has been paying a $3 dividend each year and company reports indicate that management intends to continue this dividend payment for the foreseeable future.

   (a)   If the market-determined required rate of return on Doldrum's common stock is 15%, what will be the price of a share of stock?

   (b)   Suppose that an aggressive new Chief Executive Officer, Rebecca Calvo, is hired by Doldrum. Because of the productive policies and processes instituted by Calvo, capital market participants anticipate that Doldrum's earnings and dividends will increase continuously at an 8% rate. What would be the price of a share of Doldrum common stock if the required rate of return remains at 15%?

   (c)   Instead of the 8% continuous growth rate in part (b), assume that earnings and dividends are expected to grow at a 12% rate for 6 years before declining to a constant rate of 5% growth each year thereafter. What will be the price of a share?

10-3.   The common stock of Knicely, Inc. is selling for $53 per share. If the recent dividend of $3 is expected to grow at a constant rate of 6% in the future, determine the required rate of return on the shares.

10-4.   A corporate bond bearing a 10% coupon rate will mature in 10 years.

   (a)   If the current market rate is 8%, what is the current value of the bond (assume annual interest payments)?

   (b)   If interest payments are made semiannually, what is the value of the bond?

   (c)   Under the conditions in (b), what would the price of the bond be if market interest rates rose to 12%?

10-5.   Brad Couvillion recently bought 100 shares of RDI preferred stock. The preferred stock pays $6 in dividends annually and is currently selling for $75.

   (a)   What is Brad's expected rate of return on the stock?

   (b)   If his required return of the stock was 6%, how much would he be willing to pay per share?

   (c)   If under current business conditions Brad's required real rate of return is 3%, he expects inflation to be 4% annually and he assigns a risk premium of 2% to RDI, how much would he pay for a share?

10-6. Ashleigh Williams is interested in buying some bonds of Bienville, Inc. The bonds have a 12% coupon and mature in 20 years. If the bonds have a par value of $1,000 and are currently selling for $1,160, what is the yield to maturity on the bonds?

Chapter 10: Solutions

10-1. **BJS Company**

(a) $P_p = \dfrac{D_p}{K_p} = \dfrac{\$5}{.12} = \$41.67$

(b) $P_p = \dfrac{D_p}{K_p} = \dfrac{\$5}{.10} = \$50.00$

(c) $P_p = \dfrac{D_p}{K_p} = \dfrac{\$5}{.20} = \$25.00$

10-2. **Doldrum Plastics**

(a) No growth in dividends.

$$P_0 = \frac{D_1}{K_e - g} = \frac{\$3}{.15 - 0} = \$20.00$$

(b) Dividend growth = 8%
$D_1 = D_0 (1 + g) = \$3.00 (1 + 0.08) = \$3.24$

$$P_0 = \frac{D_1}{K_e - g} = \frac{\$3.24}{.15 - .08} = \$46.29$$

(c) Changing growth rates.

$$P_0 = \frac{D_1}{(1 + K_e)^1} + \frac{D_2}{(1 + K_e)^2} + \frac{D_3}{(1 + K_e)^3} + \dots + \frac{D_6}{(1 + K_e)^6} + \frac{P_6}{(1 + K_e)^6} \quad \text{and: } P_6 = \frac{D_7}{K_e - g}$$

$D_1 = \$3.00 (1.12) = \$3.36 \qquad D_5 = \$4.71 (1.12) = \$5.28$
$D_2 = \$3.36 (1.12) = \$3.76 \qquad D_6 = \$5.28 (1.12) = \$5.91$
$D_3 = \$3.76 (1.12) = \$4.21 \qquad D_7 = \$5.91 (1.05) = \$6.21$
$D_4 = \$4.21 (1.12) = \$4.71$

$$P_6 = \frac{D_7}{K_e - g} = \frac{\$6.21}{.15 - .05} = \frac{\$6.21}{.10} = \$62.10$$

$$P_0 = \frac{\$3.36}{(1 + .15)^1} + \frac{\$3.76}{(1 + .15)^2} + \frac{\$4.21}{(1 + .15)^3} + \frac{\$4.71}{(1 + .15)^4} + \frac{\$5.28}{(1 + .15)^5} + \frac{\$5.91}{(1 + .15)^6} + \frac{\$62.10}{(1 + .15)^6}$$

$P_0 = \$2.92 + \$2.82 + \$2.77 + \$2.69 + \$2.62 + \$2.55 + \$26.83$
$P_0 = \$43.22$

10-3. **Knicely, Inc.**

$$D_1 = D_o(1 + g) = \$3.00\,(1.06) = \$3.18$$

$$K_e = \frac{D_1}{P_0} + g = \frac{\$3.18}{\$53.00} + 0.06 = 0.06 + 0.06 = 0.12 = \mathbf{12.0\%}$$

10-4. **Corporate Bond**

(a) Bond price = $100 ($IF_{PVA}$, $n = 10$, $i = 8\%$) + (IF_{PV}, $n = 10$, $i = 8\%$)
Bond price = $100 (6.710) + $1,000 (0.463)
Bond price = $671 + $463 = **$1,134**

Calculator:	P_n	=	FV	=	$1,000
	I	=	PMT	=	$100
	N	=	N	=	10
	Y	=	i	=	8%
Compute PV		=	P_b	=	**$1,134.20**

(b) Bond price = $50 ($IF_{PVA}$, $n = 20$, $i = 4\%$) + $1,000 ($IF_{PV}$, $n = 20$, $i = 4\%$)
Bond price = $50 (13.59) + $1,000 (0.456)
Bond price = $679.50 + $456 = **$1,135.50**

Calculator:	P_n	=	FV	=	$1,000
	I	=	PMT	=	$50
	N	=	N	=	20
	Y	=	i	=	4%
Compute PV		=	P_b	=	**$1,135.90**

(c) Bond price = $50 ($IF_{PVA}$, $n = 20$, $i = 6\%$) + $1,000 ($IF_{PV}$, $n = 20$, $i = 6\%$)
Bond price = $50 (11.47) + $1,000 (0.312)
Bond price = $573.50 + $312 = **$885.50**

Calculator:	P_n	=	FV	=	$1,000
	I	=	PMT	=	$50
	n	=		=	20
	Y	=	i	=	6%
Compute PV		=	P_b	=	**$885.30**

10-5. **Brad Couvillon**

(a) $$K_p = \frac{D_p}{P_p} = \frac{\$6}{\$75} = 0.08 = \mathbf{8.0\%}$$

(b) $$P_p = \frac{D_p}{K_p} = \frac{\$6}{0.06} = \mathbf{\$100.00}$$

(c) Required rate of return = 3% + 4% + 2% = 9%

$$P_p = \frac{D_p}{K_p} = \frac{\$6}{0.09} = \mathbf{\$66.67}$$

10-6. Ashleigh Williams

$$Y^I = \frac{Annual\ interest\ payment + \dfrac{Principal\ payment - Price\ of\ the\ bond}{Number\ of\ years\ to\ maturity}}{0.6\left(Price\ of\ the\ bond\right) + 0.4\left(Principal\ payment\right)}$$

$$Y^I = \frac{\$120 + \dfrac{\$1,000 - \$1,160}{20}}{0.6\left(\$1,160\right) + 0.4\left(\$1,000\right)} = \frac{\$120 + \left(-\$8\right)}{\$696 + \$400} = \frac{\$112}{\$1,096} = 0.1022 = 10.22\%$$

Calculator:	P_n	=	FV	=	$1,000
	I	=	PMT	=	$120
	N	=	N	=	20
	PV	=	P_b	=	$1,160
Compute	Y	=	$i\%$	=	**10.11%**

Chapter 11   Cost of Capital

Summary: The purpose of this chapter is to examine the processes for determining the appropriate discount rate that a firm should apply in evaluating investment opportunities. The appendices cover the CAPM and Modigliani and Miller's capital structure models.

I.   **The Overall Concept [p. 363]**

    A.   A business firm must strive to earn at least as much as the cost of the funds that it uses.

    B.   Usually a firm has several sources of funds and each source may have a different cost.

    C.   The overall cost of the funds employed is a proportionate average of the various sources.

        Assume that you borrow money from three friends in the following amounts and costs:

Source	Amount	Interest Rate
Larry	$5,000	10%
Curly	2,000	6%
Moe	3,000	8%

If the $10,000 is invested, what rate of return must be earned to enable you to pay your friends their required rate of interest?
Weighted cost of borrowing:

(1) Source	(2) Cost	(3) Amount borrowed	(4) Weighted average proportion	(5) Cost (2 × 4)
Larry	.10	$5,000	$5,000/ $10,000 = 0 .5	0.050
Curly	.06	$2,000	$2,000/ $10,000 = 0.2	0.012
Moe	.08	$3,000	$3,000/ $10,000 = 0.3	0.024
		$10,000	1.0	0.086

The average cost is 8.6%. The cost can also be found by expressing the aggregate interest cost as a ratio of the amount borrowed.

Source	Interest Rate	Amount Borrowed	Interest
Larry	.10	$ 5,000	$500
Curly	.06	2,000	120
Moe	.08	3,000	240
		$10,000	$860

$$Weighted\ cost = \frac{\$860}{\$10,000} = 0.086 = \textbf{8.6\%}$$

In order to pay your friends their required interest, you must invest the borrowed funds to earn at least 8.6%. Suppose you also invest $10,000 of your own money and seek to earn 20% on your investment, what is the required rate of return?

(1) Source	(2) Cost	(3) Amount borrowed	(4) Weighted average proportion	(5) Cost (2 × 4)
Larry	.10	$5,000	$5,000/ $20,000 = 0 .5	0.050
Curly	.06	$2,000	$2,000/ $20,000 = 0.2	0.012
Moe	.08	$3,000	$3,000/ $20,000 = 0.3	0.024
You	.20	$10,000	$10,000/ $20,000 = 0.5	0.100
		$20,000	1.0	0.143

Notice that due to financial leverage (fixed payments to lenders) the required rate of return on the total investment is less than your required return. The above computation may be validated as follows:

Dollar return required = .143 × $20,000 = $2,860
Interest payments to lenders   860
Return to you $2,000

$$Your\ rate\ of\ return = \frac{\$2,000}{\$10,000} = 0.20 = \mathbf{20.0\%}$$

D. The firm's **required rate of return** that will satisfy all suppliers of capital is called its **cost of capital.**

E. There are several steps in measuring a firm's cost of capital.

    1. Compute the cost of each source of capital.
    2. Assign weights to each source. Conversion of the historical cost capital structure to market values is most appropriate.
    3. Compute the weighted average of the component costs.

II.   **Interdependence of Valuation and Cost of Capital [p. 363-364]**

    A. To achieve the goal of the firm, maximization of shareholder's wealth, the firm's assets must be employed to earn at least the required rate of return (cost of capital).

    B. A firm's required rate of return (cost of capital) is determined in the market by the suppliers of capital.

    C. The market-determined required rate of return for each source of capital depends upon the market's perceived level of risk associated with the individual securities. The perceived risk is based on future expectations.

    D. The market allocates capital at varying rates of return based on perceptions of an individual firm's riskiness, efficiency, and expected returns.

    E. A firm's risk will be determined in part by its collection of assets.

    F. Market-determined yields on various financial instruments will equal the cost of those instruments to the firm with adjustment tax and flotation cost considerations.

III.   **The Cost of Debt [p. 364]**

A. The basic cost of debt to the firm is the effective yield to maturity. The yield to maturity is a market determined rate and can be found by examining the relationships of security price, periodic interest payments, maturity value, and length of time to maturity. The yield to maturity for a corporate bond may be found by solving for Y in the following equation:

$$P_b = \sum_{t=1}^{n} \frac{I_t}{(1+Y)^t} + \frac{P_n}{(1+Y)^n} \qquad \text{(10-1; page 323)}$$

Where:
$$
\begin{aligned}
Y &= \text{the yield to maturity} \\
P_b &= \text{the market price of the bond} \\
I_t &= \text{the periodic interest payments} \\
P_n &= \text{the principal at maturity} \\
t &= \text{the period from 1 to n} \\
n &= \text{the total number of periods}
\end{aligned}
$$

An accurate **calculator** computation is shown in the text on **page 365**.

B. Since interest is tax deductible, the actual cost of debt to the firm is less than the yield to maturity.

C. The aftertax cost of debt is:

$$K_d = Y\,(1\text{-}T) \qquad \text{(11-1}a\text{; page 366)}$$

The aftertax cost to a firm of bonds issued at par paying \$100 annually in interest would be 6 percent if the firm's marginal tax rate were 40 percent.

D. Flotation costs of a debt issue may be included by use of the formula:

$$K_d = \frac{Y\,(1\text{-}T)}{1-F} \qquad \text{(11-1}b\text{; page 367)}$$

Where: F = Flotation, or selling, cost (as a percent)

IV.   **The Cost of Preferred Stock [p. 367]**

A. Preferred stock is similar to debt in that the preferred dividend is fixed but dissimilar in that dividends are not tax deductible.

B. The cost of preferred stock to a firm may be determined by examining the relationship of its annual (usually fixed) dividend and its market determined price. Preferred stock, unlike debt, has no maturity and therefore the dividends are expected to be perpetual.

C. The cost of preferred stock K_p is computed by dividing the annual dividend payment by the net proceeds received by the firm in the sale of preferred stock.

$$K_p = \frac{D_p}{P_p - F} \qquad \text{(11-2; page 367)}$$

Where:
$$
\begin{aligned}
K_p &= \text{cost of preferred stock} \\
D_p &= \text{preferred stock dividend} \\
F &= \text{flotation costs per share} \\
P_p &= \text{market price of preferred stock}
\end{aligned}
$$

V. The Cost of Common Equity [p. 368]

A. The basis of computation of the price of common stock is the Dividend Valuation Model.

B. Assuming constant growth, the Dividend Valuation Model can be reduced to:

$$P_0 = \frac{D_1}{K_e - g}$$

and then solved for the required rate of return K_e,

$$K_e = \frac{D_1}{P_0} + g \qquad\qquad \text{(11-3; page 369)}$$

Where: K_e =   required rate of return
D_1 =   expected dividend in first year
P_0 =   price per share of stock
g =   constant growth rate in dividends

C. The equation for common stock cost is composed of two parts, the dividend yield, D_1/P_0 plus the anticipated growth rate, g, of dividends.

D. Alternative Calculation of the Required Return on Common Stock - using the Capital Asset Pricing Model (CAPM). **[p. 370]**

1. Under the CAPM, the required return for common stock can be described by the following formula:

$$K_j = R_f + \beta_j (R_m - R_f) \qquad\qquad \text{(11-4a; page 370)}$$

Where: K_j =   Required Return on Common Stock
R_f =   Risk-free rate of return; usually the current rate on Treasury bill securities
β_j =   Beta coefficient. The beta measures the historical volatility of an individual stock's return relative to a stock market index. A beta greater than 1 indicates greater volatility (price movements) than the market, while the reverse would be true for a beta less than 1.
R_m =   Return in the market as measured by an appropriate index

With flotation costs

$$K_{jn} = K_j \left(\frac{P_0}{P_n} \right) \qquad\qquad \text{(11-4b; page 371)}$$

Where: P_n =   net proceeds received on a new share issue after flotation costs and any underpricing of the share price

2. Both K_j and K_e should be equal under the case of market equilibrium with efficient markets.
3. Appendix 11A presents the capital asset pricing model in more detail for those who wish to expand the textbook coverage on this concept.

E. Common stock financing is available through the retention of earnings belonging to present shareholders or by issuing new common stock.

1. The cost of retained earnings is equivalent to the rate of return on the firm's common stock. This is the opportunity cost. Thus the cost of common equity in the form of retained earnings is:

$$K_e = \frac{D_1}{P_0} + g \qquad \text{(11-5: page 372)}$$

2. The cost of new common stock is higher than the cost of retained earnings because the firm's proceeds from sale of the stock are less than the price paid by the shareholder, due to flotation costs. The cost of new common stock, K_n is:

$$K_n = \left(\frac{D_1}{P_0} + g \right) \left(\frac{P_0}{P_n} \right) \qquad \text{(11-6; page 373)}$$

Where: P_n = net proceeds received on a new share issue after flotation costs and any underpricing of the share price

3. Earnings of a firm belong to the owners. The owners of a corporation are the shareholders. If a corporate decision is made to retain earnings, the shareholders expect a return on this indirect investment.
4. Since retained earnings are not reduced by flotation costs, the cost to the corporation is less than new common stock financing.

VI. **Optimal Capital Structure: Weighting Costs [p. 374]**

A. The firm should seek to minimize its cost of capital by employing the optimal mix of capital financing.

B. The Baker Corporation example on page 374 demonstrates the concept of weighted average cost of capital numerically while Figure 11-1 does so graphically.

C. Although debt is the cheapest source of capital, there are limits to the amount of debt capital that lenders will provide (recall the D/E relationships discussed in Chapter 3). The cost of both debt and equity financing rise as debt becomes a larger portion of the capital structure.

D. Traditional financial theory maintains that the **weighted average cost of capital** declines as lower costing debt is added to the capital structure. The optimum mix of debt and equity corresponds to the minimum point on the average cost of capital curve.

Refer to Figure 11-1, text page 376.

E. The optimal debt-equity mix varies among industries. The more cyclical the business, the lower the D/E ratio is required to be.

F. The weights applied in computing the weighted average cost should be market value weights on the presumption that this is the optimum financing mix that will be used to finance projects in the future. This will require the conversion of the historical based balance sheet to its market value equivalent before weightings are determined. (A text example is presented on **pages 377-378**).

Book value of each component of the capital structure is converted to **Market value**; assigned a weighting; and then multiplied by the **aftertax cost** of each component in the capital structure; to get a component cost. Summing these component costs = WACC.

Book value → **Market value** → **Weighting** → **Cost*** → **Cost × Weight**

* yield adjusted for taxes (debt) and flotation costs) = cost

VII. **Capital Acquisition and Investment Decision Making [p. 379]**

A. The discount rate used in evaluating capital projects should be the weighted average cost of capital. Assuming the cost of capital has been determined using the present risk characteristics of the firm it is appropriate that the capital projects evaluated have similar risk. Otherwise the discount rate should be adjusted to account for the different risk.

B. If the cost of capital is earned on all projects, the residual claimants of the earnings stream, the owners, will receive their required rate of return. If the overall return of the firm is less than the cost of capital, the owners will receive less than their desired rate of return because providers of debt capital must be paid.

C. For most firms, the cost of capital is fairly constant within a reasonable range of debt-equity mixes (flat portion of curve in Figure 11-2). Changes in money and capital market conditions (supply and demand for money), however, cause the cost of capital for all firms to vary upward and downward over time.

Refer to Figure 11-2, text page 379.

D. Cost of Capital in the Capital Budgeting Decision

1. It is the current cost of each source of funds that is important.
2. The cost of each source of capital will vary with the amount of capital derived from that source.
3. The required rate of return or discount rate for capital budgeting decisions will be the weighted average cost of capital.

VIII. **Marginal Cost of Capital [p. 381]**

A. The **marginal cost of debt** (the cost of the last amount of debt financing) will rise as more debt financing is used. The **marginal cost of equity** also rises when the shift from retained earnings to external (common stock) equity financing is necessary.

IX. **Appendix 11A: Cost of Capital and the Capital Asset Pricing Model [p. 397-404]**

A. The **Capital Asset Pricing Model (CAPM)** relates the risk-return tradeoffs of individual assets to market returns.

B. The CAPM encompasses all types of assets but is most often applied to common stock.

Refer to Figure 11A - 1, text page 399.

C. The basic form of the CAPM is a linear relationship between returns on individual stocks and the market over time. Using least squares regression analysis, the return on an individual stock K_j is:

$$K_j = a + \beta_j R_m + e \qquad\qquad \text{(11A-1; page 398)}$$

Where:
K_j = Return on individual common stock of company
α = Alpha, the intercept on the y-axis
β_j = Beta, the coefficient
R_m = Return on the stock market (an index of stock returns is used, usually the S&P/ TSX Composite Index)
e = Error term of the regression equation

D. Using historical data, the beta coefficient is computed. The beta coefficient is a measurement of the return performance of a given stock relative to the return performance of the market.

E. The CAPM is an expectational model. There is no guarantee that historical data will be repeated.

F. The CAPM evolved into a risk premium model.

1. Investors expect higher returns if higher risks are taken.
2. The minimum return expected by investors will never be less than can be obtained from a riskless asset (usually considered to be Treasury bills). The relationship is expressed as follows:

$$K_j = R_f + \beta_j (R_m - R_f) \qquad \text{(11A-2; page 400)}$$

Where:
R_f = Risk-free rate of return
β_j = Beta coefficient from Formula 11A-1
R_m = Return on the market index
$R_m - R_f$ = Premium or excess return of the market versus the risk-free rate (since the market is riskier than R_f, the assumption is that the expected R_m will be greater than R_f)
$\beta_j (R_m - R_f)$ = Expected return above the risk-free rate for the stock of Company j, given the level of risk

3. Beta measures the sensitivity of an individual security's return relative to the market.
   a. By definition, the market beta = 1.
   b. A security with a beta = 1, is expected to have returns equal to and as volatile as the market. One with a beta of 2 is twice as volatile (up or down).
4. Beta measures the impact of an asset on an individual's portfolio of assets.

G. A risk-return graph can be derived from the risk premium model. The graphed relationship between risk (measured by beta) and required rates of return is called the **Security Market Line (SML).**

Refer to Figure 11A-2, text page 404.

H. Cost of capital considerations

1. If required returns rise, prices of securities fall to adjust to the new equilibrium return level and as required returns fall, prices rise.
2. A change in required rates of return is represented by a shift in the SML.
   a. The new SML will be parallel to the previous one if investors attempt to maintain the same risk premium over the risk-free rate.
   b. If investors attempt to maintain purchasing power in an inflationary economy, the slope of the new SML may be greater than before due to an inflation premium.
   c. An investor's required rate of return and thus a firm's cost of capital will also change if investors risk preferences change. The slope of the SML would change even if the risk-free rate remained the same.

X. **Appendix 11B: Capital Structure Theory and Modigliani and Miller [p. 407-412]**

A. A capital structure that provides the lowest cost of capital and therefore the highest market value of owner's equity would be deemed to be the **optimal capital structure** for a firm. Whether such a capital structure exists is not clear and has been a focal question in the field of finance for many years.

B. Professor David Durand provided three descriptive alternative theories of cost of capital and valuation in the early 1950s.
1. Net Income (NI) Approach: The costs of debt and equity were assumed to be constant regardless of capital amounts employed.
2. Net Operating Income (NOI) Approach: Durand proposed an alternative theory that stated that although the cost of debt remained constant over varying levels of debt utilization, the cost of equity would rise in such a manner that the overall cost of capital remained constant.
3. Finally, Durand described an approach in-between the NI and NOI alternative called the Traditional Approach.

Refer to Figures 11B -1, 2, and 3, text pages 408-409.

C. Professors Franco Modigliani and Merton Miller made major contributions to capital structure theory by providing behavioral and mathematical substance rather than relying on naive assumptions.

1. Initially, M & M maintained that a firm's cost of capital and the value of the firm were independent of its capital structure. Their posture was similar to the NOI approach of Durand, but M & M provided the behavioral process and mathematical proofs to support their arguments. M & M argued that owners demand an additional risk premium as debt is employed that will exactly offset the decline in the cost of capital because debt is cheaper. If their hypothesis held, the cost of capital and value of the firm would be independent of capital structure.

$$V = \frac{EBIT}{K_a}$$ (11B-1; page 409)

2. M & M "corrected" their hypothesis to include corporate taxes. Once the tax deductibility of interest payments was included in their analysis, the market value of the firm was directly tied to the amount of debt employed. The more debt a firm used, the higher its market value would be.

$$V_L = V_U + TD$$ (11B-4; page 410)

Refer to Figure 11B-4, text page 411.

3. The next step in M & M's evolutionary consideration of capital structure was the inclusion of bankruptcy probabilities and costs. The threat of bankruptcy offsets some of the benefits from using debt and yields a U-shaped cost of capital curve. In other words, initially, debt provides market value benefits but as more debt is used, the threat of bankruptcy begins to erase the benefits. An optimal capital structure would be possible.

Refer to Figure 11B-5, text page 413.

4. Finally, in 1976, Professor Miller (without Modigliani) reverted to their original position that cost of capital and market values were independent of capital structure. His premise was based on the effect of including personal taxes in the capital structure issue. Miller said that the lower tax rates on long-term gains from stock ownership offset the tax benefits from tax deductibility of interest payments.

D. The optimal capital structure issue has not been fully reconciled. Changes in tax laws and the dynamic changes in market risk perceptions continue to impact on this question. There is general acceptance, however, of the idea that the prudent use of debt does lower the cost of capital.

E. Both professors, Modigliani and Miller, have been awarded the Nobel Prize in economics.

XI. **Review of Formulas**

See text pages 387, 404, and 412 or insert card.

Chapter 11: Multiple Choice Questions

1. The primary determinant of the value of a share of stock is the: [p. 369]
   a. Revenues of the firm.
   b. EPS of the firm.
   c. Present value of an expected stream of future dividends.
   d. Present value of expected net income.
   e. P/E ratio.

2. Which of the following is correct? [p. 363-374]
   a. The cost of retained earnings is normally higher than the cost of new common stock.
   b. The cost of preferred stock is normally lower than the aftertax cost of debt.
   c. Flotation costs raise the cost of capital.
   d. The current yield on a share of stock is the stock price divided by earnings per share.
   e. The use of debt always raises a firm's cost of capital.

3. The graphical representation of the capital asset pricing model is called the: [p. 402]
   a. CAPM.
   b. SML.
   c. IS-LM.
   d. Beta.
   e. NOI.

4. Which of the following equations is the CAPM? [p. 400]

   a. $K_e = \dfrac{D_1}{P_0} + g$

   b. $P_0 = \dfrac{D_1}{K_e - g}$

   c. $K_d = Y(1-T)$
   d. $K_j = R_f + \beta_j (R_m - R_f)$
   e. $F = \sqrt{GPA}$

5. Which of the following should be used to evaluate capital projects? [p. 380]
   a. The cost of the specific source of capital used to finance the project
   b. The cost of common equity
   c. The SML
   d. The risk-free rate + inflation premium
   e. The weighted-average cost of capital

6. When investors expect a rise in the inflation rate and also become more risk sensitive, the SML will: [p. 403]
   a. Shift upward and become more steeply sloped.
   b. Shift upward only.
   c. Become more steeply sloped but the vertical intercept will remain the same.
   d. Shift downward only.
   e. Shift downward and become less steeply sloped.

7. The firm's cost of capital is also called its: [p. 362-363]
   a. Required rate of return.
   b. Beta.
   c. K_e.
   d. NOI.
   e. M&M.

8. A firm's cost of capital is: [p. 377]
   a. Set by its board of directors.
   b. Market determined.
   c. Set by the management of the firm.
   d. The same for each firm in an industry.
   e. Set by the Securities Exchange Commission.

9. The appropriate cost of each source of capital for a firm is the: [p. 381]
   a. Average cost.
   b. Marginal cost.
   c. Historical cost.
   d. Weighted average cost.
   e. Floatation cost.

10. Which of the following statements is incorrect? [Chapter. 11]
    a. A firm's cost of capital is fairly constant within a reasonable range of debt-equity mixes.
    b. The cost of each source of capital may vary with the amount derived from that source.
    c. Owners are residual claimants on the earnings stream.
    d. When a firm earns less than its cost of capital, it has negative net income.
    e. Changes in capital market conditions cause the cost of capital of a firm to vary upward and downward over time.

Multiple Choice Answer Key: Chapter 11

| 1. | c | 2. | c | 3. | b | 4. | d | 5. | e |
| 6. | a | 7. | a | 8. | b | 9. | b | 10. | d |

Chapter 11- Problems

11-1. The aftertax cost of Par Value Corporation's outstanding bond is 6.38%. If the firm is in the 42% tax bracket, what is the *before* tax cost (yield) of that debt?

11-2. The Dowel Jones Company is planning to issue 10,000 shares of $100 preferred stock.

   (a) If flotation costs amount to 3%, what will be the net proceeds of the issue to the firm?

   (b) If the dividend is $7 annually, what will be the effective cost of preferred stock to the firm?

11-3. Stable Corporation has been paying an annual dividend of $3 per share for 10 years and is expected to continue such payment in the future.

   (a) If the firm's shares are selling for $20 per share, what is the cost of common stock?

   (b) If instead of the no-growth situation, the firm were growing at an annual rate of 5% and increasing its dividends at the same rate, what would be the price of the firm's stock (assume shareholders' desire a 15% rate of return)?

11-4.   Bond Industries issued $10,000,000 of 30-year, $1,000 bonds 20 years ago. The bonds carry a 6% coupon rate and are currently selling for $670 per bond. Bond is in a 30% tax bracket.

(a)   If Bond issued new bonds today, what would be the approximate aftertax cost of debt? (Assume new bonds are viewed as equally risky as the old bonds in the market.)

(b)   What coupon rate would they need to place on new bonds for the bonds to sell at par value?

11-5.   Alsup Manufacturing stock is selling for $28 per share. The firm's last dividend was $4 and is expected to grow at a 5% rate constantly.

(a)   What is the firm's cost of equity?

(b)   Assuming a 10% flotation cost, what is the firm's cost of new common stock?

11-6.   The characteristics of the capital sources of the Eoff Corporation are listed below.

Source	Cost	Proportion
Debt	.08	30%
Preferred stock	.09	10%
Common equity	.15	60%

Assuming Eoff's tax rate is 30%; calculate the firm's weighted-average cost of capital.

11-7.   The common stock of Soar Corporation is $100 per share. The expected dividend on its stock in the current period is $5, and the firm's cost of common stock is 12%. Determine the firm's dividend growth rate (assume that the growth rate is constant).

11-8.   Solar Utility is a rapidly expanding supplier of energy in the Western Canada. The firm has 5,000,000 shares of common stock outstanding on which it recently paid a $2 dividend. The common stock currently is priced at $30 per share. The firm wishes to maintain a payout ratio of 50%. The current earnings per share of $4 are expected to increase at an annual rate of 6% for the foreseeable future.

The firm also has a long-term bond issue outstanding. An issue of $160,000,000 bearing a 12% interest rate has been outstanding for two years, and the bonds are selling at a premium to face value. New 10-year bonds will have a coupon rate of 10% and are expected to sell for $900.

Solar Utility utilizes preferred stock as a financing source and has 400,000 shares of $100 par value preferred shares outstanding. The firm pays an annual dividend of $6 on the preferred stock which is currently selling at $75.

The firm expects to continue to provide capital financing in the future based on market value weightings. New share capital will be required.

If the issue costs of common and preferred stock average 8% and 4% of the amount issued, respectively, and the firm is in a 42% tax bracket, compute the minimum return that the firm should strive to earn. (It's WACC).

11-9. Titanic Ice Ltd. has a beta of 1.3 and has just paid a dividend of $2.40. Three years ago the dividend was $1.884. Currently the market risk premium is 8% and thirty year Government of Canada bonds pay 6%. There are presently 1,000,000 common shares outstanding.

The preferred shares are currently priced at $26 and there are 150,000 outstanding. The dividend is $0.3125 paid quarterly.

Bonds are currently priced at $1,206.11 for each $1,000 par value bond. The 20,000 bonds have 14 years to maturity and pay an annual coupon of 10%.

Flotation costs on any securities would be 4% of proceeds. Titanic has a tax rate of 40% and at present has sufficient earnings for the equity contribution for any capital projects.

Calculate Titanic Ice's WACC?

11-10. (This problem relates to the appendix.) Using the capital asset pricing model, compute the required rate of return on investment j given the following information.

(a) R_f = 8%
K_m = 14%
β_j = 1.0

(b) Recalculate the required rate of return in (a) assuming β_j is .5 and 1.8.

(c) If R_f = 6% and K_m = 12%, what value of beta (β_j) would yield a required return of 15%?

11-11. The market-determined required rate of return on the common stock of M. Hartsfield, Inc., is 18%. The expected return of the market is 12%, and the risk-free rate is currently 6%.

(a) What is the beta of M. Hartsfield?

(b) If the beta of Hartsfield were .8, what would be its required return on common stock?

Chapter 11: Solutions

11-1. **Par Value Corporation**

$$K_d = Y(1 - T)$$
$$0.638 = Y(1 - .34)$$
$$Y = \frac{0.0638}{(1 - .34)} = \frac{0.0638}{0.66} = .1100 = \textbf{11.0\%}$$

11-2. **Dowel Jones Company**

(a) 10,000 × $100 = $1,000,000
$1,000,000 (1 − 0.03) = $970,000

(b) $\dfrac{\$970,000}{10,000} = \$97 \;\; proceeds\;\; per\;\; share$

$$K_p = \frac{D_p}{P_p - F} = \frac{\$7}{\$97} \;\; or \;\; \frac{\$7 \times 10,000}{\$970,000} = 0.072 = \textbf{7.2\%}$$

11-3. **Stable Corporation**

(a) $K_e = \dfrac{D_1}{P_0} + g = \dfrac{\$3}{\$20} + 0 = 0.15 = \textbf{15\%}$

(b) $P_0 = \dfrac{D_1}{K_e - g} = \dfrac{\$3.00(1 + .05)}{.15 - .05} = \dfrac{\$3.15}{.10} = \textbf{\$31.50}$

11-4. **Bond Industries**

(a)

$$Y^1 = \frac{\$60 + \dfrac{\$1,000 - \$670}{10}}{0.6\left(\$670\right) + 0.4\left(\$1,000\right)} = \frac{\$60 + \$33}{\$402 + \$400} = \frac{\$93}{\$802} = 0.1160 = \textbf{11.60\%}$$

K_d = .1160 (1 − .3) = 0.0812 = **8.12%**

Calculator:	$FV = \$1,000$	$PV = \$670$	$PMT = \$60$	$N = 10$	$\%i =?$
Compute:	$Y = \%i = 11.79\%$				

Aftertax cost = 11.79 (1 − .3) = **8.25%**

If payment is considered on an aftertax basis as $42 [$60 (1 − .3)] the aftertax yield becomes 9.44% which is more accurate given the 10 year time period.

(b) **11.6% or 11.79% (calculator)**

11-5. **Alsup Manufacturing**

(a) $K_e = \dfrac{D_1}{P_0} + g = \dfrac{\$4(1 + .05)}{\$28} + 0.05 = \dfrac{\$4.20}{\$28} + 0.05 = 0.15 + 0.05 = 0.20 = \textbf{20\%}$

(b) $K_n = \left(\dfrac{D_1}{P_0} + g\right)\left(\dfrac{P_0}{P_n}\right) = 0.20\left(\dfrac{\$28}{\$25.20}\right) = .2222 = \textbf{22.22\%}$

140

11-6. Eoff Corporation

Source	Cost	Aftertax cost	Proportion	WACC
Debt	.08	.056	.3	.0168
Preferred stock	.09	.090	.1	.0090
Common equity	.15	.150	.6	.0900
				.1158

11-7. **Soar Corporation**

$$K_e = \frac{D_1}{P_0} + g = \frac{\$5}{\$100} + g$$

$$0.12 = 0.05 + g$$

$$g = 0.07 = \textbf{7\%}$$

11-8. **Solar Utility**

Cost of new common shares = K_n

$$K_n = \left(\frac{D_1}{P_0} + g\right)\left(\frac{P_0}{P_n}\right) = \left(\frac{\$2(1 + 0.06)}{\$30} + 0.06\right)\left(\frac{\$30}{\$30 - (0.08 \times \$30)}\right) = \left(\frac{\$2.12}{\$30} + 0.06\right)\left(\frac{\$30}{\$27.60}\right)$$

$$= 0.1307 \times 1.087 = 0.1420 = \textbf{14.20\%}$$

Note: If the firm's earnings increase at a constant rate and the payout ratio is maintained, the dividends will increase at the same rate.

Example: If the earnings per share increase by 6% in the coming year, new earnings per share will be:

$$EPS_1 = \$4\ (1.06) = 4.24$$

Maintaining the 50% payout ratio: $\qquad\qquad DPS_1 = (.5)\ (4.24) = \$2.12$

Which equals the previous dividend increased by 6%: $\quad DPS_1 = \$2\ (1.06) = \$2.12$

Cost of retained earnings = K_e

$$K_e = \frac{D_1}{P_0} + g = \frac{\$2.12}{\$30} + 0.06 = 0.0707 + 0.06 = 0.1307 = \textbf{13.07\%}$$

Cost of preferred stock = K_p

$$K_p = \frac{D_p}{P_p - F} = \frac{\$6}{\$75(1 - 0.04)} = \frac{\$6}{\$72} = 0.0833 = \textbf{8.33\%}$$

Cost of long-term debt = K_d

$$Y^I = \frac{\$100 + \dfrac{\$1,000 - \$900}{10}}{0.6\,(\$900) + 0.4\,(\$1,000)} = \frac{\$100 + \$10}{\$540 + \$400} = \frac{\$110}{\$940} = 0.1170 = \mathbf{11.70\%}$$

$K_d = Y\,(1 - T)$
$K_d = (.1170)\,(1 - .42) = 0.0679 = 6.79\%$

Calculator:	$FV = \$1,000$	$PV = \$900$	$PMT = \$100$	$N = 10$	$\%i = ?$
Compute:	$Y = \%i = \mathbf{11.75\%}$				

K_d **(aftertax cost)** $= 11.75\,(1 - .42) = \mathbf{6.82\%}$

Market values:

Equity:	$5,000,000 \times \$30 =$	$\$150,000,000$
Preferred shares:	$400,000 \times \$75 =$	$\$\ 30,000,000$

Debt:

Calculator:	$FV = \$160,000,000$ (Face value due at maturity)
	$PV = ?$ $PMT = \$19,200,000$ (Annual coupon rate @ 12%)
	$N = 10$ $\%i = 11.75\%$ (Current yield)
Compute:	$PV = \mathbf{\$162,283,407}$

Capital Structure	Market value	Weighting	Cost	Overall
Debt	$\$162,283,407$	0.4741	0.0682	.0323
Preferred shares	30,000,000	0.0877	0.0833	.0073
Equity	150,000,000	0.4382	0.1422	.0623
	$\$342,283,407$	1.0000		.1019

Weighted cost of capital = **10.19%**

11-9. **Titanic Ice**

Equity:

$K_j = R_f + \beta_j\,(R_m - R_f)$	Government bonds = riskfree rate
$K_j = 0.06 + 1.3\,(0.08)$	Market risk premium = $(R_m - R_f)$
$K_j = 0.06 + 0.104$	
$K_j = 0.164 = \mathbf{16.4\%}$	

Earnings sufficient: No adjustment for flotation costs.

Calculator:	$FV = \$2.40$	$PV = \$1.884$	$PMT = 0$	$N = 3$	$\%i = ?$
Compute:	$g = \%i = \mathbf{8.4\%}$				

$$P_0 = \frac{D_1}{K_e - g} = \frac{\$2.40\,(1 + 0.084)}{0.164 - 0.084} = \frac{\$2.60}{0.08} = \mathbf{\$32.50}$$

Market value:	$\$32.50 \times 1,000,000 =$	$\$32,500,000$

Preferreds:

$$K_p = \frac{D_p}{P_p - F} = \frac{\$0.3125 \times 4}{\$26 - (\$26 \times 0.04)} = \frac{\$1.25}{\$24.96} = 0.0501 = \textbf{5.0\%}$$

Market value: $\$26.00 \times 150,000 =$ $\$3,900,000$

Debt:

$$Y^I = \frac{\$100 + \dfrac{\$1,000 - \$1,206}{14}}{0.6\,(\$1,206) + 0.4\,(\$1,000)} = \frac{\$100 + (-\$14.71)}{\$724 + \$400} = \frac{\$85.29}{\$1,124} = 0.0759 = \textbf{7.59\%}$$

Calculator:	$FV = \$1,000$	$PV = \$1,206.11$	$PMT = \$100$	$N = 14$	$\%i = ?$
Compute:	$Y = \%i = \textbf{7.56\%}$				

$$K_d = \frac{Y\,(1 - T)}{1 - F} = \frac{0.0756(1 - .4)}{1 - .04} = \frac{0.0454}{.96} = 0.0473$$

Market value: $\$1,206.11 \times 20,000 =$ $\$24,122,200$

Capital Structure	Market value	Weighting	Cost	Overall
Debt	$\$24,122,200$	0.3986	0.0473	.0189
Preferred shares	3,900,000	0.0644	0.0500	.0032
Equity	32,500,000	0.5370	0.1640	.0881
	$\$60,522,200$	1.0000		.1102

Weighted cost of capital = **11.02%**

11-10. **CAPM**

(a) $K_j = R_f + \beta_j\,(R_m - R_f)$
       $K_j = 8\% + 1.0\,(14\% - 8\%) = \textbf{14\%}$

(b) $K_j = 8\% + .5\,(14\% - 8\%) = \textbf{11\%}$
       $K_j = 8\% + 1.8\,(14\% - 8\%) = \textbf{18.8\%}$

(c) $15\% = 6\% + \beta_j\,(12\% - 6\%)$
       $15\% - 6\% = \beta_j\,(6\%)$
       $\dfrac{9\%}{6\%} = \beta$
       $\beta_j = \textbf{1.5}$

11-11. **M. Hartsfield, Inc.**

(a) $K_j = R_f + \beta_j\,(R_m - R_f)$
       $.18 = .06 + \beta_j\,(.12 - .06)$
       $.18 - .06 = 06\,\beta_j$
       $\dfrac{.12}{.06} = \beta$
       $\beta_j = \textbf{2}$

(b) $K_j = .06 + .8\,(.12 - .06)$
       $K_j = .06 + .048 = .108 = \textbf{10.8\%}$

Summary: Capital budgeting involves planning capital expenditures that will generate future benefits. In this chapter the various techniques employed to evaluate the acceptability of capital projects are discussed and compared.

I.   **Characteristics of Capital Budgeting Decisions [p. 414]**

A. **Capital expenditures** are outlays for projects with lives extending beyond one year and perhaps for many years.

B. Intensive planning is required.

C. Capital expenditures usually require initial cash flows, often large, with the expectation of future cash inflows. The differing time periods of inflows and outflows require present-value analysis using the firms cost of capital as the basic discount rate.

D. The longer the time horizon associated with a capital expenditure, the greater the uncertainty. Areas of uncertainty are:
1. Annual costs and inflows.
2. Product life.
3. Interest rates.
4. Economic conditions.
5. Technological change.

II. **Administrative Considerations [p. 415]**

A. Search and discovery of investment opportunities

B. Collection of data

C. Evaluation and decision making

D. Reevaluation and adjustment

III. **Accounting Flows versus Resultant Cash Flows [p. 417 & 418]**

A. The capital budgeting process focuses on **cash flows** rather than income on an aftertax basis. Income figures do not reflect the cash available to a firm due to the deduction of noncash expenditures such as amortization (CCA).

B. Evaluation involves the incorporation of all **resultant cash flows (incremental and decremental)** in the capital budgeting analysis. All costs and benefits that will occur as a result of the investment decision should be included in the analysis. Sunk costs are ignored. Opportunity costs included. Cash flows that would occur regardless of the capital expenditure are non-resultant and are irrelevant to the decision.

C. Accounting flows are not totally disregarded in the capital budgeting process.

1. Investors' emphasis on earnings per share may, under certain conditions, require use of income rather than cash as the decision criterion.
2. Top management may elect to glean the short-term personal benefits of an income effect rather than the long-run cash-flow effects, which are more beneficial from the shareholder's viewpoint.

IV. **Methods for Ranking Investment Proposals [p. 421]**

   A. Average Accounting Return (AAR) **[p. 421]**
      1. The AAR is given by the following formula:

$$AAR = \frac{Average\ earnings\ aftertax}{Average\ book\ value}$$

      2. Deficiencies of the method
         a. Book values not market values are used, including accruals not cash flows.
         b. The pattern of cash flows is ignored, therefore the time value of money is not considered.

   B. Payback Period **[p. 422]**

      1. The **payback period** is the length of time necessary for the sum of the expected annual cash inflows to equal the cash investment. A cutoff period is established for comparison. Capital proposals with a payback in excess of the cutoff are rejected.
      2. Deficiencies of the method
         a. Inflows after the cutoff period are ignored.
         b. The pattern of cash flows is ignored, therefore, time value of money is not considered.
      3. Though not conceptually sound, the payback period is frequently used.
         a. Easy to use
         b. Emphasizes liquidity
         c. Quick return is important to firms in industries characterized by rapid technological development.

   C. Net Present Value (NPV) **[p. 424]**

      1. In this method, the cash inflows are discounted at the firm's cost of capital or some variation of that measure.
      2. If the present value of the cash inflows equals or exceeds the present value of the cash investment, the capital proposal is acceptable.

   D. Internal Rate of Return (IRR) **[p. 425]**

      1. The **IRR** method requires calculation of the rate that equates the cash investment with the cash inflows.
      2. The calculation procedure is the same as the yield computation presented in Chapter 9.
         a. If the inflows constitute an annuity, the IRR may be computed directly.

$$\frac{Investment}{Annuity} = PV_{IFA}$$

         The IFA may then be found in the present value of an annuity table and its correspondent interest rate (IRR).
         b. If the cash inflows do not constitute an annuity, determination of IRR is a trial-and -error process. The same framework for NPV analysis can be employed to determine the IRR. Different discount rates are used until NPV = 0.
         c. The calculator can be effective
         d. A project is acceptable if the IRR exceeds a minimum rate of return.

   E. Profitability Index **[p. 429]**

      1. **The profitability index (PI) is equal to the present value of inflows divided by the present value of outflows.**
      2. **Projects with a ratio of greater than 1 are acceptable and this method provides a means to compare relative profitability of projects.**

V. **Selection Strategy [p. 430]**

   A. All non-mutually exclusive projects having a NPV > = 0 (which also means IRR > or = cost of capital should be accepted under normal conditions).

   B. The NPV method and the IRR method always agree on the accept-reject decision on a capital proposal.

   C. A disagreement may arise between the NPV and IRR methods when a choice must be made from **mutually exclusive** proposals **[p. 430]** or all acceptable proposals cannot be taken due to capital rationing.

      1. The primary cause of disagreement is the differing discounting assumptions. The NPV method of discounts cash inflows at the cost of capital. The IRR method discounts cash inflows at the internal rate of return.
      2. The more conservative net present-value technique is usually the recommended approach when a conflict in ranking arises.

VI. **Capital Rationing [p. 433]**

   A. Management may implement **capital rationing** by artificially constraining the amount of investment expenditures.

   B. Under capital rationing, some acceptable projects may be declined due to management's fear of growth or hesitancy to use external financing.

   C. Under capital rationing, projects are ranked by NPV and accepted until the rationed amount of capital is exhausted.

VII. **Net Present Value Profile [p. 434]**

   A. The characteristics of an investment may be summarized by the use of the net present value profile.

   B. The **NPV profile** provides a graphical representation of an investment at various discount rates.

   C. Three characteristics of an investment are needed to apply the net present value profile:

      1. The net present value at a zero discount rate.
      2. The net present value of the project at the normal discount rate (cost of capital).
      3. The internal rate of return for the investment.

   D. The NPV profile is particularly useful in comparing projects when they are mutually exclusive or under conditions of capital rationing.

VIII. **Capital Cost Allowance [p. 438]**

   A. The income Tax Act of Canada allows an amortization expense from income under capital costs allowance system. A cash flow effect is created by reducing taxes payable and those tax saving must be considered in capital budgeting analysis.

   B. Several considerations determine the amount of (CCA) Capital Cost Allowance (amortization) allowable as the result of a particular capital acquisition.

      1. Each capital acquisition is assigned to a particular asset class (asset pool) which determines the rate of CCA.
      2. Only half the CCA rate is allowable in the year of acquisition.
      3. Amortization for the most part is on the declining balance method and it is the asset pool, not the individual asset that is amortized for tax purposes. As a result, if an asset pool remains open an acquired asset is effectively amortized to infinity.
      4. Therefore, tax savings result each year to infinity as a result of a capital acquisition.

5. The sale of an acquired asset reduces the amount remaining in an asset pool (its Undepreciated Capital Cost).

C. The following formula gives the present value of all the tax savings resulting from CCA of an acquired capital asset, taking into account the half rate rule assuming the asset pool continues indefinitely.

P.V. of CCA Tax Shield $\left(C - S_{pv}\right)\left(\dfrac{dT_c}{r+d}\right)\left(\dfrac{1+.5r}{1+r}\right)$ (12-1; page 444)

C = change in capital cost pool resulting from acquiring the asset
S_{pv} = change capital cost pool resulting from the salvage value
r = discount rate
d = CCA rate for the asset class
T_c = corporate tax rate
n = number of years in the future we intend to sell off the asset

D. If an asset pool ends certain tax consequences are triggered. The difference between the Undepreciated Capital Cost (UCC) and the last asset sold must be:

1. Added back to income if UCC is less than the sale price (Recaptured CCA).
2. Deducted from income if UCC exceeds the sale price (Terminal Loss).

IX. **Investment Tax Credit [p. 441]**

A. The Income Tax Act allows for tax credits on certain capital investments deemed appropriate for economic reasons by the Federal government. Cash flow consequences result.

1. A direct reduction in taxes payable by the amount of the investment tax credit.
2. A reduction in tax saving through CCA because the amount of investment tax credit is deducted from the asset pool (UCC) in the year following acquisition. The half rate rule will not apply.

X. **The Replacement Decision [p. 446]**

Refer to Tables 12-15 and 12-16, text pages 447 and 448.

XI. **Suggested Considerations for NPV Analysis [p.450]**

XII. **Review of Formulas**

See text page 452 or insert card.

Chapter 12: Multiple Choice Questions

1. Which of the following statements is incorrect? [Chapter. 12]
   a. The payback method is deficient because of its failure to incorporate the time value of money.
   b. If the NPV > 0, the proposal is acceptable.
   c. If the internal rate of return < cost of capital, the proposal should be rejected.
   d. The NPV and IRR methods always agree when evaluating mutually exclusive projects.
   e. The NPV and IRR methods always agree on the accept-reject decision.

2. Constraining investment in acceptable investments is called: [p. 433]
   a. Capital consumption.
   b. Capital rationing.
   c. Selection strategy.
   d. Technological restriction.
   e. A replacement problem.

3. In the net present value method, cash flows are discounted at: [p. 424]
   a. The cost of capital.
   b. The internal rate of return.
   c. The net profit margin.
   d. The CCA.
   e. The ITC.

4. Which of these statements comparing the NPV and IRR methods is correct? [p. 432]
   a. The NPV method assumes discounting of cash flows at the internal rate of return.
   b. The IRR method assumes discounting of cash flows at the cost of capital.
   c. The NPV method assumes discounting of cash flows at the cost of capital.
   d. The IRR assumes discounting of cash flows at the internal rate of return.
   e. Both *c* and *d* are correct statements.

5. Which of the following should be emphasized when making a capital expenditure decision? [p. 417]
   a. Resultant income
   b. Existing expenses
   c. Resultant cash flows
   d. The P/E ratio
   e. The EPS

6. The NPV and IRR methods may provide different mutually exclusive project rankings because: [p. 432-438]
   a. NPV incorporates time value of money, and IRR does not.
   b. IRR uses income, and NPV focuses on cash flow.
   c. NPV ignores cash flows beyond the crossover period.
   d. Differing discounting assumptions.
   e. IRR uses accelerated amortization and NPV does not.

7. The payback period: [p. 422]
   a. Is deficient because it ignores cash flows beyond the payback period.
   b. Ignores time value of money.
   c. May be useful to firms in industries characterized by rapid technological development.
   d. Emphasizes liquidity.
   e. All of the above are correct statements

8. The first step in the capital budgeting process is: [p. 415]
   a. Collection of data
   b. Assignment of probabilities
   c. Decision making
   d. Idea development
   e. Assessment of results

9. When the NPV of a capital expenditure proposal is > zero, the IRR: [p. 425]
   a. Will be > the cost of capital.
   b. May be > or < the cost of capital.
   c. Cannot be determined from the NPV information.
   d. Will be = the cost of capital.
   e. Will be < the cost of capital.

10. When projects are mutually exclusive or capital rationing has been imposed, the preferred capital budgeting technique is the: [p. 438]
   a. Profitability index.
   b. IRR method.
   c. NPV method.
   d. Payback method.
   e. NOI method.

Multiple Choice Answer Key: Chapter 12

1.	d	2.	b	3.	a	4.	e	5.	c
6.	d	7.	e	8.	d	9.	a	10.	c

Chapter 12: Problems

12-1. Recycle Paper Company utilizes the payback period to evaluate investment proposals. It is presently considering two investment opportunities. The first project will cost $100,000 and the second $675,000.

	Investment A Net investment = $100,000			Investment B Net investment = $500,000	
Year	Expected Cash Inflows		Year	Expected Cash Inflows	
1	$25,000		1	$125,000	
2	25,000		2	250,000	
3	25,000		3	300,000	
4	25,000		4	225,000	
5	25,000		5	100,000	
6	10,000		6	25,000	
7	5,000		7	0	

(a) Compute the payback period for each of the investments.
(b) If the firm utilized a payback cutoff standard of three years which, if either, of the investments would be acceptable?

12-2. As a recent employee of Recycle Paper Company (*12-1* above), you recognize the deficiencies of the payback period method. After deriving the firm's required rate of return (cost of capital), you desire to illustrate alternative approaches to your boss.

(a) Assuming a cost of capital of 14%, calculate the NPV of investment proposals A and B.
(b) Should Recycle accept either of the investment proposals?

12-3. Capital budgeting decisions are very sensitive to the pattern of expected cash flows and to the discount rate (cost of capital) used in the analysis.

(a) Recompute the NPV of Investment A for Recycle using a discount rate of 10%. Would investment A be acceptable at the lower required rate of return?

(b) Recompute Investment B using the 14% required rate of return but interchange the Year 3 and Year 7 cash flows. In other words, the expected cash flow in Year 3 is 0 and in Year 7, $300,000. Is investment B acceptable?

12-4. Compute the internal rate of return of an investment of $30,000 that generates the following stream of cash inflows:

Year	Cash Inflows
1	$12,500
2	12,500
3	12,500

12-5. Rework Problem *12-4* using the following stream of cash inflows:

Year	Cash Inflows
1	$17,000
2	11,000
3	9,500

12-6. The Todd Corporation expects to generate the following cash flows from a $1,000,000 investment:

Year	Net Cash Inflows
1	$100,000
2	400,000
3	500,000
4	300,000
5	100,000

(a) Compute the net present value of the investment if the firm estimates its cost of capital to be 10%.
(b) Compute the internal rate of return of the investment.
(c) Compute the profitability index.

12-7. The Noles Corporation is contemplating the purchase of a new milling machine. The machine will cost $550,000. The machine is expected to generate earnings before amortization and taxes of $200,000 each year over its five-year economic life. Mr. Noles is aware that Parliament is currently debating some tax law changes that may take effect prior to the acquisition of the new machine. Proposed changes would necessitate using a CCA rate of 15%, rather than the current 30%. Noles' tax rates would increase to 48% instead of the current 42%. Noles' cost of capital is 12%.

(a) Compute the NPV of the new machine under existing CCA and tax laws.
(b) Compute the IRR of the new machine under existing CCA and tax laws.

12-8. Compute the NPV of the milling machine for Noles Corporation (*12-7*) above) assuming the new CCA rate of 15% is required under new tax laws (tax rates remain the same).

12-9. Assume that Parliament passes tax legislation increasing the corporate tax rate of Noles (*12-7* above) to 48% and also requires a new CCA rate of 15% on equipment such as the milling machine.

(a)   Compute the NPV of the milling machine.
(b)   Compute the IRR of the milling machine.

12-10. The Tough Grip Tire Corporation is analyzing the proposed purchase of a new tire-forming machine for $60,000. The proposed machine has an estimated economic life of seven years. As a class 10 asset its CCA rate is 30 percent. The machine will increase the firm's capacity, and it is expected to contribute $15,000 annually to earnings before amortization and taxes. The firm is in a 46% tax bracket and estimates its cost of capital to be 12%. The machine qualifies for an investment tax credit of 10 percent.

(a)   Compute the payback period for the investment.
(b)   Compute the NPV of the investment.
(c)   Compute the IRR of the investment.
(d)   Should the machine be acquired?

12-11. Liquid Steel, a major steel fabricator, is evaluating a proposal to replace a major piece of equipment in its operation. The automated nature of the new equipment enables it to be operated with two less workers. Liquid Steel operates three shifts, and the purchase of the new machine will generate annual savings in salaries of $88,000. No additional maintenance costs are anticipated.

The new machine will cost $250,000 and is expected to be useful for five years. The old machine which originally cost $100,000 one year ago also has a remaining useful life of five years. The old machine can be sold to a smaller manufacturer for $70,000. Liquid Steel is in the 46% tax bracket, and its estimated cost of capital is 10%. The appropriate CCA rate is 20 percent.

Determine whether the new machine should be purchased, by using the NPV method.

12-12. Knothole Furniture is analyzing a new $45,000 computer controlled lathe that will allow the firm to substantially reduce waste of wood materials in its furniture making process. Their old lathe has a book value of $18,000 and a remaining life of three years. The new lathe is expected to reduce materials costs by $19,000 each year of its three-year useful life. At the end of three years the lathe will have a market value (salvage value) of $10,000. Both lathes have a CCA rate of 20 percent. Although the old lathe can be used for three more years, it has no market value since furniture companies prefer to buy new, modern equipment. Knothole's financial manager estimates the company's cost of capital to be 13%. The firm is in a 40% tax bracket.

(a)   Compute the net present value of the proposed lathe replacement. Should the lathe be replaced?
(b)   Compute the internal rate of return of the proposal. Does it confirm your decision in (*a*)?
(c)   Assume now that the old lathe, which was originally purchased for $25,000, could be sold for $20,000. Compute the net present value of the replacement.

12-13. You are the president of Aladdin, Inc., and an exciting new investment has come to your attention. It will require an initial capital outlay of $600,000 to acquire a building. The building will join an existing asset pool to be amortized (for tax purposes) at 4 percent per year. In 15 years the building is projected to be worth $50,000. One year from now machinery worth $400,000 will arrive, you will pay for it, and it will join an asset pool with a 30 percent CCA rate for tax purposes. Fifteen years from *now* the machinery, it is estimated, will be worth $40,000. Six years from *now* the machinery will require an additional capital outlay of $85,000.

The investment will begin to generate yearly revenues of $310,000 on terms of net 30 days, and cash flow expenses of $40,000 a year, immediately following the acquisition of the machinery for a total of 14 years. These same cash flows will continue until 15 years from *now*. Aladdin has a tax rate of 43 percent, and its cost of capital is 13 percent.

Should Aladdin invest in this project?

12-14. Abracadabra Arcades owns and operates a number of boutiques for video games across the country. It now has an opportunity to open the River of Dreams Boutique at Whistler. It has just the right line of video machines that were purchased last year for $120,000 but have yet to be seen by the public. They are presently in secret storage facilities.

Unfortunately, new technological innovations have reduced the market value of the video machines to $90,000. Furthermore, the machines have not yet been amortized for tax purposes because they have not yet been put into use.

The River of Dreams Boutique will lease its premises for $14,500 per month and will spend $20,000 for computer hardware and its related systems software. In seven years, when the lease expires, the project will end and the computer will be worthless.

Monthly cash flow before amortization, taxes, and lease expenses is projected to be $22,000. Due to the novelty of the new games, in the first two years there will be an extra $3,000 per month in cash flow. Annual administrative and repair costs will be approximately $60,000. In seven years' time, the video machines will likely be sold to collectors for $12,000. To operate the boutique, an investment of $33,333 in working capital is required.

Abracadabra Arcades has a tax rate of 43 percent, and its cost of capital is 13 percent. The CCA rate on its computer will be 30 percent, and the CCA rate on video machines is 40 percent.

(a)   Should Abracadabra proceed with its River of Dreams Boutique?
(b)   What is the justification for using the cost of capital for the discount rate in this analysis?
(c)   If all markets are efficient (see Chapter 14) and your analysis reveals a positive net present value, what might this suggest about your analysis?

Chapter 12: Solutions

12-1.   **Recycle Paper Company**

(a)   Payback period

$$PP(A) = \frac{\$100,000}{\$25,000} = \textbf{4 years}$$

PP (B) =			
	$125,000	$125,000	Year 1
	250,000	375,000	Year 2
$\frac{125,000}{300,000} = 0.42$		500,000	**Year 2.42**

(b)   **Investment B**

12-2. Recycle (continued)

(a) **Investment A**

Tables:
NPV = $25,000 (3.433) + $10,000 (.456) + $5,000 (.400) – $100,000
NPV = $92,385 – $100,000 = **– $7,615**

Calculator:	$FV = 0$	$PV = ?$	$PMT = \$25,000$	$N = 5$	$\%i = 14\%$
Compute:	$PV = \$85,827.02$				

Calculator:	$FV = \$10,000$	$PV = ?$	$PMT = 0$	$N = 6$	$\%i = 14\%$
Compute:	$PV = \$4,555.87$				

Calculator:	$FV = \$5,000$	$PV = ?$	$PMT = 0$	$N = 7$	$\%i = 14\%$
Compute:	$PV = \$1,998.19$				

NPV = $85,827.02 + $4,555.87 + $1,998.19 – $100,000 = **– $7,619**

Investment B

Tables:
NPV = $125,000 (.877) + $250,000 (.769) + $300,000 (.675) + $225,000 (.592) + $100,000 (.519) + $25,000 (.456) – $500,000
NPV = $700,875 – $500,000 = **$200,875**

Calculator:	$FV = \$125,000$	$PV = ?$	$PMT = 0$	$N = 1$	$\%i = 14\%$
Compute:	$PV = \$109,649.12$				

Calculator:	$FV = \$250,000$	$PV = ?$	$PMT = 0$	$N = 2$	$\%i = 14\%$
Compute:	$PV = \$192,366.88$				

Calculator:	$FV = \$300,000$	$PV = ?$	$PMT = 0$	$N = 3$	$\%i = 14\%$
Compute:	$PV = \$202,491.46$				

Calculator:	$FV = \$225,000$	$PV = ?$	$PMT = 0$	$N = 4$	$\%i = 14\%$
Compute:	$PV = \$133,218.06$				

Calculator:	$FV = \$100,000$	$PV = ?$	$PMT = 0$	$N = 5$	$\%i = 14\%$
Compute:	$PV = \$51,936.87$				

Calculator:	$FV = \$25,000$	$PV = ?$	$PMT = 0$	$N = 6$	$\%i = 14\%$
Compute:	$PV = \$11,389.66$				

NPV = 109,649.12 + 192,366.88 + 202,491.46 + 133,218.06+ 51,936.87+ 11,389.66 – $500,000.00
= $701,052.05 – $500,000.00
= $201,052

(b) Recycle should accept **Investment B**.

12-3. **Recycle (again)**

(a)   **Investment A**

Tables:
NPV = $25,000 (3.791) + $10,000 (.564) + $5,000 (.513) – $100,000
NPV = $102,980 – $100,000 = **$2,980**

Calculator:	$FV = 0$	$PV =?$	$PMT = \$25,000$	$N = 5$	$\%i = 10\%$
Compute:	$PV = \$94,769.67$				

Calculator:	$FV = \$10,000$	$PV =?$	$PMT = 0$	$N = 6$	$\%i = 10\%$
Compute:	$PV = \$5,644.74$				

Calculator:	$FV = \$5,000$	$PV =?$	$PMT = 0$	$N = 7$	$\%i = 10\%$
Compute:	$PV = \$2,565.79$				

NPV = $94,769.67 + $5,644.74 + $2,565.79 – $100,000 = **$2,980.20**

Investment A is acceptable under these conditions.

(b)   **Investment B**

Tables:
NPV = $125,000 (.877) + $250,000 (.769) + $0 (.675) + $225,000 (.592) + $100,000 (.519) + $25,000 (.456) + $300,000 (.400) – $500,000
NPV = $618,375 – $500,000 = **$118,375**

Calculator:	$FV = \$300,000$	$PV =?$	$PMT = 0$	$N = 7$	$\%i = 14\%$
Compute:	$PV = \$119,891.20$				

NPV = 109,649.12 + 192,366.88 + 0 + 133,218.06 + 51,936.87 + 11,389.66 + 119,891.20 – $500,000
  = $618,475.79 – $500,000.00
  = **$118,475.79**

Investment B is still acceptable, but the NPV is considerably reduced.
An easier calculation to determine the change in NPV of Investment B follows:
$$\Delta NPV = \$300,000\ (Year\ 3\ PV_{IFA} - Year\ 7\ PV_{IFA})$$
$$= \$300,000\ (.400 - .675)$$
$$= \$300,000\ (- .275)$$
$$= -\ \mathbf{\$82,500}$$

Calculator:	3rd year	$202,491.46
	7th year	119,891.20
		$ 82,600.26

This can be confirmed by subtracting the original NPV from the recomputed NPV.
$$\Delta NPV = \$118,452 - \$201,052 = \mathbf{-\$82,600}$$

12-4. The stream of expected cash inflows constitutes an annuity.

$$\frac{Investment}{Annuity} = PV_{IFA} = \frac{\$30,000}{\$12,500} = 2.4$$

Refer to present value of an annuity table; 3 years, $PV_{IFA} = 2.4$.
IRR = approximately 12%

Calculator:	$FV = 0$	$PV = \$30,000$	$PMT = \$12,500$	$N = 3$	$\%i = ?$
Compute:	$\%i = 12.04\%$				

12-5. Since the expected cash inflows do not constitute an annuity, the IRR must be determined by a trial and error process.

(1)   Average the inflows:

$$\frac{\$17,000 + \$11,000 + \$9,500}{3} = \$12,500$$

(2)   Divide the investment by the average annuity

$$\frac{\$30,000}{\$12,500} = 2.4$$

(3)   Refer to the present value of annuity table. The IRR indicated is approximately 12%, the same rate indicated in Problem *12-4*. Notice, however, that the returns take place sooner than in the previous situation. It should be expected that the actual rate of return will be greater than previously determined.

(4)   Trial and error process.
Try 18%

Year	18%			Calculator
1	$ 17,000 × .847	=	$14,399	$14,407
2	11,000 × .718	=	7,898	7,900
3	9,500 × .609	=	5,786	5,782
			$28,083	$28,089

The amount $28,089 is less than the investment of $30,000; therefore, another "guess" must be made. The basic equation that is being used is:

$$\$30,000 = \frac{\$17,000}{(1+r)^1} + \frac{\$11,000}{(1+r)^2} + \frac{\$9,500}{(1+r)^{31}}$$

We seek to find the value of r, the internal rate of return that makes the equation hold. To increase the right side we lower the denominator or, in other words, select a lower rate.

Try 14%

Year	14%			Calculator
1	$ 17,000 × .877	=	$14,909	$14,912
2	11,000 × .783	=	8,459	8,464
3	9,500 × .675	=	6,413	6,412
			$29,781	$29,788

Try 13%

Year	13%			Calculator
1	$ 17,000 × .885	=	$15,045	$15,044
2	11,000 × .783	=	8,613	8,615
3	9,500 × .693	=	6,548	6,584
			$30,242	**$30,243**

The rate lies **between 13% and 14%**.

Calculator:	Cf_i = – 0; 17,000; 11,000; 9,500;	%i =?
Compute:	**IRR = 13.53%**	

12-6. Todd Corporation

(a)   *Net present value = present value of inflows – present value of outflows*

Present value of inflows

Year	10%			Calculator
1	$100,000 × .909 =	$	90,900	$ 90,909
2	$400,000 × .826 =		330,400	330,579
3	$500,000 × .751 =		375,500	375,657
4	$300,000 × .683 =		204,900	204,904
5	$100,000 × .621 =		62,100	62,092
			$1,063,800	$1,064,141

Present value of inflows	$1,063,800	$1,064,141
Present value of outflows	1,000,000	1,000,000
Net present value	**$ 63,800**	**$ 64,141**

(b)   Note: The NPV and IRR approaches may disagree on the ranking of projects, but they always agree on the accept-reject decision. Whenever you are asked to compute both NPV and IRR, it will be wise to compute the NPV first in order to have some direction in making your first trial-and-error guess. Since the NPV of this investment is positive, the IRR must be greater than the cost of capital.

Try 12%

Year	12%			Calculator
1	$100,000 × .893 =	$	89,300	$ 89,286
2	$400,000 × .797 =		318,800	318,878
3	$500,000 × .712 =		356,000	355,890
4	$300,000 × .636 =		190,800	190,655
5	$100,000 × .567 =		56,700	56,743
			$1,011,600	**$1,011,452**

$1,011,600 exceeds investment of $1,000,000 so a higher rate (13%) should be selected.

Year	13%			Calculator
1	$100,000 × .885 =	$	88,500	$ 88,496
2	$400,000 × .783 =		313,200	313,259
3	$500,000 × .693 =		346,500	346,525
4	$300,000 × .613 =		183,900	183,996
5	$100,000 × .543 =		54,300	54,276
			$ 986,400	**$ 986,552**

The IRR lies between 12% and 13%.

(c)

$$\text{Profitability index (PI)} = \frac{present\ value\ of\ inflows}{present\ value\ of\ outflows} = \frac{\$1,064,141}{\$1,000,000} = \mathbf{1.0641}$$

12-7. Noles Corporation

(a)   NPV

Year	Event	Expected Cash Flow	Aftertax Cash Flow	Present Value
0	Purchase machine	($550,000)	---	($550,000)
1-5	Earnings	200,000	116,000	418,154
	CCA (PV of tax savings)	$(550,000)\left(\dfrac{.3\times.42}{.12+.3}\right)\left(\dfrac{1+.5(.12)}{1+.12}\right)$		156,161
			NPV =	**$ 24,315**

(b)   IRR

Since the NPV is positive, try a higher discount rate than 12%.

Try 14%:

Year	Event	Expected Cash Flow	Aftertax Cash Flow	Present Value
0	Purchase machine	($550,000)	---	($550,000)
1-5	Earnings	200,000	116,000	398,238
	CCA (PV of tax savings)	$(550,000)\left(\dfrac{.3\times.42}{.14+.3}\right)\left(\dfrac{1+.5(.14)}{1+.14}\right)$		147,829
			NPV =	($ 3,933)

The internal rate of return is determined when the NPV = 0.

At   12%   NPV = $24,315
    ?   NPV =   0   } 24,315   } 28,248
   14%   NPV = ($3,933)

IRR is approximately: $12\% + \dfrac{24,315}{28,248}(2\%) = 12\% + 0.86(2\%) = \mathbf{13.72\%}$

NPV > 0, IRR > 12%, Decision: Yes!

12-8.   **Noles Corporation (continued)**

NPV

Year	Event	Expected Cash Flow	Aftertax Cash Flow	Present Value
0	Purchase machine	($550,000)	---	($550,000)
1-5	Earnings	200,000	116,000	418,154
	CCA (PV of tax savings)	$(550,000)\left(\dfrac{.15 \times .42}{.12 + .15}\right)\left(\dfrac{1 + .5(.12)}{1 + .12}\right)$		121,458
			NPV =	($ 10,388)

12-9.   Noles Corporation (continued)

(a)   NPV

Year	Event	Expected Cash Flow	Aftertax Cash Flow	Present Value
0	Purchase machine	($550,000)	---	($550,000)
1-5	Earnings	200,000	104,000	374,897
	CCA (PV of tax savings)	$(550,000)\left(\dfrac{.15 \times .48}{.12 + .15}\right)\left(\dfrac{1 + .5(.12)}{1 + .12}\right)$		138,810
			NPV =	**($ 36,293)**

(b)   IRR
Since the NPV is negative, try a lower discount rate than 12%.

Try 10%:

Year	Event	Expected Cash Flow	Aftertax Cash Flow	Present Value
0	Purchase machine	($550,000)	---	($550,000)
1-5	Earnings	200,000	104,000	394,242
	CCA (PV of tax savings)	$(550,000)\left(\dfrac{.15 \times .48}{.10 + .15}\right)\left(\dfrac{1 + .5(.10)}{1 + .10}\right)$		151,200
			NPV =	**($ 4,558)**

The internal rate of return is determined when the NPV = 0.

At   12%   NPV =   ($36,293) ⎫
                                ⎬ 31,735 ⎫
      10%   NPV =   ($4,558) ⎭   ⎬ 36,293
      ?   NPV =   0   ⎭

IRR is approximately: $12\% - \dfrac{36,293}{31,735}(2\%) = 12\% - 1.144(2\%) = \textbf{9.71\%}$

NPV < 0, IRR < 12%, Decision: No!

12-10. Tough Grip Tire Corporation

(a)   Payback

Year	Event	Expected Cash Flow		Aftertax Cash Flow
0	Cash Investment	($60,000)		($60,000)
1	ITC	6,000		6,000
1	Earnings	15,000	(1 – .46)	8,100
	CCA	9,000	(.46)	4,140
2	Earnings	15,000	(1 – .46)	8,100
	CCA	13,500	(.46)	6,210
3	Earnings	15,000	(1 – .46)	8,100
	CCA	9,450	(.46)	4,347
4	Earnings	15,000	(1 – .46)	8,100
	CCA	6,615	(.46)	3,043
5	Earnings	15,000	(1 – .46)	8,100
	CCA	4,631	(.46)	2,130

By the end of the 4th year $56,140 is paid back.
By the end of the 5th year $66,370 is paid back.
Payback occurs in the 5th year.

CCA Schedule

Year	(UCC) Amortization Base	Calculation	(CCA) Amortization
1	$60,000	60,000 (.30) (.5)	$ 9,000
2	45,000*	45,000 (.30)	13,500
3	31,500	31,500 (.30)	9,450
4	22,050	22,050 (.30)	6,615
5	15,435	15,435 (.30)	4,631
6	10,804	10,804 (.30)	3,241

This schedule continues as long as asset pool is open.
*ITC is taken out of the pool in the 2nd year.

(b)   NPV

Year	Event	Expected Cash Flow	Aftertax Cash Flow	Present Value
0	Cash investment	($60,000)	---	($60,000)
1	ITC	6,000		5,357
1-7	Earnings	15,000	(1 −.46) 8,100	36,966
	CCA (PV of tax savings)	$(60,000)\left(\dfrac{.30 \times .46}{.12 + .30}\right)\left(\dfrac{1 + .5(.12)}{1 + .12}\right)$		18,658
	CCA lost when ITC enters pool	$(-5,357)\left(\dfrac{.30 \times .46}{.12 + .30}\right)$		(1,760)
			NPV =	($ 779)

(c)   IRR

Since NPV is negative but near zero. Try a rate slightly below the cost of capital

Year	Event	Expected Cash Flow	Aftertax Cash Flow	Present Value
0	Cash investment	($60,000)	---	($60,000)
1	ITC	6,000		5,405
1-7	Earnings	15,000	(1 −.46) 8,100	38,169
	CCA (PV of tax savings)	$(60,000)\left(\dfrac{.30 \times .46}{.11 + .30}\right)\left(\dfrac{1 + .5(.11)}{1 + .11}\right)$		19,194
	CCA lost when ITC enters pool	$(-5,405)\left(\dfrac{.30 \times .46}{.11 + .30}\right)$		(1,819)
			NPV =	$ 949

The internal rate of return is determined when the NPV = 0.

At	12%	NPV =	($779)		
				1.728	
	?	NPV =	0		949
	11%	NPV =	949		

IRR is approximately: $11\% + \dfrac{949}{1,728}(1\%) = 11\% + 0.55(1\%) = \textbf{11.55\%}$

NPV < 0, IRR < 12% (hurdle rate), Decision: No!

12-11. Liquid Steel

(a)   NPV

Year	Event	Expected Cash Flow	Aftertax Cash Flow	Present Value
0	Purchase new machine	($250,000)	---	($250,000)
0	Sell old machine	70,000	---	70,000
1-5	Annual savings	88,000	(1 – .46) 47,520	180,138
	CCA (PV of tax savings)	$(250{,}000 - 70{,}000)\left(\dfrac{.20 \times .46}{.10 + .20}\right)\left(\dfrac{1 + .5(.10)}{1 + .10}\right)$		<u>52,691</u>
			NPV =	**$ 52,829**

Decision: Replacement machine should be purchased as NPV > 0.

12-12. Knothole Furniture

(a)   NPV

Year	Event	Expected Cash Flow	Aftertax Cash Flow	Present Value
0	Purchase new machine	($45,000)	---	($45,000)
1-3	Annual savings	19,000	(1 – .40) 11,400	26,917
3	Salvage lathe	10,000		6,931
	CCA (PV of tax savings)	$(45{,}000 - 6{,}931)\left(\dfrac{.20 \times .40}{.13 + .20}\right)\left(\dfrac{1 + .5(.13)}{1 + .13}\right)$		<u>8,698</u>
			NPV =	**($ 2,454)**

Decision: Do not purchase replacement lathe, as NPV < 0.

(b)   IRR

Since the NPV was negative, the IRR must be less than the cost of capital.
Try 10%

Year	Event	Expected Cash Flow	Aftertax Cash Flow	Present Value
0	Purchase new machine	($45,000)	---	($45,000)
1-3	Annual savings	19,000	(1 – .40) 11,400	28,350
3	Salvage lathe	10,000		7,513
	CCA (PV of tax savings)	$(45,000 - 7,513)\left(\dfrac{.20 \times .40}{.10 + .20}\right)\left(\dfrac{1 + .5(.10)}{1 + .10}\right)$		9,542
			NPV =	$ 405

The internal rate of return is more than 10% [but less than 11%; NPV = (586) at 11%] which is less
than the cost of capital. Decision in (a) confirmed.

(c)   NPV (old machine sold for $20,000)

Year	Event	Expected Cash Flow	Aftertax Cash Flow	Present Value
0	Purchase new machine	($45,000)	---	($45,000)
0	Sell old lathe	20,000	---	20,000
1-3	Annual savings	19,000	(1 - .40) 11,400	26,917
3	Salvage lathe	10,000		6,931
	CCA (PV of tax savings)	$(45,000 - 20,000 - 6,931)\left(\dfrac{.20 \times .40}{.13 + .20}\right)\left(\dfrac{1 + .5(.13)}{1 + .13}\right)$		4,129
			NPV =	$ 12,977

Decision: Purchase the replacement lathe, as NPV > 0.

12-13. Aladdin Inc.

$n = 15$ $T = 43\%$ $r = 13\%$ d (machinery) $= 30\%$
d (buildings) $= 4\%$

Year	Event	Expected Cash Flow	Aftertax Cash Flow	Present Value @ 13%
0	Purchase building	(600,000)	–	($600,000)
1	Purchase machinery	(400,000)	–	(353,982)
1	Working capital	$310,000 \times 30/365$ = (25,479)	–	(22,548)
2-15	Revenues	310,000	176,700 1,113,650	985,531
2-15	Expenses	(40,000)	22,800 143,697	(127,165)
6	Machinery outlay (capitalized)	(80,000)	–	(38,425)
15	Sell building	50,000	–	7,995
15	Sell machinery	40,000	–	6,396
15	Recovery WC	24,658	–	4,074

CCA (PV of tax savings) machinery $\left(353,982 + 38,425 - 6,396\right)\left(\dfrac{.30 \times .43}{.13 + .30}\right)\left(\dfrac{1 + .5(.13)}{1 + .13}\right) = 109,142$ CCA PV

of tax savings) building $\left(600,000 - 7,995\right)\left(\dfrac{.04 \times .43}{.13 + .04}\right)\left(\dfrac{1 + .5(.13)}{1 + .13}\right) = 56,452$ **NPV =**

$27,470

Aladdin should proceed with this project. Value will be added to the firm.

12-14. **Abracadabra Arcades**

(a) $n = 7$ $T = 43\%$ $r = 13\%$ d (video machines) = 40%
                                                        d (computer)   = 30%

Year	Event	Expected Cash Flow	Aftertax Cash Flow	Present Value @ 13%
0	Use video machines (opportunity cost) (market value)	$(90,000)	–	$(90,000)
0	Purchase computer	(20,000)	–	(20,000)
0	Working capital	(33,333)	–	(33,333)
1-7	Cash flow	22,000 × 12 = 264,000	150,480	665,514
1-2	Extra cash flow	3,000 × 12 = 36,000	20,520	34,229
1-7	Expenses	14,500 × 12 + 60,000 = (234,000)	(133,380)	(589,888)
7	Sell machines	12,000	–	5,101
7	Sell computer	0		0
7	Recovery WC	33,333	–	14,169

CCA (PV of tax savings) videos

$$(90,000 - 5,101)\left(\frac{.40 \times .43}{.13 + .40}\right)\left(\frac{1 + .5(.13)}{1 + .13}\right) = 25,967 \quad \text{CCA(PV}$$

of tax savings) computer

$$(20,000)\left(\frac{.30 \times .43}{.13 + .30}\right)\left(\frac{1 + .5(.13)}{1 + .13}\right) = \underline{5,655} \quad \textbf{NPV =}$$

$17,414

Abracadabra should proceed with its River of Dreams Boutique.

(b)   The cost of capital is justified in analysis if the investments are of the same risk as other investments. Since this is one of several video game boutiques we may assume the risk is similar from the point of view of Abracadabra.

(c)   If the market for video game operation is efficient we should expect a NPV = 0. Since we have a positive NPV this might suggest that some of the expected cash flows are incorrect or the selection of the discount rate does not fully reflect the risk exposure. In addition, we must question the efficiency of the markets for computers and leasing premises at Whistler.

Chapter 13

**Risk and
Capital Budgeting**

Summary: In this chapter the definitions of risk, its measurement and incorporation into the capital budgeting process, and the basic tenets of portfolio theory are examined.

I.   **Risk in Capital Budgeting [p. 470]**

    A. Management's ability to achieve the goal of owner's wealth maximization will largely depend on success in dealing with risk.

    B. Definition: Variability of possible outcomes. The wider the distribution of possible outcomes for a particular investment, the greater its **risk**.

Refer to Figure 13-1, text page 470.

    C. **Risk aversion** is a basic assumption of financial theory. Investors require a higher expected return the riskier an investment is perceived to be. Certainty is preferred to uncertainty.

II. **The Measurement of Risk [p. 472]**

    A. The basic risk measurement is the **standard deviation**, which is a measure of dispersion around an expected value. A numerical example appears on page 473-474.

        1. The **expected value** is a weighted average of the possible outcomes of an event times their probabilities.

$$\overline{D} \text{ (expected value)} = \sum DP \qquad \text{(13-1; page 473)}$$

        2. The formula for computing the standard deviation is:

$$\sigma \, (standard \; deviation) = \sqrt{\sum (D - \overline{D})^2 P} \qquad \text{(13-2; page 473)}$$

    B. The Coefficient of Variation

        1. The standard deviation is limited as a risk measure for comparison purposes. Two projects A and B may both be characterized by a standard deviation of $10,000 but A may have an expected value of $50,000 and B $100,000.

        2. The size problem is eliminated by employing the **coefficient of variation**, V, which is the ratio of the standard deviation of an investment to its expected value. The higher the coefficient of variation, the higher the risk.

$$Coefficient \; of \; variation \, (V) = \frac{\sigma}{\overline{D}} \qquad \text{(13-3; page 475)}$$

$$V_A = \frac{\$10,000}{\$50,000} = 0.20 \qquad V_B = \frac{\$10,000}{\$100,000} = 0.10$$

    C. **Beta (β) is** another measure of risk that is widely used in portfolio management. Beta measures the volatility of returns on an individual stock relative to a stock market index of returns. (See Appendix 11A for a thorough discussion.)

III. **Risk and the Capital Budgeting Process [p. 476]**

A. The expected inflows from capital projects usually are risky - they are not certain.

B. Cash flows of projects bearing a normal amount of risk undertaken by the firm should be discounted at the cost of capital.

C. The required rate of return of lenders and investors increases as the risk they are subjected to increases.

D. The cost of capital is composed of two components: the **risk-free rate** (time value of money only) and a **risk premium** (risk associated with usual projects of a business).

E. Adjustments must be made in the evaluation process for projects bearing risk levels (more or less) other than normal.

   1. **Risk-adjusted discount rate approach**: The discount rate is adjusted upward for a more risky project and downward for projects bearing less than normal risk. A firm may establish a risk-adjusted discount rate for each of various categories of investment such as new equipment, new market, etc.

Refer to Figure 13-5, text page 477.

   2. The **CAPM** may be helpful in establishing an appropriate discount rate based on a project's risk.

   3. **Certainty equivalent approach [p. 481]**: recognition of differing risk levels is made by multiplying the expected cash flow by a percentage figure indicating degree of certainty and discounting at the risk-free rate.

   4. "Seat of the pants" approach is based on experience and preference of the decision maker.

F. Increasing risk over time: Our ability to forecast diminishes as we forecast farther out in time.

G. Qualitative measures may mean that management makes up various risk classes for projects having similar characteristics.

IV. **Simulation Models [p. 482]**

A. The uncertainty associated with a capital budgeting decision may be reduced by projecting and preparing for the various possible outcomes resulting from the decision. Simulation models and decision trees enhance management's initial capital budget decision efforts and also expedite intermediate decisions (Whether to continue, etc.) once the initial decision has been made.

B. Simulation models - various values for economic and financial variables affecting the capital budgeting decision are randomly selected and used as inputs in the simulation model. Although the process does not ensure that a manager's decision will be correct (in terms of actual events), decisions can be made with a greater understanding of possible outcomes. Sensitivity analysis adjusts the model one variable at a time, identifying key variables for further investigation.

C. **Decision trees** - the sequential pattern of decisions and resulting outcomes and associated probabilities (managerial estimates based on experience and statistical processes) are tracked along the branches of the decision tree. Tracing the sequence of possible events in this fashion is a valuable analytical tool in the decision making process.

V.   **The Portfolio Effect [p. 485]**

   A.   A risky project may actually reduce the total risk of the firm through the **portfolio effect**.

Refer to Figure 13-9, text page 485.

   B.   Projects that move in opposite directions in response to the same economic stimulus are said to be negatively correlated. Since the movement of negatively correlated projects is in opposite directions, the total deviation is less than the deviations of the projects individually.

   C.   The relationship between project movements is expressed by the **coefficient of correlation** which varies from the extremes of - 1 (perfectly negative) to +1 (perfectly positive) correlation. Non - correlated projects have a correlation coefficient of zero.

   D.   Although projects with correlation coefficients of - 1 are seldom found, some risk reduction will occur, however minor, when projects are negatively correlated or have low positive correlation.

   E.   The firm should strive to achieve two objectives in combining projects according to their risk-return characteristics.

      1.   Achieve the highest possible return at a given risk level.
      2.   Allow the lowest possible risk at a given return level.

   F.   The various optimal combinations of projects are located along a risk-return line referred to as the **"efficient frontier."**

Refer to Figure 13-11, text page 489.

   G.   The possible benefit of the portfolio effect suggests that an adjustment to the discount rate used in capital budgeting (particularly the cost of capital) may be in order.

VI.   **The Share Price Effect [p. 490]**

   A.   Higher earnings do not necessarily contribute to the firm's goal of owner's wealth maximization. The firm's earnings may be discounted at a higher rate because investors perceive that the firm is pursuing riskier projects to generate the earnings.

   B.   The risk aversion of investors is verified in the capital market. Firms that are very sensitive to cyclical fluctuations tend to sell at lower P/E multiples.

VII.   **Review of Formulas**

   See text page 491 or insert card.

Chapter 13: Multiple Choice Questions

1.   When employing the certainty equivalent approach in capital budgeting: [p. 481]
   a.   Flows are discounted at the risk-adjusted discount rate.
   b.   Flows are discounted at the weighted-average cost of capital.
   c.   Flows are discounted at the marginal cost of capital.
   d.   Flows are discounted at the risk-free rate.
   e.   Flows are not discounted.

2. If investors perceive that a firm has become more risky: [p. 477]
   a. They will lower their discount rate when valuing the firm's stock.
   b. They will raise their discount rate when valuing the firm's stock.
   c. They may raise or lower their discount rate when valuing the firm's stock.
   d. They will require a lower rate of return from the stock.
   e. None of the answers above are correct.

3. The coefficient of variation is computed by: [p. 475]
   a. Dividing the expected value by the standard deviation.
   b. Multiplying the firm's beta by its coefficient of correlation.
   c. Dividing the standard deviation by the expected value.
   d. Squaring the standard deviation.
   e. Squaring the probability of graduating from college.

4. A basic assumption of financial theory is that investors are: [p. 471]
   a. Risk averse.
   b. Risk neutral.
   c. Risk seekers.
   d. Risk ignorant.
   e. Positively correlated with risk.

5. The returns of securities A and B have a zero correlation coefficient. The returns are: [p. 486-487]
   a. Slightly positively correlated.
   b. Negatively correlated.
   c. Slightly negatively correlated.
   d. Positively correlated.
   e. Independent.

6. Optimal combinations of risk-return characteristics of investments are located along the: [p. 489]
   a. Risk-free curve.
   b. Efficient frontier.
   c. Certainty equivalent curve.
   d. Yield curve.
   e. Normal distribution.

7. Reduction in risk by combining risky securities with appropriate risk-return characteristics is called: [p. 485]
   a. Risk aversion.
   b. Correlation.
   c. The portfolio effect.
   d. The share price effect.
   e. The "seat of the pants" approach.

8. Which of the following is the correct relationship (choose the *best* answer). [p. 470]
   a. High risk, high return
   b. High risk, low return
   c. High risk, high required return
   d. Low risk, high return
   e. High risk, low required return

9. Firms (and investors) strive to combine projects (investments) such that they: [p. 488]
   a. Achieve the highest return at the highest risk.
   b. Achieve the highest return at a given level of risk.
   c. Allow the lowest possible risk at a given level of return.
   d. Answers *a* and *c* are correct.
   e. Answers *b* and *c* are correct.

10. Risk-adjusted discount rates are composed of: [Chapter 13]
    a. The risk-free rate minus a risk premium.
    b. The risk-free rate plus beta.
    c. The required rate of return x beta plus the risk-free rate.
    d. The risk-free rate plus a risk premium.
    e. The risk premium minus the risk-free rate.

Multiple Choice Answer Key: Chapter 13

1.	d	2.	b	3.	c	4.	a	5.	e
6.	b	7.	c	8.	c	9.	e	10.	d

Chapter 13: Problems

13-1.   Zappa Manufacturing is evaluating an investment opportunity that would require an outlay of $100,000. The annual net cash inflows are estimated to vary according to economic conditions.

Economic Conditions	Probability	Cash Flow
very good	.10	40,000
good	.45	32,000
fair	.30	20,000
poor	.15	4,000

The firm's required rate of return is 14%. The project has an expected life of six years. Compute the expected NPV of the proposed investment.

13-2.   Calculate the coefficient of variation of the cash flows of Zappa Manufacturing (*13-1* above).

13-3.   Ringgold, Inc. is planning advertising campaigns in three different market areas. The estimates of probability of success and associated additional profits are provided below:

	Market 1		Market 2		Market 3	
	Profit	Probability	Profit	Probability	Profit	Probability
Fair	10,000	.40	5,000	.20	16,000	.50
Normal	18,000	.50	8,000	.60	20,000	.30
Excellent	25,000	.10	12,000	.20	25,000	.20

(a)   Compute the expected value and standard deviation of profits resulting from advertising campaigns in each of the market areas.
(b)   Rank the three markets according to riskiness using the coefficient of variation.
(c)   Is one area clearly superior and why?

13-4. The Alphabet Soup Company is seeking to diversify its operations and is considering acquisition of three firms in unrelated fields. Alphabet's cost of capital is approximately 10% and the coefficient of variation associated with its usual investments averages .3. Using the information below, determine which, if any, of the three proposed acquisitions are acceptable investments.

(1)

Firm	Blue Boy Supermarkets	Acey-Ducey Electronics	Wild Cat Drilling
Required investment	$25,000,000	$40,000,000	$22,000,000
Expected life	12 years	8 years	6 years
Expected annual aftertax returns	3,000,000	8,000,000	5,000,000
Estimated standard deviation of returns	300,000	3,000,000	3,000,000

(2) Required rates of return on company investments:

Coefficient of variation	less than .2	.2 to .40	.4 to .55	above .55
Required rate of return	8%	10%	15%	20%

13-5. Moonshot, Inc., a venture capital firm, is considering investing in either a new space movie, *Star Raiders*, or sponsoring the development of an energy saving device that will be used in heavy manufacturing. Each project can be funded for $30 million. Using the information below, compute the net present value of each of these projects.

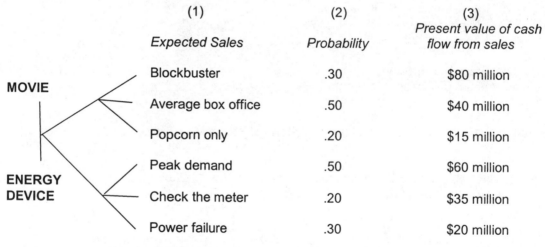

	(1) Expected Sales	(2) Probability	(3) Present value of cash flow from sales
MOVIE	Blockbuster	.30	$80 million
	Average box office	.50	$40 million
	Popcorn only	.20	$15 million
ENERGY DEVICE	Peak demand	.50	$60 million
	Check the meter	.20	$35 million
	Power failure	.30	$20 million

Author's note: This problem does not incorporate the time value of money, but if called for, the discount rate used should be the risk free rate.

13-6. Plummer Chemicals employs the internal rate of return method to evaluate capital expenditure proposals. Plummer adjusts its acceptable rate of return to accommodate varying degrees of risk. The cash flow characteristics of a capital proposal and required rate of return are presented below.

Coefficient of variation of cash flow	Required rate of return
.10 to .15	.12
.16 to .35	.14
.36 to .50	.18
> .5	.24

Expected cash flows each year from proposal for 10 years	Probability
$400,000	.20
600,000	.40
800,000	.30
900,000	10

The capital expenditures proposal will require a cash investment of $3,000,000. Utilizing the internal rate of return method and the information above, should Plummer accept the proposal?

Chapter 13: Solutions

13-1. Zappa Manufacturing
Expected Annual Net Cash Inflow

Conditions	Probability	Cash inflows	Expected annual flow
Very good	.10	$40,000	$ 4,000
Good	.45	32,000	14,400
Fair	.30	20,000	6,000
Poor	.15	14,000	2,100
			$26,500

$NPV = \$26,500 \times PV_{IFA}(n = 6, r = 14\%) - \$100,000$
$NPV = \$26,500 \times 3.889 - \$100,000$
$NPV = \$103,058.50 - \$100,000 = \textbf{\$3,058.50}$

13-2. Zappa Manufacturing (continued)

D	$\overline{D}$	$D - \overline{D}$	$(D - \overline{D})^2$	P	$(D - \overline{D})^2 P$
$40,000	$26,500	$13,500	$182,250,000	.10	$18,225,000
32,000	26,500	5,500	30,250,000	.45	13,612,500
20,000	26,500	(6,500)	42,250,000	.30	12,675,000
14,000	26,500	(12,500)	156,250,000	.15	23,437,500
					$67,950,000

$\sigma \ (standard\ deviation) = \sqrt{\$67,950,000} = \textbf{\$8,243} \ (rounded)$

$Coefficient\ of\ variation\ (V) = \dfrac{\sigma}{\overline{D}} = \dfrac{\$8,243}{\$26,500} = \textbf{0.31}$

13-3. **Ringgold, Inc.**

(a)   *Exp. Val. Mkt. 1* = 10,000 (.40) + 18,000 (.50) + 25,000 (.10)
      Exp. Val. Mkt. 1 = 4,000 + 9,000 + 2,500 = **15,500**

Standard deviation of profits in Market 1:

$$\sigma = \sqrt{(.4)(10,000 - 15,500)^2 - (.5)(18,000 - 15,500)^2 - (.1)(25,000 - 15,500)^2}$$
$$\sigma = \sqrt{12,100,000 + 3,125,000 + 9,025,000}$$
$$\sigma = \sqrt{24,250,000} = \textbf{4,924}$$

Exp. Val. Mkt. 2 = (5,000) (.2) + (8,000) (.6) + (12,000) (.2)
Exp. Val. Mkt. 2 = 1,000 + 4,800 + 2,400 = **$8,200**

Standard deviation of profits in Market 2:

$$\sigma = \sqrt{(.2)(5,000 - 8,200)^2 - (.6)(8,000 - 8,200)^2 - (.2)(12,000 - 8,200)^2}$$
$$\sigma = \sqrt{2,048,000 + 24,000 + 2,888,000}$$
$$\sigma = \sqrt{4,960,000} = \textbf{2,227}$$

Exp. Val. Mkt. 3 = 16,000(.5) + 20,000(.3) + 25,000(.2)
Exp. Val. Mkt. 3 = 8,000 + 6,000 + 5,000 = **19,000**

Standard deviation of profits in Market 3:

$$\sigma = \sqrt{(.5)(16,000 - 19,000)^2 - (.3)(20,000 - 19,000)^2 - (.2)(25,000 - 19,000)^2}$$
$$\sigma = \sqrt{4,500,000 + 300,000 + 7,200,000}$$
$$\sigma = \sqrt{12,000,000} = \textbf{3,464}$$

(b)   Coefficient of variation:

$$Market\ 1\ (V) = \frac{\sigma}{D} = \frac{\$4,924}{\$15,500} = \textbf{0.32}$$

$$Market\ 2\ (V) = \frac{\sigma}{D} = \frac{\$2,227}{\$8,200} = \textbf{0.27}$$

$$Market\ 3\ (V) = \frac{\sigma}{D} = \frac{\$3,464}{\$19,000} = \textbf{0.18}$$

(c)   Market area 3

      Highest NPV
      Lowest risk

13-4. Blue Boy Supermarkets

$$V = \frac{\sigma}{\overline{D}} = \frac{\$300,000}{\$8,000,000} = \textbf{0.10}$$ Required rate of return = 8%

$NPV =$ $3,000,000 (N = 12, %i = 8) – $25,000,000
$NPV =$ $22,608,234 – $25,000,000 = – **$2,391,766**

Supermarket investment is unacceptable even though the required rate of return, 8%, is less than normally required of investments.

Acey-Ducey Electronics

$$V = \frac{\sigma}{\overline{D}} = \frac{\$3,000,000}{\$8,000,000} = \textbf{0.375}$$ Required rate of return = 10%.

$NPV =$ $8,000,000 (N = 8, %i = 10) – $40,000,000
$NPV =$ $42,679,410 – $40,000,000 = **$2,679,410**

Acey-Ducey Electronics is an acceptable investment.

Wild Cat Drilling

$$V = \frac{\sigma}{\overline{D}} = \frac{\$3,000,000}{\$5,000,000} = \textbf{0.60}$$ Required rate of return = 20%.

$NPV =$ $5,000,000 (N = 6, %i = 20) – $22,000,000
$NPV =$ $16,627,551 – $22,000,000 = – **$5,372,449**

Wild Cat Drilling is an unacceptable investment.

13-5. Moonshot, Inc.

	(1) Expected Sales	(2) Prob	(3) Present Value of Cash Flow from Sales	(4) Initial Invest.	(5) NPV (3-4)	(6) Expected NPV (2x5)
MOVIE	Blockbuster	.30	$80 mil.	$30 mil.	$50 mil.	$15 mil.
	Avg box office	.50	$40 mil.	$30 mil.	$10 mil.	$ 5 mil.
	Popcorn only	.20	$15 mil.	$30 mil.	$(15) mil.	$(3) mil.
						$17 mil.
ENERGY DEVICE	Peak demand	.50	$60 mil.	$30 mil.	$30 mil.	$15 mil.
	Check meter	.20	$35 mil.	$30 mil.	$ 5 mil.	$ 1 mil.
	Power failure	.30	$20 mil.	$30 mil.	$(10) mil.	$(3) mil.
						$13 mil.

13-6. Plummer Chemicals

Expected Cash Flow Each Year

$400,000	× .20	=	$ 80,000	
600,000	× .40	=	240,000	
800,000	× .30	=	240,000	
900,000	× .10	=	90,000	
			$650,000	

Internal Rate of Return

$PV_A = A \times PV_{IFA}\,(n = 10,\ i =?)$

$3,000,000 = \$650,000/\ PVA_{IFA}$

$$PVA_{IFA} = \frac{\$3,000,000}{\$650,000} = 4.615$$

IRR is **between 17% and 18%**.

Calculator:	$FV = 0$	$PV = \$3,000,000$	$PMT = \$650,000$	$N = 10$	$\%i =?$
Compute:	$\%i = \textbf{17.26\%}$				

Standard Deviation of Cash Flows

D	$\overline{D}$	$D - \overline{D}$	$\left(D - \overline{D}\right)^2$	P	$\left(D - \overline{D}\right)^2 P$
$400,000	$650,000	($250,000)	$62,500,000,000	.20	$12,500,000,000
600,000	650,000	(50,000)	2,500,000,000	.40	1,000,000,000
800,000	650,000	150,000	22,500,000,000	.30	6,750,000,000
900,000	650,000	250,000	62,500,000,000	.10	6,250,000,000
					$26,500,000,000

$$\sigma\,(standard\ deviation) = \sqrt{\$26,500,000,000} = \textbf{\$162,788}\ (rounded)$$

$$Coefficient\ of\ variation\,(V) = \frac{\sigma}{\overline{D}} = \frac{\$162,788}{\$650,000} = \textbf{0.25}$$

The required rate of return of the project is 14% according to Plummer's schedule. The IRR of this proposal which is 17.26% exceeds the requirement. **The proposal is acceptable**.

Chapter 14   Capital Markets

Summary: The role of the various participants in the capital market and its structure are discussed in this chapter.

I.   **Money and Capital Markets [p. 506]**

    A.   **Money market**: Short-term market for securities maturing in a year or less.

    B.   **Capital market**: Long-term market for securities with maturities greater than one year.

    C.   More often, companies search all capital markets including world markets for capital at the lowest cost.

    D.   The markets allocate funds to the most efficient users.

II.   **International Capital Markets [p. 507]**

    A.   Competition for low cost funding is worldwide.

    B.   Money flows between countries based on the best perceived risk-return tradeoffs.

III.   **Competition for Funds in the Capital Markets [p. 507]**

    A.   Overall

        1.   Corporations compete for funds in the capital and money markets with the federal and provincial governments.
        2.   Although a return to longer capital funding occurred in the 90s the money markets had contributed almost 50 percent of new funding in the late 80s.
        3.   The overall size of the money market has remained relatively constant over the last 10 years. Commercial paper and asset backed securities are becoming increasingly important. Treasury bills although still dominant, are less so.
        4.   In the last decade corporations have increased their outstanding bond obligations significantly, relative to governments.
        5.   The Canadian equity market, centred in Toronto, in the 1990s surpassed the bond market in book value of securities.
        6.   The Canadian bond market represents only about 2 percent of the world bond market. Therefore we find foreign currency bond obligations equal to domestic obligations for corporations.

    B.   Government Securities **[p. 509]**

        1.   The federal debt approximated $588 billion in 1997. Non-residents hold 19% of federal debt. Since then annual federal surpluses have reduced capital and money market funding requirements. Treasury bills outstanding have dropped 50 percent. This has caused some liquidity problems in the money markets. The average term of federal debt has lengthened to 6.5 years. Marketable debt in 2001 was $418 billion.
        2.   Provincial governments collectively had accumulated debt of $380 billion in 2000, 38 percent denominated in foreign currencies. Traditionally long term borrowers, the provinces have borrowed short term through treasury bills.
        3.   Municipal governments are small borrowers in the capital markets and their issues are relatively illiquid. About $2 billion was raised in 1991, a high water mark. Today net borrowings are negative

C. Corporate Securities **[p. 511]**

Refer to Figure 14-4, text page 511.

1. New bond financings have been volatile from one year to the next, varying with market conditions. In 1993 and 1994 equity issues were predominant but by the late 1990s bonds were dominating. Large financings were done outside of Canada in the 80s, but there has been a return to the Canadian markets in the 90s. The economic slowdown of 1992 is illustrated in Figure 14-4.
2. Preferred stock is a relatively important source of corporate financing in Canada. The tax treatment of dividends and holding company ownership account for this prevalence of preferred stock. Recent tax changes and disruptions in corporate ownership have seen preferred financings decline in recent years.
3. Common stock is a significant source of corporate financing, varying with market conditions. More equity capital is being raised abroad. (A concern).

D. It appears that managers tend to time their issue of common stock to take advantage of higher valuations. This accounts for the large variances in funding sources from year to year. In 1994, 78% was raised through equity and in 2000, 77% through debt. (Figure 14-4).

1. Corporate managers don't appear to believe in rational markets and their behavior suggests they believe underpricing/ overpricing occurs.
2. With increased market value, more debt is possible, yet managers substitute equity for debt.

E. Historically, internally generated funds (retain earnings and depreciation) have been the major source of funds to the corporation. Inflation has accounted for the greater reliance on external financing in recent years.

F. The majority of internally generated funds are not included in reported earnings. Funds from operations, but not included in reported earnings through the amortization process, provide the primary "source" of internal funding.

IV. **The Supply of Capital Funds [p. 516]**

A. Business and government have been net demanders of funds and the household sector the major supplier of funds in our **three-sector economy**.

B. Household sector savings are usually channeled to the demanders of funds through financial intermediaries such as chartered banks, trust companies, mortgage companies, and credit unions.

C. Other intermediaries in the flow-of-funds process include mutual funds, pension plans, and insurance firms.

Refer to Figure 14-8, text page 516.

D. The international saver/investor has become a very important supplier of capital to the Canadian economy.

V. **The Role of the Security Markets [p. 518]**

Refer to Figure 14-10, text page 517.

A. Securities markets aid the allocation of capital between the sectors of the economy. The money and bond markets dwarf the stock market in daily trading volumes.

B. Security markets enable the demanders of capital to issue securities by providing the necessary liquidity for investors in two ways :

1. Corporations are able to sell new issues of securities rapidly at fair competitive prices.
2. The markets allow the purchaser of securities to convert the securities to cash with relative ease and speed in the **secondary market**.

VI. **The Organization of the Security Markets [p. 519]**

A. The Organized Exchanges **[p. 519]**

1. Exchanges facilitate the trading of various securities through a competitive auction market that establishes prices by supply and demand conditions. Registered brokers transact orders on behalf of buyers and sellers.
2. The Toronto Stock Exchange (TSX) is Canada's most important exchange with about 1,400 listings. Montreal is a derivatives exchange. Winnipeg is basically a commodity exchange. The Venture Exchange (TSX-V) owned by the TSX is a junior exchange.
3. To be listed on the TSX, firms must meet certain minimum requirements pertaining to pretax cash flow, working capital, net tangible, number of shareholders, number of publicly held shares, and market value.

B. Foreign Exchanges **[p. 519]**

1. Canada represents about 2% of the world's capital market value. Many Canadian companies are listed on foreign exchanges (Table 14-1). Daily trading volumes rank the TSX 12th in the world for stock exchanges.

C. Over the Counter Markets (OTC) **[p. 521]**

1. The OTC market is a network of brokers and dealers linked by computer display terminals, telephones, and teletypes.
2. Few OTC stocks could obtain listing on the TSX and because of lower average prices trading volume on the OTC is much less than the organized exchanges.
3. A reporting system on about 1,000 designated unlisted stocks is maintained by the Investor Dealers Association and the Ontario Securities Commission.
4. Bonds and debentures trade in the OTC market. Bond and money market securities volumes are at least 10 times the volume (each) on the organized equity exchanges.

VII. **Recent Developments in Trading [p. 522]**

A. The Canadian securities markets face several challenges.

1. Competition from the liquid capital markets of the world, in particular the U.S.
2. 'Upstairs trading', bypassing the stock exchanges.
3. Alternative trading platforms using the Internet.

B. Securities markets are more competitive.

1. Commissions are no longer fixed. Discount brokers now execute a significant amount of trades.
2. Chartered banks and foreign investment houses operate brokerage services in Canada.

C. There are efforts to make the markets more liquid.

   1. Computer Assisted Trading Systems (CATS) that had executed trades on the TSX has been replaced. Canadian Over-The-Computer Automated Trading Systems (COATS) has been in place since 1986. Floor trading no longer occurs at the TSX and it is fully automated
   2. Dealers are acting more as principals rather than brokers as the Canadian markets have had few buyers and sellers relatively; they are 'thin.'
   3. Markets now operate 24 hours a day.
   4. The TSX will become a public company.

VIII. **Market Efficiency [p. 523]**

   A. Criteria of Efficiency

      1. Rapid adjustment of prices to new information.
      2. Continuous market; successive prices are close.
      3. Market is capable of absorbing large dollar amounts of securities without destabilizing the price.

   B. The more certain the income stream, the less volatile price movements will be and the more efficient the market will be. This is because of the tremendous liquidity and volume of trades in these securities.

   C. The efficiency of the stock market is stated in three forms.

      1. **Weak form**: Past price information is unrelated to future prices; trends cannot be predicted and taken advantage of by investors.
      2. **Semi-strong form**: Prices reflect all public information.
      3. **Strong form**: Prices reflect all public and private information.

   D. A fully efficient market, if it exists, precludes insiders and large institutions from making profits from security transactions in excess of the market in general. Transactions in an efficient market are said to have an NPV = 0. That is, investors are appropriately compensated for the risk they assume in purchasing a financial asset.

   E. The efficiency of the market is debatable, but most would agree that the movement is toward greater efficiency. This suggests that the possibility of abnormal returns should be investigated carefully. These returns should not be obtainable in an efficient market.

IX. **Securities Regulation [p. 528]**

   A. Regulation of the securities industry is a provincial responsibility. Regulations of the Ontario Securities Commission (OSC) tend to be adopted by most provinces. The stock exchanges and the Investment Dealers Association carry out self-regulation.

   B. There has been erosion of the separate functions of the four pillars of Canadian finance; banking, trust companies, insurance companies and securities dealers. As well, the real sector and financial sector have now overlapped under one corporate roof in some instances.

   C. Banks now dominate the securities business in Canada and seek to remain competitive in the world financial markets.

   D. Foreign interests can also own up to 100 percent of the investment dealers and do play a significant role in the underwriting of issues by Canadian firms.

   E. There is a need for a coordinated approach to securities regulation amongst governments and for greater deregulation across investment sectors.

Chapter 14: Multiple Choice Questions

1. In the Canada, the largest outstanding money market security is: [p. 545]
    a. Commercial paper.
    b. Treasury bills.
    c. Bankers' acceptances.
    d. Asset-backed securities.
    e. Common shares.

2. Which of the following levels of market efficiency is based on past price information being unrelated to future prices? [p. 526]
    a. Weak form
    b. Strong form
    c. Illegal form
    d. Insider trading
    e. Semi-strong form

3. The over-the-counter market is primarily regulated by the: [p. 521]
    a. OTC.
    b. TSX.
    c. OSC.
    d. Bank of Canada.
    e. Investment Dealers Association.

4. The largest secondary market daily trading in Canada is in: [p. 517]
    a. Canada bonds.
    b. Treasury bills.
    c. Commercial paper.
    d. Bankers' acceptances.
    e. Equities.

5. The primary benefit provided investors by security markets is: [p. 518]
    a. Guaranteed returns.
    b. Liquidity.
    c. Riskless trading.
    d. Costless trading.
    e. Access to all relevant security information.

6. Non-residents holdings are most significant in the[p. 517]]
    a. Stock market.
    b. Money market
    c. Bond market.
    d. Toronto market.
    e. Winnipeg commodity market.

7. The markets are generally considered to be: [p. 527]
    a. Weak form efficient.
    b. Inefficient.
    c. Semi-strong form efficient.
    d. Abnormally efficient.
    e. Strong form efficient.

8. The market for securities having maturities of more than one year is called the: [p. 506]
   a. Intermediate market.
   b. Money market.
   c. International market.
   d. Capital market.
   e. Domestic market.

9. The level of market efficiency most impacted by insider trading is the: [p. 526]
   a. Strong form.
   b. Semi-weak form.
   c. Doubly strong form.
   d. Semi-strong form.
   e. Weak form.

10. Which of the following owns securities and seeks to earn a profit from buying and selling? [p. 521]
    a. Brokers.
    b. OSC.
    c. OTC.
    d. Dealers.
    e. Canadian Dealing Network (CDN).

Multiple Choice Answer Key: Chapter 14

1.	b	2.	a	3.	e	4.	a	5.	b
6.	c	7.	c	8.	d	9.	a	10.	d

Investment Underwriting: Public and Private Placement

Summary: This chapter discusses the role of the investment dealer, the advantages and disadvantages of selling securities to the public, and the private placement of securities with various institutions.

I. **The Role of Investment Underwriting [p. 535]**

   A. The investment dealer serves as a middleperson in channeling funds from the investor to the corporation.

II. **Functions of the Investment Dealer [p. 535]**

   A. **Underwriter:** The risk-taking function. The underwriter bears the risk of fluctuations in the selling price of the security issue.

      1. Best efforts (marketed deal) or bought deal
      2. Seasoned of initial public offering

   B. **Market maker:** The investment dealer may engage in buying and selling of a security to ensure an available market.

   C. **Advising:** Corporations may seek an investment dealer's advice on the size, timing, and marketability of security issues. Advice is also rendered pertaining to merger and acquisition decisions, leveraged buyouts, and corporate restructuring.

   D. **Agency functions:** As an agent, the investment dealer assists in the private placement of security issues and in the negotiating process of merger and acquisition transactions.

III. **The Distribution Process [p. 537]**

   A. The **managing investment dealer** forms an underwriting syndicate of investment dealers to increase marketability of the issue and spread the risk.

   B. Syndicate members, acting as wholesalers, sell the securities to brokers and dealers who eventually sell the securities to the public.

   Refer to figure 15-1, text page 538.

   C. The **spread** is the difference in the price of a security to the public and the amount paid to the issuing firm and represents the compensation of those participating in the distribution.

      1. The spread is divided among the distribution participants. The lower a party falls in the distribution hierarchy, the lower the portion of the spread received.
      2. Usually, the larger the dollar values of an issue, the smaller the spread.
      3. The spread on equity issues is greater than on debt issues because of the greater price uncertainty.
      4. A corporation will also incur other flotation costs such as printing and legal expenses in raising funds.
      5. Spread is calculated with the public price as the base, although the return to the underwriter should be calculated on the base of funds received (pages 538-539).

IV.   **Pricing the Security [p. 540]**

A. Several factors must be considered by the managing investment dealer when negotiating the issue price of a security of a first-time issuer.

1. Experience of the firm in the market.
2. Financial position of the issuing firm.
3. Expected earnings and dividends.
4. P/E multiples of firms in the same industry.
5. Anticipated public demand.

B. The issue price of securities of firms with existing securities outstanding is usually determined by "underpricing."

1. Price is set slightly below current market value.
2. Underpricing is partially a result of the dilutive effect of spreading earnings over a greater number of shares of stock.

C. **Dilution:** When new common stock is sold, the new shares issued immediately cause earnings per share to decline until the earnings can be increased from the investment of new funds.

D. **Market Stabilization:** The managing investment dealer seeks to stabilize the market (keep the sales price up) by repurchasing securities while at the same time selling them.

E. **Aftermarket:** Research has indicated that initial public offerings often do well in the immediate aftermarket.

V.   **Changes in the Investment Industry [p. 542]**

A. Growth

1. The growth in functions other than underwriting was the primary cause of increased revenues in recent years. These include corporate finance, mergers and acquisitions, derivatives and bond trading.
2. In addition to domestic growth, many investment firms are expanding their international operations.

B. Consolidation

1. Need for larger capital bases (Canadian investment houses are small internationally).
2. Investment dealers going public; entry of Canadian banks and foreign financial institutions into markets. Consolidation of investment and banking operations within the chartered banks has occurred.
3. Development of financial conglomerates.
4. Combining the trading operations of banks on immense trading floors.
5. Global trading units, particularly U.S. expansion.

VI.   **Underwriting Activity in Canada [p. 544]**

Refer to figure 15-3, text page 544.

A. Equity underwritings dropped in 2001 due to weak equity markets. Debt financings became significant particularly in foreign capital markets.

B. Asset backed securities have become a significant underwriting activity.

VII. **Public versus Private Financing [p. 545]**

    A. Advantages of being public

        1. Greater availability of funds.
        2. Prestige.
        3. Higher liquidity for shareholders.
        4. Established price of public issues aids a shareholder's estate planning.
        5. Enables a firm to engage in merger activities more readily.

    B. Disadvantages of being public

        1. Company information must be made public through Securities Commissions.
        2. Accumulating and disclosing information is expensive in terms of dollars and time.
        3. Short-term pressure from security analysts and investors.
        4. Embarrassment from public failure.
        5. High cost of going public.

    C. **Initial Public Offerings (IPOs)** are distinguished from **seasoned** offerings as the first time a firm sells equity in the market by. The price performance of these shares is particularly volatile because of the minimal information available in comparison to shares already trading in the markets. **[p. 546]**

    D. **Private placement** refers to selling securities directly to insurance companies, pension funds, and others rather than going through security markets. **[p. 547]**

        1. Used more for debt than equity issues.
        2. Advantages.
            a. Eliminates the lengthy, expensive registration process with the Securities Commissions.
            b. Greater flexibility in negotiating terms of issue.
            c. Costs of issue are less.
        3. The usually higher interest cost on a privately placed debt instrument is a disadvantage.

    E. Firms that elect to go private are usually small companies that are seeking to avoid large auditing and reporting expenses. In the 1980's, however, larger firms have been going private to avoid the pressure of pleasing analysts in the short term. There are two basic ways to go private. The public firm can be purchased by a private firm or the company can repurchase all publicly traded shares from the shareholders.

    F. Many firms have gone private through **leveraged buyouts**. Management or some external group borrows the needed cash to repurchase all the shares of the company. Frequently the management of the private firm must sell off assets in order to reduce the heavy debt load.

    G. Several firms that have gone privately during the 1980's have restructured and returned to the public market at an increased market value. In some cases the firm was divided and the divisions were sold separately. The "breakup value" of some firms was substantially higher than the market value of the unified entity.

    H. The lack of leveraged buyout activity in Canada can be attributed to more tightly controlled corporations (as to ownership) and the cyclical nature of the cash flow of the corporations.

VIII. **Largest Investment Deals [p. 549]**

    A. In 2002 the PanCanadian/ Alberta Energy merger was one of the largest M & A deals. Activity decreased considerably in the weak capital markets.
    B. Privatization: The 1990s have been the decade for many state owned companies around the world issuing ownership securities to private individuals.
    C. Table 15-3 lists the biggest international privatization deals country by country.

Chapter 15: Multiple Choice Questions

1. Setting a price of a new security below current market value is called: [p. 542]
   a. Syndicating.
   b. Underwriting.
   c. Stabilizing.
   d. Spreading.
   e. Underpricing.

2. Many firms have gone private through: [p. 548]
   a. Prompt offering qualification system (POP).
   b. Leverage buyouts.
   c. Consolidation.
   d. Syndicating.
   e. Merger.

3. Selling securities directly to firms such as insurance companies is called: [p. 547]
   a. Private placement.
   b. Public placement.
   c. Syndication.
   d. Intermediation.
   e. Best efforts.

4. Which of the following is an investment dealer's risk-bearing function? [p. 536]
   a. Buying and selling to insure a market.
   b. Price support.
   c. Underwriting.
   d. Providing size and timing advice.
   e. Accepting deposits.

5. A managing investment dealer may seek to spread the risk by: [p. 537]
   a. Underpricing.
   b. Utilizing a leveraged buyout.
   c. Spreading.
   d. Forming a syndicate.
   e. Going public.

6. Which of the following is not an advantage of being a publicly traded firm? [p. 546]
   a. Prestige
   b. Higher liquidity for shareholders
   c. Frequent securities commission filings
   d. Greater availability of funds
   e. Increased ability to engage in merger activity

7. If the investment dealer does not bear the risk of fluctuations in the selling price of the security issue, the issue is handled: [p. 536]
   a. On a best-efforts basis.
   b. By syndication.
   c. By a prompt offering prospectus.
   d. By underwriting.
   e. By consolidation.

8. Permission to large firms by the securities commission to file a short form prospectus to shorten the waiting time required to issue securities is called: [p. 538]
   a. Private placement.
   b. Stabilizing the market.
   c. Market making.
   d. Prompt offering qualification system.
   e. Pre-selling.

9. Which of the following types of securities is most often involved in a private placement? [p. 547]
   a. Corporate bonds
   b. Common stock
   c. Preferred stock
   d. Treasury bills
   e. Municipal bonds

10. A firm that elects to buy-in all shares of stock in the public's hands is said to be: [p. 548]
   a. Consolidating.
   b. Leveraging.
   c. Going private.
   d. Spreading.
   e. Shrinking.

Multiple Choice Answer Key: Chapter 15

1.	e	2.	b	3.	a	4.	c	5.	d
6.	c	7.	a	8.	d	9.	a	10.	C

Chapter 15: Problems

15-1. The Timms Corporation expects earnings of $8,000,000 in the current year on 6,000,000 shares of common stock. The company is considering the effects on reported earnings of issuing an additional 2,000,000 shares of common stock.

(a)   What will be the initial dilution in earnings per share?
(b)   If the firm sells the stock for a net price of $23 per share and is able to earn 6% *aftertax* on the proceeds before year end, what will be the earnings per share?

15-2. Eighteen Wheeler Corporation has recently received approval from regulatory authorities to expand its territory. The firm needs $30,000,000 to acquire trucks and other equipment for their expanded route.

Company officials are confident that a 12-year term loan can be negotiated with a national insurance firm at an annual rate of 10%. Alternatively, an investment dealer has indicated that it will underwrite a common stock issue for a gross spread of 5%. The firm currently has 2,000,000 shares of stock outstanding.

(a)   If Eighteen's stock can be sold for $30, how many shares of stock must be sold to *net $30,000,000* assuming out-of-pocket costs are $600,000?

(b)   If the firm's earnings before interest and taxes increase to $10,000,000 and the applicable tax rate is 34%, what would the earnings per share be under each financing alternative? (Assume annual interest before financing of $1,000,000.)

(c)   Compute the approximate market price of the common stock if the P/E ratio remains at 10 if stock is issued but falls to 9.5 if debt is privately placed. This decline in P/E ratio may occur because with increased debt the firm is perceived to be riskier.

15-3. S. O'Neal Dunkin Donuts is planning a multiple security issue to raise $50,000,000. Following the advice of an investment dealer, the company will seek to issue $20,000,000 in 20-year corporate bonds with a 9% coupon rate and $10,000,000 (par value at $100 per share) of preferred stock with a $5 per share fixed dividend. The remainder of the $50,000,000 will come from the sale of common stock. The firm's common stock is currently selling at $32 per share.

    (a)   If the current yield to maturity on similar bonds is 11% and the management estimates flotation costs to be 2%, what amount will S. O'Neal Dunkin Donuts receive from the sale of bonds?

    (b)   The yield demanded in the market on comparable preferred stock is 8%. What is the expected selling price of the preferred stock? If the floatation cost of preferred stock averages 10%, what will be the net proceeds to the firm?

    (c)   If the investment dealer agrees to handle the common stock issue for a commission of $1.50 per share and advises S. O'Neal that underpricing of $2 per share will be necessary to sell the new stock, how many shares of common stock must be sold?

15-4. Prior to the issuance of the securities indicated (*15-3* above); S. O'Neal projected its operating earnings to be $18,000,000 for the coming year. It had annual interest payments of $2,200,000 and 4,000,000 shares of common stock outstanding. The firm had not issued preferred stock previously. The firm is in the 34% tax bracket.

    (a)   What was the projected EPS prior to the issuance of the securities indicated in *Problem 15-3*?

    (b)   At what before tax rate must the $50,000,000 be invested to maintain EPS available to common stock?

    (c)   If the P/E ratio falls from 15 to 12 due to the market's risk perception, what will be the percentage decline in the price per share?

Chapter 15: Solutions

15-1.   **Timms Corporation**

    (a)   Initial dilution

        Projected EPS prior to issue of new stock:

$$e.p.s. = \frac{earnings}{number\ of\ shares} = \frac{\$8,000,000}{6,000,000} = \mathbf{\$1.33}$$

        Projected EPS after issue of new stock:

$$e.p.s. = \frac{earnings}{number\ of\ shares} = \frac{\$8,000,000}{8,000,000} = \mathbf{\$1.00}$$

        The dilution effect = $1.33 – $1.00 = **$0.33 per share**

$$dilution\ effect = \frac{\$0.33}{\$1.33} = \mathbf{0.25} = \mathbf{25\%}$$

(b)　　*Net proceeds* = $23 × 2,000,000 = $46,000,000
　　Additional aftertax earnings = $46,000,000 × .06 = $2,760,000

New earnings per share:

$$e.p.s. = \frac{earnings}{number\ of\ shares} = \frac{\$8,000,000 + \$2,760,000}{8,000,000} = \textbf{\$1.345}$$

15-2.　Eighteen Wheeler Corporation

(a)　　$30.00
　　　<u>　1.50　</u>　(5% spread)
　　　$28.50　　proceeds/share of stock issued

$$number\ of\ shares\ that\ must\ be\ issued = \frac{\$30,000,000 + \$600,000}{\$28.50} = \textbf{1,073,684}$$

(b)

Stock		*Debt*	
EBIT	$10,000,000	EBIT	$10,000,000
Interest	<u>1,000,000</u>	Interest	<u>4,000,000</u>
Taxable income	9,000,000	Taxable income	$ 6,000,000
Taxes	<u>3,060,000</u>	Taxes	<u>2,040,000</u>
Net income	<u>$ 5,940,000</u>	Net income	<u>$ 3,960,000</u>

$$e.p.s. = \frac{earnings}{number\ of\ shares} = \frac{\$5,940,000}{3,073,684} = \textbf{\$1.93} \qquad \frac{\$3,960,000}{2,000,000} = \textbf{\$1.98}$$

(c)　　Share
　　　Share price = 10 × $1.93 = **$19.30**

　　　Debt
　　　Share price = 9.5 × $1.98 = **$18.81**

Note the possible conflict between maximizing EPS and maximizing the market value of shareholders' equity (market price).

15-3.　S. O'Neal Dunkin Donuts

(a)　　P_b = $90 (7.963) + $1,000 (.124)
　　　P_b = $716.67 + $124 = $840.67

Calculator:	P_n	=	FV	=	$1,000
	I	=	PMT	=	$90
	N	=	N	=	20
	Y	=	i	=	11%
Compute PV		=	P_b	=	**$840.73**

$$Number\ of\ bonds\ sold = \frac{\$20,000,000}{\$1,000} = 20,0000$$

Net proceeds per bond = $840.73 × (1 − .02) = $823.49
Total proceeds from sale of bonds = 20,000 × $823.49 = **$16,469,800**

(b)

$$P_p = \frac{D_p}{K_p} = \frac{\$5}{0.08} = \$62.50$$

Net proceeds per preferred stock share = $62.50 × (1 − .1) = $56.25

$$Number\ of\ preferred\ shares\ sold = \frac{\$10,000,000}{\$100} = 100,0000$$

Net proceeds from sale of preferred stock = 100,000 × $56.25 = **$5,625,000**

(c)   Amount that must be raised from the sale of common stock:

$50,000,000	amount needed
− 16,469,800	net proceeds from sale of bonds
− 5,625,000	net proceeds from sale of preferred stock
$27,905,200	amount to be raised from selling common stock

Net proceeds per share of common stock = $32.00 − $2.00 − $1.50 = $28.50

Number of common stock shares needed to be sold = $27,905,200/ $28.50 = **979,130** (rounded)

15-4.   **S. O'Neal Dunkin Donuts**

(a)   EPS prior to raising $50,000,000

$18,000,000	projected operating earnings (EBIT)
2,200,000	annual interest payments
15,800,000	taxable income
5,372,000	Taxes (34%)
$10,428,000	net income

$$e.p.s.\ (projected) = \frac{earnings}{number\ of\ shares} = \frac{\$10,428,000}{4,000,000} = \$2.61\ (rounded)$$

(b)   Number of common shares after financing = 4,000,000 + **979,130** = 4,979.130
Required net income to maintain EPS = 4,979,130 × $2.61 = $12,995,529 (rounded)

Since the $50,000,000 is to be acquired from multiple sources, the payments to each source must be considered.

Annual interest on the <u>new</u> bonds = .09 × $20,000,000 = $1,800,000
Annual dividend payments on preferred shares = 100,000 × $5 = $500,000

The preferred stock dividends, however, are not tax deductible as are the interest payments. To determine the amount of before tax earnings necessary, the dividend payments must be divided by (1 − tax rate).

Before tax earnings to pay preferred dividends = $500,000/ (1 − .34) = $757,576

Required increase in net income = $12,995,529 − $10,428,000 = $2,567,529
The required increase in before tax income will be $2,567,529/ (1 − .34) = $3,890,195.

Before tax required return on the $50,000,000 to maintain EPS =

$$\frac{\$1,800,000 + \$757,576 + \$3,890,195}{\$50,000,000} = \frac{\$6,447,771}{\$50,000,000} = 0.1290 = \mathbf{12.9\%}$$

This calculation can be confirmed as follows:

$24,447,771	EBIT = ($18,000,000 + $6,447,771)
4,000,000	interest = ($2,200,000 + $1,800,000)
20,447,771	taxable income
6,952,242	taxes (34%)
13,495,529	net income
500,000	preferred dividends
$12,995,529	net income available to common shareholders

$$e.p.s. = \frac{earnings}{number\ of\ shares} = \frac{\$12,995,529}{4,979,130} = \mathbf{\$2.61}\ (rounded)$$

(c)   Price of stock before raising $50,000,000:
$P = 15 \times \$2.61 = \$39.15$ *(rounded)*

Price of stock after issue of new securities:
$P = 12 \times \$2.61 = \$31.32$

$$decline\ in\ share\ price = \frac{\$39.15 - \$31.32}{\$39.15} = 0.20 = \mathbf{20\%}$$

Summary: This chapter considers the importance of debt in the Canadian economy, the nature of long-term debt instruments, the mechanics of bond yield and pricing, the bond refunding decision, and the use of leasing as a special case of long-term debt financing.

I.   **The Expanding Role of Debt [p. 561]**

   A.   Corporate debt has expanded dramatically over the years.

   B.   The rapid expansion of corporate debt is the result of:

      1.   Rapid business expansion.
      2.   Inflation.
      3.   At times, inadequate funds generated from the internal operations of business firms.
      4.   A relatively weak stock market at times.

   C.   Corporations have suffered a decline in interest coverage in the last two decades, although the 1990s saw a restoration of healthier coverage ratios.

II.   **Debt Contract Terminology and Provisions [p. 561-567]**

   A.   **Par Value**: the face value of a bond.

   B.   **Coupon Rate**: the actual interest rate on a bond; annual interest/par value (semiannual installments usually).

   C.   **Maturity Date**: the final date on which repayment of the debt principal is due.

   D.   **Indenture**: lengthy, legal agreement detailing the issuer's obligations pertaining to a bond issue. The indenture is administered by an independent trustee.

   E.   **Restrictive covenants**: promises that limit management flexibility but protect investor, contained in indenture. Also known as negative pledges.

   F.   Security provisions

      1.   **Secured claim**: specific assets are pledged to bondholders in the event of default.
      2.   **Mortgage agreement**: real property is pledged as security for loan.
      3.   Senior claims require satisfaction in liquidation proceedings prior to **junior** claims.
      4.   New property may become subject to a security provision by an **"after acquired property clause."**

   G.   Unsecured debt

      1.   **Debenture**: an unsecured, long-term corporate bond
      2.   **Subordinated debenture**: an unsecured bond in which payment will be made to the bondholder only after the holders of designated senior debt issues have been satisfied.
      3.   **Junk bond**: debt obligation of questionable quality. Speculative in nature with a high expected yield, sometimes used in leveraged buyouts. Technically a bond with a rating below investment grade (BBB).

H. Methods of Repayment of Principal

1. Lump-sum payment at maturity
2. **Serial payments**: bonds are paid off in installments over the life of the issue; each bond has a predetermined maturity date.
3. **Sinking fund**: the issuer is required to make regular contributions to fund under the trustee's control. The trustee purchases (retires) bonds in the market with the contributions.
4. **Conversion**: retirement by converting bonds into common stock; this is the option of the holder but it may be forced. (See Chapter 19.)
5. **Call Feature**: an option of the issuing corporation allowing it to retire the debt issue prior to maturity. This feature requires payment of a call premium over par value of 5 percent to 10 percent to the bondholder. The call is often exercised by the firm when interest rates have fallen.

I. Generally the greater the protection afforded the bondholder (security, protective covenants), the lower the interest rate (yield) they must accept.

III. **Bond Prices, Yields, and Ratings [p. 568]**

A. Bond prices are largely determined by the relationship of their coupon rate to the going market rate and the number of years until maturity.

1. If the market rate for the bond exceeds the coupon rate, the bond will sell below par value. If the market rate is less than the coupon rate, the bond will sell above par value.
2. The more distant the maturity date of a bond, the farther below or above par value the price will be given the coupon rate and market rate relationship.

B. Bond yields are quoted on three different bases. Assume a $ 1,000 par value bond pays $ 100 per year interest for 10 years. The bond is currently selling at $900 in the market. **[p. 610]**

1. **Coupon rate (nominal yield)**: Stated interest payment divided by par value $100/ $1,000 = 10%.
2. **Current yield**: Stated interest payment divided by the current price of the bond, $100/ $900 = 11.11%.
3. **Yield to Maturity**: The interest rate that will equate future interest payments and payment at maturity to current market price (the internal rate of return). The yield to maturity may be computed by the following formula and solving for Y:

$$P_b = \sum_{t=1}^{n} \frac{I_t}{(1+Y)^t} + \frac{P_n}{(1+Y)^n}$$

(10-1, page 323)

Calculator:	P_n	=	FV	=	$1,000
	I	=	PMT	=	$100
	N	=	N	=	10
	PV	=	P_b	=	$1,200
Compute	Y	=	$i\%$	=	7.13%

C. Bond ratings **[p. 570]**

1. There are two major bond rating agencies - Dominion Bond Rating Service and Standard and Poor's Rating Service.
2. The higher the rating, the lower the interest rate that must be paid.
3. The ratings are based on:
   a. the firm's ability to make interest payments.
   b. its consistency of performance.
   c. its size.
   d. its debt/equity ratio.
   e. its working capital position.
   f. and other factors.

D. Examining actual bond ratings: See Table 16-3 (page 571) and accompanying discussion.

IV. **The Refunding Decision [p. 573-577]**

A. The process of calling outstanding bonds and replacing them with new ones is termed refunding. This action is most likely to be pursued by businesses during periods of declining interest rates.

B. Interest savings from refunding can be substantial over the life of a bond but the costs of refunding can also be very large.

C. A **refunding** decision is a capital budgeting problem. The refunding costs constitute the investment and the net reduction in annual cash expenditures are the inflows.

D. A major difference in evaluating a capital expenditure for refunding is that the discount rate applied is the aftertax cost of debt rather than the cost of capital because the annual savings are known with greater certainty.

E. Calculation of NPV:

> **Refer to summary of refunding decision on page 576.**

1. Investment costs include:
   a. Call premium, non-tax deductible.
   b. Issue expenses (underwriting, legal, accounting, printing) are tax deductible at 20 percent a year over 5 years.
   c. Overlap interest costs less interest revenue, both on an aftertax basis.
2. Annual benefit (cost savings).
   a. The annual interest savings from a lower interest rate on an aftertax basis (1 – tax rate) discounted at the appropriate rate. (AFTERTAX COST OF NEW DEBT)
3. Issue discounts are tax deductible at the time of redemption.

V. **Other Forms of Bond Financing [p. 577]**

A. Zero-Coupon Rate Bond

1. Do not pay interest; sold at deep discounts from face value.
2. These bonds provide immediate cash inflow to the corporation (sell bonds) without any outflow (interest payments) until the bonds mature.
3. Since the difference between the selling price and the maturity value is amortized for tax purposes over the life of the bond, a tax reduction benefit occurs without a current cash outflow.
4. Although these have limited appeal in Canada because of tax rulings, the Eurobond market has been more receptive.

B. Stripped bond **[p. 577-578]**

1. The investment dealer strips coupons from face value of bond and sells differing maturities to investors based on their time preferences.
2. No reinvestment rate risk.
3. An illustration is given in the text on pages 577-578.

C. Floating rate bond

1. The interest rate varies with market conditions.
2. Unless market rates move beyond floating rate limits, the price of the floating rate bond should not change, therefore, the investor is assured (within limits) of the market value of his investment.

D. Real return bond

    1. These securities provide a return above the inflation rate.

E. Revenue bond

    1. In 1996 Nav Canada issued the first revenue bonds in Canada, based on its stream of cash flows from controlling air traffic within Canada, not based on its assets.

VI. **Eurobond Market [p. 579]**

A. A Eurobond is a bond in a unit of currency other than the currency of that country in which the bond is issued. Usually denominated in U.S. dollars but not always. Disclosure is less stringent than in domestic country.

B. Allows access to the large international capital market for Canadian corporations.

VII. **Advantages and Disadvantages of Debt [p. 580]**

A. Benefits of Debt

    1. Tax deductibility of interest.
    2. The financial obligation is specific and fixed (with the exception of floating rate bonds).
    3. In an inflationary economy, debt may be repaid with "cheaper dollars."
    4. Prudent use of debt may lower the cost of capital.

B. Drawbacks of Debt

    1. Interest and principal payments must be met when due regardless of the firm's financial position.
    2. Burdensome bond indenture restrictions.
    3. Imprudent use of debt may depress stock prices.

VIII. **Intermediate Term Loans and Medium Term Notes [p. 581]**

A. Financial intermediaries may extend credit to a corporation by way of a term loan based on a capital asset as security. The loan is not payable on demand unless the legal covenants are violated.

B. MTN (Medium term note) financings exceeded $24 billion in 2002. These notes allow corporations to raise funds on a shorter time frame, through the capital markets, than the traditional debt financing.

IX. **Leasing as a Form of Debt [p. 582-586]**

A. A long-term, noncancellable lease has all the characteristics of a debt obligation.

B. The Canadian Institute of Chartered Accountants (CICA) requires that certain types of long-term lease obligations be included on the balance sheet as if the asset was purchased and a long-term debt obligation incurred.

C. Leases that substantially transfer all the benefits and risks of ownership from the owner to the lessee must be capitalized. A **capital lease** is required whenever any one of the following conditions exists.

    1. Ownership of the property is transferred to the lessee by the end of the lease term.
    2. The lease contains a bargain purchase price (sure to be purchased) at the end of the lease.
    3. The lease term is equal to 75 percent or more of the estimated life of the leased property.
    4. The present value of the minimum lease payments equals or exceeds 90 percent of the fair value of the leased property at the beginning of the lease.

D. A lease that does not meet any of the four criteria is an **operating lease.**

   1. Usually short-term.
   2. Often cancelable at the option of the lessee.
   3. The lessor frequently provides maintenance.
   4. Capitalization and presentation on the balance sheet is not required.

E. Impact of capital lease on the income statement

   1. The intangible leased property under capital lease (asset) amount is amortized and written off over the life of the lease.
   2. The obligation under capital lease (liability) is written off through amortization with an "implied" interest expense on the remaining balance.

F. Advantages of leasing

   1. Lessee may not have sufficient funds to purchase or have borrowing capability.
   2. Provisions of lease may be less restrictive.
   3. May be no down payment.
   4. Expert advice of leasing (lessor) company.
   5. Creditor claims on certain types of leases are restricted in bankruptcy and reorganization procedures.
   6. Tax considerations
       a. Obtain maximum benefit of tax advantages.
       b. Tax deductibility of lease payments for land.
   7. Infusion of capital through a sale-leaseback.

G. **Lease versus Purchase Decision [p. 586-588]**

   1. Leasing as a means of financing is often compared to borrow-purchase arrangements when assets are to be acquired. This procedure is particularly appropriate for comparing an operating lease to purchasing. Most capital leases are treated the same for tax purposes as borrowing to purchase.
   2. The present value of all after-tax cash outflows associated with each form of financing is computed. The procedure requires consideration of all tax shields for each method. Since all outflows are fixed by contract, the discount rate employed in computing the present value of the outflows is the aftertax cost of debt. A possible salvage value has greater uncertainty as a cash flow, and the cost of capital is used to acknowledge this greater uncertainty within the analysis.
   3. Although qualitative factors must be considered, the usual decision criterion is to accept the financing method, leasing or borrow-purchase that has the lowest present value of cash outflows. The cash inflows should be the same whether the asset is leased or purchased.
   4. PV of CCA tax shield

$$\frac{Cdt}{r+d}\left[\frac{1+.5r}{1+r}\right]$$

X. **Appendix 16A: Financial Alternatives for Distressed Firms [p. 601]**

A. Financial Distress **[p. 601]**

   1. **Technical Insolvency:** firm has positive net worth but is unable to pay its bills as they come due.
   2. **Bankruptcy:** a firm's liabilities exceed the value of its assets-negative net worth.

B. Out-of-court Settlements **[p. 600]**

   1. **Extension:** creditors allow the firm more time to meet its financial obligations.
   2. **Composition:** creditors agree to accept a fractional settlement on their original claim.
   3. **Creditor committee:** a creditor committee is established to run the business in place of the existing management.
   4. **Assignment:** a **liquidation** of the firm's assets without going through formal court action.

C. In-court Settlements: Formal Bankruptcy **[p. 601]**

1. Bankruptcy proceedings may be initiated voluntarily by the firm or forced by the creditors: involuntary bankruptcy.
2. The decisions of a court appointed referee who arbitrates the bankruptcy proceedings are final subject to court review.
3. Reorganization: a fair and feasible plan to reorganize the bankrupt firm.
   a. **Internal reorganization**: necessitates an evaluation of existing management and policies. An assessment and possible redesign of the firm's capital structure is also required.
   b. **External reorganization**: a financially strong and managerially competent merger partner is found for the bankrupt firm.
4. Liquidation: if reorganization of the firm is determined to be infeasible, the assets of the firm will be sold to satisfy creditors. Common shareholders rank last in bankruptcy.

Chapter 16: Multiple Choice Questions

1. Which of the following is a long-term unsecured bond? [p. 564]
   a. First mortgage bond
   b. Commercial paper
   c. Indenture
   d. Serial bond
   e. Debenture

2. Which of the following is usually a characteristic of an operating lease? [p. 583]
   a. The lessee provides maintenance.
   b. The lease term is equal to 75% or more of the estimated life of the property.
   c. It is cancellable by lessee.
   d. Capitalization is required.
   e. Ownership is transferred to lessee at end of lease.

3. The bond yield found by dividing the annual interest payment by the current price of a bond is called the: [p. 569]
   a. Current yield.
   b. Yield to maturity.
   c. Approximate yield to maturity.
   d. Coupon rate.
   e. Historical yield.

4. New property may become subject to a security provision by a(n): [p. 563]
   a. Acceleration clause.
   b. Debenture.
   c. Subordinated debenture.
   d. After acquired property clause.
   e. Sinking fund.

5. Which of the following debt instruments is most likely to maintain a constant price? [p. 578]
   a. Strip bond
   b. Floating rate bond
   c. Convertible bond
   d. Revenue bond
   e. Eurobond

6. An issuer may be required to fund the retirement of a bond issue by a: [p. 565]
   a. Conversion.
   b. Call feature.
   c. Mortgage agreement.
   d. Sinking fund.
   e. Refunding.

7. Which of the following indicates the status of a firm which has positive net worth but is unable to pay its bills? [p. 600]
   a. Extension
   b. Composition
   c. Technical insolvency
   d. Bankruptcy
   e. Assignment

8. The legal agreement that details a security issuer's obligation is called a(n): [p. 562]
   a. Indenture.
   b. Trustee.
   c. Covenant.
   d. Pledge.
   e. Assignment.

9. In a liquidation of a firm's assets, which of the following will have the highest priority of claim? [p. 603]
   a. Legal fees.
   b. Federal taxes.
   c. Common shareholders.
   d. Wages of workers.
   e. Secured creditors.

10. The call premium that a firm pays when refunding a bond issue is: [p. 576]
    a. Spread over the life of the new issue for tax purposes.
    b. A noncash cost.
    c. A non-tax deductible expense at the time of refunding.
    d. Required by law.
    e. A tax deductible expense at the time of refunding.

Multiple Choice Answer Key: Chapter 16

1.	e	2.	c	3.	a	4.	d	5.	b
6.	d	7.	c	8.	a	9.	a	10.	c

Chapter 16: Problems

16-1. The Williams Sisters Corporation issued $1,000-thirty-year bonds which pay $120 annually in interest. The bonds are currently selling at $1,100.

   (a)   What is the coupon rate?
   (b)   What is the current price of the bonds?
   (c)   What is the current yield?
   (d)   What is the yield to maturity?

16-2. Referring to Table 16-1 in the text which highlights Bombardier, answer the following questions.

(a)   When does its 5.75% bond mature?

(b)   What is the currency of its 5.75% bonds?

(c)   How often is interest paid on the 5.75% issue??

(d)   What are the conditions of redemption on the 6.58% bonds??

16-3. CBA Corporation issued a 20-year bond 10 years ago. The bond, which pays $80 interest annually, was issued at par.

(a)   What was the yield to maturity on the bond at time of issue?

(b)   If the bond is currently selling for $820, is its yield to maturity greater or less than the coupon rate?

(c)   What is the yield to maturity on the bond at the present time?

(d)   If the firm were to issue a similar bond today, approximately what yield to maturity would be required for the bond to sell at par?

(e)   What is the current yield on the bond if the bond price is $820?

16-4. What would be the market price of a 20-year bond that pays $80 interest annually if the market rate of interest on bonds of similar risk were (a) 6%, (b) 8%, and (c) 10%?

16-5. In 1998, National Utility issued $60,000,000 of 10% 25-year bonds at par. The current market rate on bonds with the same rating is 8%. The bond contract will allow refunding of these bonds in 2003. Company officers have estimated the flotation costs of a 20-year refunding bond issue to be $1,500,000. The underwriting costs on a best-efforts basis will be 3 percent of the issue price. The terms of the current bond contract require the payment of a 6% call premium. Short term money market rates are 6% and a one month overlap period is expected.

(a)   Assuming that the utility firm's tax rate is 40%; would a decision to refund the outstanding bonds be acceptable?

(b)   Would your answer be the same if there was only 10 years left to maturity?

16-6. The Cap-Short Corporation is debating whether to acquire an asset through an operating lease arrangement or to borrow funds and purchase the asset. The purchase price of the asset, $100,000, can be financed with a four-year, 15% bank loan. If purchased, the asset will be placed in a CCA class of 30% with no expected salvage, at the end of its four-year life. Alternatively, the firm can obtain the use of the asset with an operating lease of four years. The lease payments would be $30,000 per year. The firm's tax rate is approximately 40%. Lease payments are payable at the beginning of each year and tax savings are available at the end of the year. Which alternative should be selected based on minimizing the present value of aftertax costs?

Chapter 16: Solutions

16-1. **Williams Sisters Corporation**

(a) $Coupon\ rate = \dfrac{Stated\ interest\ rate}{Par\ value} = \dfrac{\$120}{\$1,000} = .1200 = \textbf{12.0\%}$

(b) *Bonds are selling at par* = **$1,000**

(c) $Current\ yield = \dfrac{Stated\ interest\ rate}{Current\ (market)\ price} = \dfrac{\$120}{\$1,100} = .1091 = \textbf{10.91\%}$

(d) **Calculator:**

P_n	=	FV	=	$1,000
I	=	PMT	=	$120
N	=	N	=	30
PV	=	P_b	=	$1,100
Compute Y	=	i %	=	**10.86%**

16-2. **Bombardier**

(a) **February 22, 2008**
(b) Euros
(c) Annually
(d) Redeemable at any time at the greater of U.S. Treasury Yield + 0.50% and par.

16-3. **CBA Corporation**

(a) The bond was issued at par; therefore, the yield to maturity was equal to the coupon rate, 8%. The rate can be verified by the approximate yield to maturity formulation.

$$Y^1 = \dfrac{Annual\ interest\ payment + \dfrac{Principal\ payment - Price\ of\ the\ bond}{Number\ of\ years\ to\ maturity}}{0.6\ (Price\ of\ the\ bond) + 0.4\ (Principal\ payment)}$$

$$Y^1 = \dfrac{\$80 + \dfrac{\$1,000 - \$1,000}{20}}{0.6\ (\$1,000) + 0.4\ (\$1,000)} = \dfrac{\$80 + \$0}{\$600 + \$400} = \dfrac{\$80}{\$1,000} = 0.0800 = \textbf{8.0\%}$$

Calculator:

P_n	=	FV	=	$1,000
I	=	PMT	=	$80
N	=	N	=	20
PV	=	P_b	=	$1,000
Compute Y	=	i %	=	**8.0%**

(b) The yield to maturity is **greater** than the coupon rate as it will always be when the bond is selling at a discount (below face value).

(c)   Yield to maturity:

$$Y^{l} = \frac{\$80 + \dfrac{\$1,000 - \$820}{10}}{0.6\,(\$820) + 0.4\,(\$1,000)} = \frac{\$80 + \$18}{\$492 + \$400} = \frac{\$98}{\$892} = 0.1099 = \mathbf{10.99\%}$$

Calculator:	P_n	=	FV	=	$1,000
	I	=	PMT	=	$80
	N	=	N	=	10
	PV	=	P_b	=	$820
Compute	**Y**	=	**i %**	=	**11.06%**

(d)   **11.06%** (The best estimate of the yield to maturity required on a new bond would be the yield on the outstanding bond. If, however, the riskiness of the firm were increased by the new issue, the required yield might be greater, etc.)

(e) $Current\ yield = \dfrac{Stated\ interest\ rate}{Current\ (market)\ price} = \dfrac{\$80}{\$820} = .0976 = \mathbf{9.76\%}$

16-4.   **Bond pricing**

$$P_b = \sum_{t=1}^{n} \frac{I_t}{(1+Y)^t} + \frac{P_n}{(1+Y)^n}$$

(a) $BP = \$80\ (11.47) + \$1,000\ (.312)$
       $BP = \$917.60 + \$312 = \$1,229.60$

Calculator:	P_n	=	FV	=	$1,000
	I	=	PMT	=	$80
	N	=	N	=	20
	Y	=	i	=	6%
Compute PV		=	P_b	=	**$1,229.40**

(b) $BP = \$80\ (9.818) + \$1,000\ (.215)$
       $BP = \$785.44 + \$215 = \$1,000.44$ (bond sells at par; coupon rate = market rate)

Calculator:	P_n	=	FV	=	$1,000
	I	=	PMT	=	$80
	N	=	N	=	20
	Y	=	i	=	8%
Compute PV		=	P_b	=	**$1,000.00**

(c) $BP = \$80\ (8.514) + \$1,000\ (.149)$
       $BP = \$681.12 + \$149 = \$830.12$

Calculator:	P_n	=	FV	=	$1,000
	I	=	PMT	=	$80
	N	=	N	=	20
	Y	=	i	=	10%
Compute PV		=	P_b	=	**$829.73**

16-5.   **National Utility**

(a)   STEP A:Computation of costs (outflows):

Note: discount rate   = .08 (1 – .4)
   = .048 or 4.8% (aftertax borrowing rate on new debt)

1. Call premium   .06 × $60,000,000 $3,600,000
    (no tax deduction)

2. Borrowing expenses
    Flotation costs $1,500,000
    Underwriting expense (.03 × $60,000,000) =   1,800,000
    Total borrowing expense $3,300,000
    Amortization of expense   ($3,300,000/ 5) (.40)
                              = $660,000 (.40)
                              = $264,000 tax savings per year

    Actual expenditure $3,300,000
    PV of future tax savings $264,000 (n = 5, i = 4.8%)   1,149,329
    Net cost of borrowing expenses of new issue $2,150,671   2,150,671

3. Interest on old bonds during overlap
    (Aftertax) .10 × $60,000,000 (1 – .4) × 1/12   300,000
    Interest revenue during overlap
    .06 × $60,000,000 (1 – .4) × 1/12   180,000
                                                        $ 120,000   120,000
                                                                                $5,870,671

Step B: Computation of benefits (present value of annual Inflows):

4. Annual cost savings in lower interest rates
    .10 × $60,000,000   = $6,000,000
    .08 × $60,000,000 =   4,800,000
                                   $1,200,000

    Aftertax (1 – .4) $ 720,000

    PV of annual interest savings
    $720,000 (n = 20, i = 4.8%) = $9,126,924

Step C: Summary

    Present value of interest savings less investment
    NPV = $9,126,924 – $5,870,671 = $3,256,253

    Decision: Since the NPV > 0, **refund the issue**

16-6.   Cap-Short Corporation

Discount rate for analysis should be the aftertax borrowing rate.
In this case: .15 (1 − .4) = .09 = 9%

NPV of Borrow to Purchase

Cost of asset (PV of loan payments and tax savings on interest)   ($100,000)
Tax shield from CCA

$$\frac{Cdt}{r+d}\left[\frac{1+.5r}{1+r}\right] = \frac{\$100{,}000 \times .30 \times .40}{.09+.30}\left[\frac{1+.5\times.09}{1+.09}\right] = \underline{29{,}499}$$

Total   **($ 70,501)**

NPV of Lease

Lease payments at time 0   ($ 30,000)
Lease payments at times 1, 2, 3
       $30,000 (n = 3, i = 9%)   (75,939)
Tax savings
       $30,000 (.4) = $12,000 for 4 years
       $12,000 (n = 4, i = 9%)   <u>38,877</u>
Total   **($ 67,062)**

Decision: Lease because the cost of leasing is less by $70,501 − $67,062 =   **$3,439**

Note: Lease payments can also be considered at 4 year annuity (in advance).
       $30,000 (n = 4, i = 9%) (BGN or DUE)   ($105,939)

Chapter 17

Summary: The characteristics of common and preferred stock and the rights pertaining to the ownership of each are considered in this chapter.

I.   **Common Stock and Common Shareholders [p. 608]**

    A.   Directly or indirectly through mutual funds 49 percent of Canadians own shares.

    B.   Although management controls the corporation on a daily basis, ultimate control of the firm resides in the hands of the shareholders.

    C.   Management has become increasingly sensitive to the growing institutional ownership of common stock. Mutual funds, pension funds, insurance companies and bank trust accounts are examples of financial institutions that in combination own a large percentage of many leading corporations.

II.   **Common shareholders' claim to income [p. 609]**

    A.   Common shareholders have a **residual claim** on the income stream; the amount remaining after creditors and preferred shareholders have been satisfied belongs to the owners (common shareholders) whether paid in dividends or retained. There is no legal claim to dividends.

    B.   A corporation may have several **classes of common stock** that differ in regard to voting rights and claim on the earnings stream (e.g. Canadian Tire, Bombardier).

III.   **The Voting Right [p. 610]**

    A.   Owners of common stock have the right to vote on all major issues including election of the board of directors.

    B.   **Majority voting**: holders of majority of stock can elect all directors.

    C.   In some firms, different classes of stock are entitled to elect a specified percentage of the board of directors.

    D.   **Cumulative voting**: possible for minority shareholders (own less than 50 percent of stock) to elect some of the directors. **[p. 611-613]**

        1.   The shareholder can cast one vote for each share of stock owned times the number of directors to be elected.
        2.   The following formula may be employed to determine the number of shares needed to elect a given number of directors under cumulative voting.

$$Shares\ required = \frac{(\#\ of\ directors\ desired) \times (Total\ \#\ of\ shares\ outstanding)}{Total\ \#\ of\ directors\ to\ be\ elected + 1} + 1 \qquad \text{(17-1; page 612)}$$

        3.   By staggering director's terms, with only a few elected each year, minority interests can be denied board representation.

    E.   The type of voting process has become more important to both shareholders and management because of challenges to management=s control of the firm.

F. The majority of Canadians do not own shares directly. However through large and growing mutual and pension funds, Canadians indirectly have a large stake in corporate Canada and its performance.

IV. **The Right to Purchase New Shares [p. 613]**

A. The shareholder may have the right to maintain his percentage of ownership, voting power, and claim to earnings through the preemptive right provision which requires that existing shareholders be given the first option to purchase new shares.

B. Financing through rights offerings.

> Refer to Figure 17-1, text page 615 for a time line.

1. Even if the **preemptive right** provision is not required, the corporation may finance through a rights offering.
2. Each shareholder receives one right for each share of stock owned, and is allowed to buy new shares of stock at a reduced price (below market value) plus the required number of rights/share.
3. The number of rights required to purchase a new share equals the ratio of shares outstanding to the new shares issued.

$$\text{Number of rights required} \atop \text{to purchase one new share} \quad = \quad \frac{\text{Number of shares outstanding}}{\text{Number of shares to be issued}}$$

4. Rights have market value since they entitle the holder to purchase shares of stock at less than market price.
   a. Initially, after the rights offering announcement, stock trades **"rights-on."** The formula for the value of a right during the rights-on period is:

$$R = \frac{P_0 - S}{N + 1}$$
(17-3; page 616)

   P_0 = Market value of stock, rights-on
   S = Subscription price
   N = Number of rights required to purchase a new share of stock

   b. After a certain period, the right no longer trades with the stock but may be bought and sold separately. On the **"ex-rights"** date the stock price falls by the theoretical value of a right. The ex-rights value of a right is:

$$R = \frac{P_e - S}{N}$$
(17-4; page 616)

   P_e = Market value of stock, ex-rights

5. Existing shareholders usually do not have a monetary gain from a rights offering. The gain from purchasing shares at less than market price is eliminated by dilution of previously owned shares.

6. A shareholder has three options when presented with a rights offering.
   a. Exercise the rights; no net gain or loss
   b. Sell the rights; no net gain or loss
   c. Allow the rights to lapse; a loss will be incurred due to the dilution of existing shares that is not offset by value of unsold or unexercised rights.

C. Desirable features of rights offerings **[p. 617]**

1. Protects shareholders' voting position and claim on earnings
2. Existing shareholders provide a built-in market for new issues; distribution costs are lower
3. May create more interest in stock than a straight offering
4. Lower margin requirements

D. American Depository Receipts (ADRs) **[p. 618]**
1. ADRs are shares of foreign stock held in trust by U.S. Banks that issue a claim on these trust receipts.
2. ADRs allow foreign companies to raise funds in U.S. markets, the world=s largest capital market, and provide investors with annual reports using U.S. GAAP accounting.

E. Poison Pills **[p. 618]**
1. A **"poison pill"** is a rights offering made to existing shareholders of a company with the sole purpose of thwarting an acquisition attempt by another company. The increased number of shares may dilute the ownership percentage of the firm pursuing the takeover.
2. Some investors feel that a poison pill strategy is contrary to the goal of maximizing the wealth of the owners.

V. **Preferred Stock Financing [p. 619]**

A. Characteristics of preferred stock

1. Stipulated dividends must be paid before dividends on common stock but are not guaranteed or required.
2. Dividends are not tax-deductible.

B. Preferred stock contributes to capital structure balance by expanding the capital base without diluting common stock or incurring contractual obligations. Under the Bank Act of 1980 preferred stock qualifies for capital adequacy tests for Canadian banks.

C. Primary purchasers of preferred stock are corporate investors, insurance companies and pension funds. Dividend income received by corporations in most cases is exempt from taxation. To the individual investor the dividend tax credit reduces the amount of tax payable on dividend income. Bond interest is usually fully taxable. Preferreds are of greater significance in Canadian markets than U.S. markets.

D. Provisions associated with preferred stock **[p. 622]**

1. Cumulative dividends
2. Conversion feature
    a. Convertible preferred stock is convertible to common stock at the option of the preferred shareholder. (See Chapter 19 for a thorough discussion of the conversion feature associated with debt.)
    b. Convertible preferreds include a recent innovation--**convertible exchangeable preferreds** that allow the firm to force conversion from convertible preferred stock into convertible debt.
3. Call feature
4. Retractable feature (bondholder option)
5. Participation provision
6. Floating rate
    a. Investors purchase floating rate preferreds to minimize risk of price changes and to take advantage of tax benefits.
    b. Price stability makes preferred stock the equivalent of a safe, short-term investment.
7. Par value
8. Dutch auction preferred stock
    a. Similar to floating rate preferred but is a short-term security.
    b. Preferred stock is issued to bidders willing to accept lowest yield.
    c. Security matures every seven weeks and is re-auctioned at a subsequent bidding.

Comparing Features of Common and Preferred Stock and Debt

Refer to Table 17-1, and Figure 17-2, text page 625.

VII. **Review of Formulas**

See text page 627 or insert card.

Chapter 17: Multiple Choice Questions

1. Which type of voting allows minority shareholders to elect some of the directors of a corporation? [p. 611]
   a. Majority
   b. Preferred
   c. Common
   d. Cumulative
   e. Preemptive

2. The number of rights required to purchase one new share in a rights offering is found by: [p. 614]
   a. Dividing the subscription price by the ex-rights value of a right.
   b. Dividing the number of shares outstanding by the number of shares to be issued.
   c. Multiplying the subscription price by N.
   d. Subtracting the subscription price from the ex-rights price of the stock.
   e. Adding the rights-on right value to the ex-rights right value.

3. A shareholder may be protected against dilution of percentage of ownership by: [p. 613]
   a. Cumulative voting.
   b. A call option.
   c. A participation provision.
   d. A preemptive right.
   e. A convertible feature.

4. Which of the following has the lowest claim to assets in bankruptcy? [p. 625]
   a. Common stock
   b. Convertible preferred stock
   c. Preferred stock
   d. Corporate bonds
   e. Convertible exchangeable preferred stock

5. Which of these securities is short term? [p. 624]
   a. Convertible preferred stock
   b. Corporate bonds
   c. Dutch auction preferred stock
   d. Common stock
   e. Municipal bonds

6. The purpose of a "poison pill" rights offering is to: [p. 618]
   a. Thwart a takeover attempt.
   b. Get rid of the current management.
   c. Maximize the wealth of the owners.
   d. Lower margin requirements.
   e. Force conversion of convertible preferred stock.

7. Which of the following statements about a rights offering is incorrect? [p. 616-617]
   a. A shareholder may exercise rights.
   b. A shareholder will normally be able to buy stock at a price less than the market price.
   c. A shareholder will always have a gain on a rights offering.
   d. A shareholder may sell rights.
   e. A shareholder may allow rights to lapse.

8. The ultimate goal of a corporation resides in the hands of the: [p. 625]
   a. Management.
   b. Board of directors.
   c. Bondholders.
   d. Preferred shareholders.
   e. Common shareholders.

9. Theoretically, the price of a share of stock should: [p. 615]
   a. Rise by $N \times$ the value one right on the ex-rights date.
   b. Fall by the value of one right on the ex-rights date.
   c. Fall by the value of one right on the rights-on date.
   d. Rise by $N \times$ the value of one right on the rights-on date.
   e. Not be affected on the ex-rights date.

10. Which of the following statements is correct? [p. 625]
    a. Preferred stock dividends are tax deductible.
    b. Common stock dividends are tax deductible.
    c. Intercorporate interest is tax exempt.
    d. The cost of distribution is highest for corporate bonds.
    e. Intercorporate dividends are tax exempt to the receiving firm.

Multiple Choice Answer Key: Chapter 17

1.	d	2.	b	3.	d	4.	a	5.	c
6.	a	7.	c	8.	e	9.	b	10.	e

Chapter 17: Problems

17-1. The Lotsa-Luck Gold Mining Company is seeking to raise $10,000,000 through a rights offering. The company presently has 1,000,000 shares of common stock outstanding at a current market price of $25 per share.

   (a) How many new shares must be sold via the rights offering if the subscription price is $20?

   (b) How many new shares could a shareholder owning 100 shares purchase?

   (c) What is the value of one right?

   (d) What will be the approximate price of the stock ex-rights?

17-2. Suppose you owned 100 shares of Lotsa Luck Gold Mining stock. Assuming that you have sufficient cash to purchase the number of shares available to you from the rights offering (*17-1* above), indicate your position under each of the following circumstances:

(a)   You exercise your rights.
(b)   You sell your rights.
(c)   You neither exercise nor sell your rights.

17-3. The TVG Corporation has not paid dividends on its $3 preferred stock for the previous two years. There are 1,000,000 shares of preferred stock outstanding. How much can the firm pay to common shareholders if it limits dividends to current earnings under each of the following circumstances?

(a)   Current earnings are $1,000,000.
(b)   Current earnings are $9,000,000.
(c)   Current earnings are $12,000,000 and the firm wishes to retain 50% of earnings available to common shareholders.

17-4. The Slip-n-Slide Corporation has experienced several consecutive years of declining profits. D. S. Satisfied and several other shareholders are seeking to replace as many corporate directors as possible. The disgruntled shareholders own 18,001 shares of 72,000 outstanding voting shares.

(a)   If the company employs the cumulative voting procedure, how many directors can they elect to an 11-member board?

(b)   How many additional shares must the dissident shareholders acquire to enable them to elect five directors?

(c)   Suppose the company would choose to rotate the directors on a yearly basis and elect only 4 members to the board yearly. How many directors could the disgruntled shareholders then be guaranteed to elect?

Chapter 17: Solutions

17-1.   Lotsa-Luck Gold Mining Company

(a) $\# \ of \ new \ shares \ required = \dfrac{\$10,000,000}{\$20} = \textbf{500,000}$

(b) $\# \ of \ rights \ required \ for \ 1 \ new \ share = \dfrac{1,000,000}{500,000} = \textbf{2} \ rights$

Each shareholder receives one right per share of stock. A holder of 100 shares of stock would receive 100 rights.

$\# \ of \ shares \ that \ shareholder \ can \ purchase = \dfrac{\# \ of \ rights \ owned}{\# \ of \ rights \ required} = \dfrac{100}{2} = \textbf{50} \ new \ shares$

(c) $R = \dfrac{P_0 - S}{N+1} = \dfrac{\$25 - \$20}{2+1} = \dfrac{\$5}{3} = \textbf{\$1.67}$

(d) $\$25 - 1.67 = \textbf{\$23.33}$

17-2. **Lotsa-Luck Gold Mining Company (continued)**

(a)   *Cash required to purchase 50 shares* = 50 × $20 = $1,000

Position at time of rights offering announcement:

Cash	$1,000
100 shares at $25	2,500
Total value	$3,500

Position if rights are exercised:

Cash	$ 0.00
150 shares at $23.33	3,499.50
	$3,499.50 (approximately $3,500)

(b)

100 shares at $23.33	$2,333
Proceeds, sale of 100 rights	167
Cash	1,000
Total	**$3,500**

(c)

100 shares at $23.33	$2,333
Cash	1,000
	$3,333

Doing nothing results in a loss of wealth.

17-3. **TVG Corporation**

(a)   *Annual preferred dividends* = $3 × 1,000,000 = $3,000,000
      Dividends in arrears = 2 (years) × $3,000,000 = $6,000,000

Preferred dividends due:		
	Current dividends	$3,000,000
	Pf. dividends in arrears	6,000,000
		$9,000,000

No dividends could be paid to common shareholders.

(b)

Current earnings	$ 9,000,000
Preferred dividends due	9,000,000
Earnings available to common shareholders	$ -0-

(c)

Current earnings	$12,000,000
Preferred dividends due	9,000,000
Earnings available to common shareholders	$ 3,000,000
Payout ratio (50%)	0.50
Common stock dividends	**$ 1,500,000**

17-4. **Slip-n-Ride Corporation**

(a) *Number of directors that can be elected =*

$$\left[\begin{array}{c} \#\ of\ directors \\ that\ can\ be\ elected \end{array}\right] = \frac{\begin{array}{c}(Shares\ owned\ -1)\times \\ (Total\ \#\ of\ directors\ to\ be\ elected\ +1)\end{array}}{Total\ \#\ of\ shares\ outstanding}$$

$$= \frac{(18{,}001-1)\times(11+1)}{72{,}000} = \frac{18{,}000\times12}{72{,}000} = \frac{216{,}000}{72{,}000} = \mathbf{3}\ \ director$$

(b) *Shares required:*

$$Shares\ required = \frac{\begin{array}{c}(\#\ of\ directors\ desired)\times \\ (Total\ \#\ of\ shares\ outstanding)\end{array}}{Total\ \#\ of\ directors\ to\ be\ elected\ +1} + 1$$

$$= \frac{5\times72{,}000}{11+1} + 1 = \frac{360{,}000}{12} + 1 = \mathbf{30{,}001}\ \ shares$$

Additional shares needed = 30,001 – 18,001 = **12,000**

(c) *Number of directors that can be elected =*

$$\left[\begin{array}{c} \#\ of\ directors \\ that\ can\ be\ elected \end{array}\right] = \frac{\begin{array}{c}(Shares\ owned\ -1)\times \\ (Total\ \#\ of\ directors\ to\ be\ elected\ +1)\end{array}}{Total\ \#\ of\ shares\ outstanding}$$

$$= \frac{(18{,}001-1)\times(4+1)}{72{,}000} = \frac{18{,}000\times5}{72{,}000} = \frac{90{,}000}{72{,}000} = 1.25 = \mathbf{1}\ \ director$$

Chapter 18

Dividend Policy and
Retained Earnings

Summary: The Board of Directors of a corporation must decide what portion of the firm's earnings will be paid to the shareholders. This chapter examines the many factors that influence the dividend policy decision and processes.

I. **The Marginal Principle of Retained Earnings [p. 639]**

   A. According to the passive **residual theory of dividends**, earnings should be retained as long as the rate earned is expected to exceed a shareholder's rate of return on the distributed dividend.

   B. The residual dividend theory assumes a lack of preference for dividends by investors. **[p. 640].** There is much disagreement as to investors' preference for dividends or retention of earnings.

   C. Irrelevance of dividend argument [p. 641]

      1. The homemade dividend argument suggests dividend policy is irrelevant to firm valuation.

   D. Relevance of dividends arguments **[p. 642]**

      1. Resolves uncertainty
      2. Information content
      3. Payout ratios suggest firms view dividends as relevant (Table 18-1; page 644)

   E. Dividend yields are significant for Canadian traded companies (Table 18-2; page 645).

      Dividends / market share price

II. **Corporate Dividend Policy: Dividend Stability [p. 645]**

   A. Growth firms with high rates of return usually pay relatively low dividends.

   B. Mature firms follow a relatively high payout policy.

   C. The stable dividend policy followed by Canadian corporations indicates that corporate management feels that shareholders have a preference for dividends.

III. **Other Factors Influencing Dividend Policy [p. 646-648]**

   A. Legal rules: laws have been enacted protecting corporate creditors by forbidding distribution of the firm's capital in the form of dividends. Dividends are also prohibited if the firm will become insolvent as a result.

   B. Cash position: the firm must have cash available regardless of the level of past or current earnings in order to pay dividends.

   C. Access to capital markets: the easier the access to capital markets, the more able the firm is to pay dividends rather than retain earnings. Some large firms have borrowed to maintain dividend payments.

   D. Desire for control

      1. Small, closely-held firms may limit dividends to avoid restrictive borrowing provisions or the need to sell new stock.
      2. Established firms may feel pressure to pay dividends to avoid shareholders' demand for change of management.

E. Tax position of shareholders (clientele effect)

   1. High tax-bracket shareholders may prefer retention of earnings.
   2. Lower tax-bracket individuals, institutional investors, and corporations receiving dividends prefer higher dividend payouts.
   3. Shareholders preference for dividends or capital gains fosters investor behavior called the clientele effect. High tax bracket investors often invest in growth-oriented firms that pay no or low dividends. Low tax bracket investors often purchase stocks with high dividend payouts.
   4. The dividend tax credit lowers the effective tax rate on dividend income. See example on page 649 of text.

IV. **Life Cycle Growth and Dividends [p. 650]**

   A. The corporate growth rate in sales is a major influence on dividends.

   B. A firm's dividend policy will usually reflect the firm's stage of development.

   1. Stage I: small firm, initial stage of development -- no dividends.
   2. Stage II: successful firm, growing demand for products and increasing sales, earnings and assets: stock dividends followed later by cash dividends.
   3. Stage III: cash dividends rise as asset expansion slows and external funds are more readily available -- stock dividends and stock splits also common.
   4. Stage IV: the firm reaches maturity and maintains a stable sales growth rate and cash dividends tend to be 40-60 percent of earnings.

V. **Dividend Payment Procedures [p. 651]**

   A. Dividends are usually paid quarterly.

   B. Three key dividend dates:

   1. **Dividend record date**: the date the corporation examines its books to determine who is entitled to a cash dividend.
   2. **Ex-dividend date**: two business days prior to the holder of record date. If an investor buys a share of stock after the second day prior to the holder of record date, the investor's name would not appear on the firm's books.
   3. **Payment date**: approximate date of mailing of dividend checks.
   4. Time line (page 651).

Refer to Figure 18-4, text page 651 for a time line.

VI. **Stock Dividends and Stock Splits [p. 652]**

   A. **Stock dividends**: an additional distribution of stock shares, typically about 10 percent of outstanding amount.

   1. An accounting transfer is required at fair market from retained earnings. The remainder of the stock dividend is transferred to the common stock account.
   2. Unless total cash dividends increase, the shareholder does not benefit from a stock dividend.
   3. Use of stock dividends
       a. Informational content: retention of earnings for reinvestment
       b. Camouflage inability to pay cash dividends
   4. Tax legislation requires that stock dividends be taxable as if they were regular cash dividends.

B. **Stock split [p. 654]:** a distribution of stock that increases the total shares outstanding by 20-25 percent or more.

    1. Accounting transfer from retained earnings is not required. The number of shares increases proportionately.
    2. Benefits to shareholders, if any, are difficult to identify.
    3. Primary purpose is to lower stock price into a more popular trading range.

VII. **Repurchase of Stock [p. 656]**

    A. Alternative to payment of dividends

        1. Most often used when the firm has excess cash and inadequate investment opportunities.
        2. With the exception of a lower capital gains tax (in certain circumstances) the shareholder would be as well off with a cash dividend.

    B. Other reasons for repurchase

        1. Management may deem that stock is selling at a very low price and is the best investment available.
        2. Use for stock options or as part of a tender offer in a merger or acquisition.
        3. To reduce the possibility of being "taken over."

VIII. **Dividend Reinvestment Plans [p. 658]**

    A. Begun during the 1970s, plans provide investors with an opportunity to buy additional shares of stock with the cash dividend paid by the company.

    B. Types of plans

        1. The company sells authorized but unissued shares. The stock is often sold at a discount since no investment or underwriting fees have to be paid. This plan provides a cash flow to the company.
        2. The company's transfer agent buys shares of stock in the market for the shareholder. This plan does not provide a cash flow to the firm but is a service to the shareholder.

    C. Plans usually allow shareholders to supplement dividends with cash payments up to $1,000 per month in order to increase purchase of stock.

Chapter 18: Multiple Choice Questions

1. One of the arguments for the relevancy of dividends is the: [p. 642]
    a. Resolution of uncertainty.
    b. Residual theory of dividends.
    c. Tax deductibility of dividends.
    d. Management entrenchment.
    e. TSE requirements.

2. A firm that follows a residual dividend policy will probably have: [p. 640]
    a. High dividends per share.
    b. Low dividends per share.
    c. Widely fluctuating dividends per share.
    d. Stable dividends per share.
    e. A high payout ratio.

3. Corporate creditors are protected against distribution of a firm's capital by: [p. 647]
   a. The cash position of the firm.
   b. The securities commission.
   c. Legal rules.
   d. The TSE.
   e. Dividend reinvestment plans.

4. The date on which a shareholder must be listed on the firm's books as the owner in order to receive declared dividends is the: [p. 651]
   a. Holder of dividend record date.
   b. Payment date.
   c. Ex-dividend date.
   d. Dividend declaration date.
   e. Legal date.

5. Growth firms with high rates of return usually have: [p. 650]
   a. High dividends.
   b. A high payout rate.
   c. A low retention rate.
   d. A high retention rate.
   e. A high proportion of shareholders who prefer dividends.

6. Which of the following requires an accounting transfer at fair market value from retained earnings? [p. 652]
   a. Stock split
   b. Repurchase of stock
   c. Dividend reinvestment plans
   d. Stock dividends
   e. Declaration of a cash dividend

7. Shareholder preference for dividends or capital gains often leads to: [p. 649]
   a. A residual dividend policy.
   b. A clientele effect.
   c. Stock dividends.
   d. A repurchase of stock.
   e. High taxes.

8. Which of the following statements about Canadian corporations is correct? [p. 646]
   a. Dividends are more volatile than corporate earnings.
   b. There is no relationship between corporate earnings and dividends.
   c. All stock exchange listed firms must distribute at least 10% of earnings.
   d. Dividends yields in the 1990s were high by historical standards.
   e. Corporate earnings are more volatile than dividends.

9. A firm with excess cash and inadequate investment opportunities may elect to: [p. 656]
   a. Declare a stock dividend.
   b. Split its stock.
   c. Reduce its cash dividends.
   d. Repurchase stock.
   e. Retain all earnings.

10. The payout ratio of corporations such as Inco in the1990s has been [p. 644]
   a. stable due to management directives.
   b. stable due to earnings variation.
   c. variable due to management directives.
   d. variable due to earnings variation.
   e. non-existent.

Chapter 18: Problems

18-1.   The stock of Jennifer Plummer Dance Academy is currently trading at $25 per share. The firm's dividend yield is 10%.

    (a)   If the firm distributes 40% of its earnings, what are the earnings per share?

    (b)   What is the firm's P/E ratio?

18-2.   The Watkins' Corporation has current aftertax earnings of $6,000,000.

    (a)   If the firm follows a 60% payout policy, what amount of earnings will it retain?

    (b)   How much will it retain under a residual dividend policy if it has the following acceptable investment opportunities: (1) $0; (2) $4,000,000; (3) $8,000,000.

18-3.   The Bungling Brothers Circus Company recently experienced a 2-for-1 stock split. Its partial balance sheet after the split is presented below.

After

Common stock (12,000,000 shares)	$16,000,000
Retained earnings	10,000,000
	$26,000,000

    (a)   Reproduce Bungling's partial balance sheet that existed before the stock split.

    (b)   If the partial balance sheet above is the result of a 20% stock dividend, determine the pre-stock dividend balance sheet. The price of Bungling's stock was $3 when the new stock was issued.

18-4.

D.I.V. CORPORATION
Balance Sheet

Cash	$ 2,000,000	Current liabilities	$18,000,000
Accounts receivable	10,000,000	Long-term debt	15,000,000
Inventory	25,000,000	Common stock	19,000,000
Plant & equipment	40,000,000	Retained earnings	25,000,000
	$77,000,000		$77,000,000

(a) How much can D.I.V. Corporation legally pay in dividends?

(b) What is the probable maximum dividend the firm can pay if it seeks to maintain a minimum cash balance of $1,000,000 and other asset balances at present levels?

(c) Assume that D.I.V. is a rapidly growing firm that faces severe difficulty in raising needed capital. If substantial additional credit sales have been approved, is the passing (not paying) of dividends likely or unlikely?

18-5. You own 900 shares of Magfin Corporation which recently announced a 3-for-1 stock split. At the time of the announcement, the firm's stock price of $60 per share represented a P/E ratio of 20. The firm follows a 50% payout dividend policy.

(a) What was the market value of your stock holdings when the stock split was announced?

(b) Assuming that the $60 price has not impeded trading of the stock, what will be the likely price per share of your stock after the split?

(c) Compute the earnings per share before and after the stock split.

(d) Compute the dividends per share before and after the stock split.

(e) If the $60 stock price has retarded trading of the stock, are you likely to benefit from the split?

18-6. Rising Star Corporation plans to enlarge its capacity during the coming period. The increase in capacity will require $40,000,000 in additional assets. The firm anticipates net income of $20,000,000 and follows a 60% dividend payout policy. If Rising Star desires to maintain its debt/assets ratio of 40%, how much external equity and debt financing will be required?

Chapter 18: Solutions

18-1. **Jennifer Plummer Dance Academy**

(a)

$$Dividend\ yield = \frac{Dividends\ per\ share}{Market\ share\ price} = \frac{Dividends}{\$25.00} = .10 = \textbf{10\%}$$

$$Dividends = 0.10 \times \$25 = \textbf{\$2.50}$$

$$Payout\ ratio = \frac{Dividend\ per\ share}{Earnings\ per\ share} = .40$$

$$e.p.s. = \frac{\$2.50}{.40} = \textbf{\$6.25}$$

(b) $P/E\ ratio = \dfrac{Market\ per\ share}{Earnings\ per\ share} = \dfrac{\$25}{\$6.25} = \mathbf{4} \times$

18-2. Watkins Corporation

(a) *Retention ratio* = 1 – payout rate
Retention ratio = 1 – .60 = 0.40

Retained earnings = 0.40 × $6,000,000 = **$2,400,000**

(b)
1. **None. All earnings will be distributed.**
2. *Retained earnings* = $6,000,000 – $4,000,000 = **$2,000,000**
3. **All earnings will be retained.**

18-3. Bungling Brothers Circus Company

(a)   *Before 2-for-1 Split*

Common stock (6,000,000 shares at $2 par)	$16,000,000
Retained earnings	10,000,000
	$26,000,000

(b)   *Before 20% Stock Dividend*

Common stock (10,000,000 shares)	$10,000,000
Retained earnings	16,000,000
	$26,000,000

Calculations:

$$\#\ of\ previously\ existing\ shares = \dfrac{12,000,000}{1.20} = 10,000,000$$

Change in retained earnings = number of new shares × market value/ share
Change in retained earnings = 2,000,000 × $3 = $6,000,000

18-4. D.I.V. Corporation

(a) **$25,000,000**

(b) **$1,000,000**

(c) **Very likely**

18-5. **Magfin Corporation**

(a)   900 × $60 = **$54,000**

(b)   Likely price = $60/ 3 = **$20/ share**

(c)   Before split: P/E = 20

$$P/E\ ratio = \frac{Market\ per\ share}{Earnings\ per\ share} = \frac{\$60}{eps} = \mathbf{20} \times$$

$$eps = \frac{\$60}{20} = \mathbf{\$3.00}$$

After split (assuming P/E remains at 20)

$$P/E\ ratio = \frac{Market\ per\ share}{Earnings\ per\ share} = \frac{\$20}{eps} = \mathbf{20} \times$$

$$eps = \frac{\$20}{20} = \mathbf{\$1.00}$$

(d)   Assuming 50% payout
Dividend/ share = (.50) (*eps*) = (.50) ($3.00) = **$1.50 before**
Dividend/ share = (.50) ($1) = $0.**50 after**

(e)   **Yes**

18-6. **Rising Star Corporation**

$20,000,000	net income
.60	payout ratio
$12,000,000	dividends

$40,000,000	financing required
8,000,000	internal equity financing (earnings retention)
$32,000,000	**external financing** required

$40,000,000	
.40	
$16,000,000	**debt financing required** to maintain debt/assets ratio = .4

$32,000,000	external financing required
−16,000,000	debt financing
$16,000,000	**external equity financing needed**

Chapter 19

Summary: In this chapter the characteristics and uses of convertibles and warrants as issued securities are explained. The use of derivatives to reduce risk is explored.

I.   **Introduction [p. 671]**

    A.   Derivatives are contracts that give the holder the right to buy or sell a particular commodity or asset, at an established price, at some time in the future.

    B.   Derivatives allow the holder to reduce or hedge their risk from the volatile price changes of commodities, foreign exchange, and interest rates. The derivatives markets are huge. See also chapters 8 and 21.

    C.   Derivatives take the form of forwards, futures, or options. Derivatives are side bets on the performance of corporations, commodities and other assets. Options are available on corporation shares, but are sold through exchanges independently of the firm.

    D.   Convertibles, warrants, and rights (from chapter 17) are options issued by corporations to raise money.

II.   Forwards [p. 672]

    A.   Forward are customized contracts that fix the price of some commodity for delivery at a specified place and a specified time in the future.

    B.   The use of a forward is demonstrated with a simple example on page 674.

III.   Futures [p. 676]

    A.   Futures are standardized contracts that fix the price of some commodity for delivery at a specified place and a specified time in the future.

    B.   Futures are available on commodities, interest rates, market indexes, and currencies and are often sold through exchanges.

    C.   The use of a future is demonstrated with a simple example on page 677.

IV.   Options [p. 678]

    A.   A beginning knowledge of options requires understanding a few key terms, from page 678-679.

    B.   Options are standardized contracts that fix the price of some commodity for delivery at a specified place and a specified time in the future. Unlike forwards and futures, options can expire. The holder does not have to exercise it.

    C.   The use of a call option is demonstrated with a simple example, on pages 679-680. The market price relationships are illustrated in Figure 19-1.

    D.   The use of a put option is demonstrated with a simple example, on page 682. The market price relationships are illustrated in Figure 19-2.

    E.   Options versus futures for hedging is discussed, and the options issued the corporation are introduced.

V.   **Convertible Securities [p. 683]**

A.   A convertible is a fixed income security, bond, or preferred stock that can be converted at the option of the holder into common stock. (The chapter focuses on convertible bonds.) Convertible securities are only a small percentage of Canadian capital market activity (Figure 15-3; page 581).

B.   Convertible terminology **[p. 684-685]**

1.   **Conversion ratio**: number of shares of common stock into which the security may be converted.
2.   **Conversion price**: face value of bond divided by the conversion ratio.
3.   **Conversion value**: conversion ratio times the market price per share of common stock.
4.   **Conversion premium**: market value of convertible bond minus the conversion value.
5.   **Pure bond value**: the value of the convertible bond as a straight bond; the present value of the annual interest payment and maturity payment discounted at the market rate of interest.
6.   Face value = Conversion value × Conversion ratio   (19-1; page 684)

C.   Value of a convertible bond **[p. 684]**

Refer to Figure 19-3, text page 685.

1.   At issue, investors pay a conversion premium and the price of the convertible exceeds both the pure bond value and the conversion value.
2.   If the market price of the common stock exceeds the conversion price, the market value of the bond will rise above its par value to the conversion value or higher.
3.   The convertible bond's value is limited on the downside by its pure bond value, which is considered the "floor value."

D.   Is this Fool's Gold? Disadvantages to the Investor **[p. 686]**

1.   All downside risk is not eliminated. When the conversion value is very high, the investor is subject to much downward price movement.
2.   The pure bond value will fall if interest rates rise.
3.   Interest rates on convertibles are less than on nonconvertible straight bonds of the same risk.
4.   Convertibles are usually subject to the call provision.

E.   Advantages to the Corporation **[p. 687]**

1.   Lower interest rate than a straight bond.
2.   May be only means of gaining access to the capital market.
3.   Enables the sale of stock at higher than market price.

F.   Forcing conversion **[p. 688]**

1.   Conversion may be forced if the company calls the convertible when the conversion value exceeds the call price.
2.   Conversion is encouraged by a "step-up" provision in the conversion price.
3.   The convertible bond's value is limited on the downside by its pure bond value.

G.   Convertible preferred shares **[p. 690]**

1.   Table 19-3 (page 691) shows a few convertible preferred shares that offer attractive dividend yields.

VI. Accounting Considerations with Convertibles (and Warrants) [p. 688-690 & 694]

A. Prior to 1970 the possible dilution effect of convertible securities on earnings per share was not adequately reflected in financial reports.

B. Currently earnings per share must be reported as if common shares related to conversion had occurred at the beginning of the accounting period.

$$\text{Fully diluted earnings per share} = \frac{\text{Adjusted aftertax earnings}}{\text{Fully diluted shares}}$$ (19-2; page 689)

1. Numerator adjustment includes dividends payable on convertible preferred shares, aftertax interest on convertible debt.
2. Denominator adjustment includes all common shares outstanding and equivalent shares of all convertible preferreds and bonds and common shares issued if rights, warrants and options exercised and then the proceeds used to repurchase share at the market price.

VII. Warrants [p. 690

A. A **warrant** is an option to buy a stated number of shares of stock at a specified price over a given period.
   1. Sweetens a debt issue
   2. Usually detachable
   3. Speculative; value dependent on market movement of stock

B. Value of a warrant **[p. 692**

1. Applying this formula, the minimum value of a warrant may be found:

$$I = (M - E) \times N$$ (19-3; page 692

Where:
   I = Intrinsic value of a warrant
   M = Market value of a common stock
   E = Exercise price of a warrant
   N = Number of shares each share entitles the holder to purchase

> Refer to Figure 19-4, text page 693.

2. Intrinsic value can not be negative.
3. The actual price of the warrant may substantially exceed the formula value due to the speculative nature of warrants. The amount above the intrinsic value is a speculative premium.

$$S = (W - I)$$ (19-4; page 692)

Where:
   S = Speculative premium
   W = Warrant price
   I = Intrinsic value of warrant

C. Use of warrants for corporate financing **[p. 694]**

1. Enhances a debt issue.
2. Add-on in a merger or acquisition.
3. Cannot be forced with a call, but option price is sometimes "stepped-up."
4. Equity base expands when warrants are exercised but the underlying debt remains.

D. Potential dilution of earnings per share upon exercise of warrants must be disclosed in financial reports.

VIII.   **Use of Warrants in Corporate Finance**

    A.   Warrants are effective in growth companies where free cash flow is limited. Warrants keep the cost of debt down and allow for future cash infusion if and when the warrants are exercised.

IX.   **Review of Formulas**

    See text page 695 or insert card.

Chapter 19: Multiple Choice Questions

1. The difference between the price of a warrant and the warrant's intrinsic value is the: [p. 692]
    a. Exercise price.
    b. Conversion premium.
    c. Speculative premium.
    d. Pure bond value.
    e. Conversion ratio.

2. The floor value of a convertible bond is the: [p. 685]
    a. Conversion premium.
    b. Conversion value.
    c. Conversion price.
    d. Market price of common stock × conversion ratio.
    e. Pure bond value.

3. The pure bond value of a convertible will _____ when interest rates fall and the conversion value will ____ when the underlying stock price increases. [p. 685-686]
    a. Rise, fall
    b. Fall, rise
    c. Fall, fall
    d. Rise, rise
    e. Not change, rise

4. The Templeton Company recently issued convertible bonds. The conversion price is $50 and its common stock is currently selling for $45 per share. The conversion ratio and conversion value of the bonds are: [p. 684]
    a. 50 and $1,000.
    b. 20 and $900.
    c. 20 and $1,000.
    d. 20 and $45.
    e. 50 and $900.

5. Which of the following statements about convertible bonds and warrants are correct? [Chapter 19]
    a. A firm receives cash when warrants are exercised and when bonds are converted.
    b. A firm's equity base is increased when warrants are exercised and bonds are converted.
    c. Conversion may be forced when the call price exceeds the conversion value.
    d. Warrants normally sell below intrinsic value.
    e. The conversion option is usually detachable from a convertible bond.

6. Which of the following statements about the downside risk of a convertible bond is true? [p. 686]
    a. The conversion option eliminates downside risk.
    b. Downside risk is usually greatest at the time of issue of the convertible.
    c. Downside risk is greatest when the conversion value is high.
    d. Downside risk is greatest when the conversion value is below the pure bond value.
    e. Downside risk is greatest when the market price of a convertible is below its pure bond value.

7. A convertible bond: [p. 683]
   a. Is convertible at the option of the bond owner.
   b. Is convertible at the option of the bond issuer.
   c. Is automatically converted when the conversion price is stepped up.
   d. Has no value when the market price of the underlying stock is less than the conversion price.
   e. Usually has a higher coupon rate than a pure bond of equal risk.

8. Which of the following describes a difference in warrants and convertible bonds? [p. 794]
   a. Warrants sweeten an issue.
   b. The conversion option is always exercised.
   c. Debt is eliminated when convertibles are converted but remains when warrants are exercised.
   d. The pure bond value falls when interest rates rise on a bond with warrants attached but not on convertible bonds.
   e. Warrants are callable.

9. The impact of convertible securities may be considered in computing: [p. 689]
   a. dividends per share.
   b. the coupon rate.
   c. the share price.
   d. fully diluted EPS.
   e. retained earnings.

10. A warrant is selling for $5. The warrant will allow a holder to purchase one share of stock for $60. The current price of the stock is $60. The intrinsic value and speculative premium of this warrant are: [p. 692]
    a. $60 and $60.
    b. $0 and $0.
    c. $60 and $5.
    d. $0 and $5.
    e. $5 and $0.

11. Futures contracts are similar to forward contracts because they [p. 672-676]
    a. trade on an organized exchange.
    b. are marked to market every day.
    c. allow delivery any day of the delivery month.
    d. allow delivery or purchase of an asset at a future date.
    e. allow only the delivery of an asset at a future date.

12. A put option gives the holder the right [p. 678]
    a. but not the obligation to sell an asset at a predetermined price.
    b. but not the obligation to buy an asset at a predetermined price.
    c. and the obligation to sell an asset at a predetermined price.
    d. and the obligation to buy an asset at a predetermined price.
    e. It gives no rights.

Multiple Choice Answer Key: Chapter 19

1.	c	2.	e	3.	d	4.	b	5.	b	6.	c
7.	a	8.	c	9.	d	10.	d	11.	d	12.	a

Chapter 19: Problems

19-1.   Blackwell Lumber Company has an outstanding convertible bond that is currently quoted at $900 in the bond market. The bond has a coupon rate of 9% and matures in 15 years. The conversion price is $50, and the common stock is currently selling at $40.

   (a)   How many shares of stock can the convertible bondholders obtain by converting?

   (b)   Why is the bond selling for an amount larger than its conversion value?

   (c)   If the stock price has not changed since the bond was first issued and the pure bond value was $750, what was the conversion premium at the issue date if the bonds were sold at their $1,000 face value?

   (d)   If the stock rises to $60 per share, what will be the approximate price of the bond?

19-2.   Roemer Engineering has warrants outstanding that entitle the holder to purchase one new share of common stock for $23. The stock is currently selling for $38. The warrant is quoted at $20.

   (a)   What is the intrinsic value of the warrant?

   (b)   How much is the speculative premium on the warrant?

   (c)   As the warrant nears maturity, will the speculative premium increase or decrease?

   (d)   Suppose you bought a share of the firm's common stock at $38. If the stock price rises to $57, what would be your percentage gain? If you had bought a warrant for its intrinsic value instead, what would be your percentage gain?

   (e)   If the price of the stock were $19, what would be the intrinsic value of the warrant? Will the warrant sell at this price?

19-3.   Flintstone, Inc., has a convertible bond outstanding bearing a coupon rate of 10%. The bond which matures in 10 years is convertible into 20 shares of common stock. The common stock is presently selling at $40 per share.

   (a)   If the current interest rate on bonds of the same risk class is 12%, what will be the pure bond value of this bond?

   (b)   What is the conversion price?

   (c)   What will be the price of the bond under the condition stated above?

   (d)   Assuming a call price of 110, would Flintstone be able to force conversion when the stock was selling for $52?

19-4. The JMA Corporation produced net income of $10,000,000 during the past year. The firm has 3,000,000 shares of common stock outstanding. JMA also has a $25,000,000 issue of convertible bonds outstanding which pays 8% interest annually. The average A (low) bond yield when the convertible bonds were issued was 10%. The firm is in the 46% tax bracket. The conversion price of the $1,000 convertible bonds is $40.

(a) Compute the fully diluted earnings per share for the firm.

(b) Compute the primary earnings per share for the firm.

(c) Assume the bonds carried an interest rate of 6% when issued, and compute the firm's primary earnings per share.

19-5. Ultimate Webster share prices have been up and down in price since its initial public offering. Currently call and put options are available on the common shares at an exercise price of $45.00. We expect that both types of options will trade at speculative premiums of $5.00 in one month's time.

(a) Calculate the price of both options if the price of Ultimate Webster is trading at $70.00 in one month's time.

(b) Calculate the price of both options if the price of Ultimate Webster is trading at $25.00 in one month's time.

19-6. Tulsa Drilling Company has $1 million in 11 percent convertible bonds outstanding. Each bond has a $1,000 par value. The conversion ratio is 40, the stock price is $32, and the bond matures in 10 years. The bonds are currently selling at a conversion premium of $70 over the conversion value.

(a) If the price of Tulsa Drilling Company common stock rises to $42 on this date next year, what would your rate of return be if you bought a convertible bond today and sold it in one year? Assume that on this date next year, the conversion premium has shrunk from $70 to $20.

(b) Assume the yield on similar nonconvertible bonds has fallen to 8 percent at the time of sale. What would the pure bond value be at that point? (Use semiannual analysis.) Would the pure bond value have a significant effect on valuation then?

Chapter 19: Solutions

19-1. **Blackwell Lumber Company**

(a) Face value = Conversion value × Conversion ratio
$1,000 = $50 × Conversion ratio
Conversion ratio = 20 (shares)

(b) *Conversion value = market share price × conversion ratio*
Conversion value = $40 × 20 = $800

The bond is selling above conversion value because **the convertible bond's value as a pure bond is greater than its conversion value**.

(c) *Conversion premium = market value of bond – conversion value of bond*
Conversion premium = $1,000 – $800 = **$200**

(d) The price of the bond will rise above $1,000 as the stock price rises above the conversion price. If the share price rises to $60, the bond will sell at approximately **$1,200** = 20 × $60.

19-2. **Roemer Engineering**

    (a)   *Intrinsic value of a warrant = [market value of common stock – exercise price of warrant] × number of shares warrant entitles holder to purchase*

$$I = (M - E) \times N$$
$$I = [\$38 - \$23] \times 1 = \mathbf{\$15}$$

    (b)   *Speculative premium of warrant = market price of warrant - intrinsic value of warrant*

$$S = (W - I)$$
$$S = \$20 - \$15 = \mathbf{\$5}$$

    (c)   **Decrease**

    (d)   Buy stock:

$$Rate\ of\ return = \frac{\$57 - \$38}{\$38} = 0.50 = \mathbf{50\%}$$

Buy warrant:
Intrinsic value of warrant after stock price rises:
Intrinsic value of warrant = (57 – 23) × 1 = 34

$$Rate\ of\ return = \frac{\$34 - \$15}{\$15} = 1.27 = \mathbf{127\%}$$

    (e)   *Intrinsic value of warrant = ($19 – $23) × 1 = – **$4 (We assign zero).***
No. The warrant cannot sell below zero. A price of -$4 would mean that the holder would pay $4 for someone to take the warrant; an unlikely occurrence!

19-3. **Flintstone, Inc.**

    (a)   *Bond price = present value of interest stream + present value of lump-sum payment*
Bond price = A × PV_{IFA} (n = 10, i = 12%) + FV × PV_{IF} (n = 10th, i = 12%)
Bond price = 100 (5.65) + 1,000 (.322)
BP = $565 + $322
BP = **$887**

Calculator:	P_n	=	FV	=	$1,000
	I	=	PMT	=	$100
	n	=		=	10
	Y	=	i	=	12%
Compute PV		=	P_b	=	**$887.00**

    (b)   Face value = Conversion value × Conversion ratio
$1,000 = Conversion value × 20
Conversion value = $50

    (c)   *Conversion value = 20 × $40 = $800*
Price of bond will be **$887**. The pure bond value is greater than the conversion value.

    (d)   *Conversion value = 20 × $52 = $1,040*
No, convertible bondholders would probably accept the call.

19-4.   JMA Corporation

(a)

$$\text{Fully diluted earnings per share} = \frac{\text{Adjusted aftertax earnings}}{\text{Fully diluted shares}}$$

Adjusted earnings aftertax = current net income + interest savings income

Interest saving = annual interest × (1 – tax rate)
Interest savings = ($25,000,000 × .08) × (1 – .46)
Interest savings = $2,000,000 × .54 = $1,080,000

Adjusted earnings aftertaxes = $10,000,000 + $1,080,000
Adjusted earnings aftertaxes = $11,080,000

Face value = Conversion value × Conversion ratio
$1,000 = $40 × Conversion ratio
Conversion ratio = 25 (shares)

$$\text{\# new shares if all bonds converted} = 25 \times \frac{\$25,000,000}{\$1,000} = \mathbf{625,000}$$

Adjusted shares = 3,000,000 + 625,000 = 3,625,000

$$\text{Fully diluted earnings per share} = \frac{\$11,080,000}{3,625,000} = \mathbf{\$3.06}$$

19-5.   Ultimate Webster

(a)   Call option gives the right to buy at $45.00
Current market price of shares is $70.00

Intrinsic or minimum value =	$70.00 – $45.00 = $35.00
Market value of call =	$35.00 + $5.00 = **$40.00**

Put option gives the right to sell at $45.00

Intrinsic or minimum value =	$45.00 – $70.00 = 0
Market value of put =	0 + $5.00 = **$5.00**

(b)   Call option gives the right to buy at $45.00
Current market price of shares is $25.00

Intrinsic or minimum value =	$25.00 – $45.00 = 0
Market value of call =	0 + $5.00 = **$5.00**

Put option gives the right to sell at $45.00

Intrinsic or minimum value =	$45.00 – $25.00 = $20.00
Market value of put =	$20.00 + $5.00 = **$25.00**

19-6. **Tulsa Drilling Company**

(a)   First find the price of the convertible bond. The conversion value is $1,280 ($32 × 40). The value, $1,280, plus the premium, $70, equals $1,350, the current market price of the convertible bond.

Next, you find the price of the convertible bond on this day next year.

$42 share price × 40 conversion ratio = $1,680 conversion value
$1,680 conversion value + $20 premium = $1,700 market value of the convertible bond.

Then determine the rate of return.

$$Rate\ of\ return = \frac{\$1,700 - \$1,350}{\$1,350} = \frac{\$350}{\$1,350} = 0.2593 = \textbf{25.93\%}$$

(b)   **Calculator:**

P_n	=	FV	=	$1,000
I	=	PMT	=	$55 ($110/ 2)
N	=	N	=	18 (9 × 2)
Y	=	i	=	4% (8%/ 2)
Compute PV		=	P_b =	**$1,189.89**

Because the pure bond value of $1,189.89 is still well below the conversion value of $1,680 and the market value is $1,700, it would not have a significant effect on valuation.

Summary: This chapter focuses on the significant financial and management variables influencing the merger decision including the price to pay, the accounting implications, the stock market effect and the motivation of the participating parties.

I. **The International and Canadian Merger Environment [p. 706]**

   A. Heavy merger activity returned in the 1990s fueled by low interest rates, changing regulations, competition and evolving technology.

   B. The 1960s and 1970s saw mergers attempting to achieve the benefits of diversification. The 1980s saw divestiture activity, particularly in Canada as a result of the National Energy Program. The 1990s saw strategic positioning and convergence of technology firms.

   C. Divestitures are a component of this topic. In the 1990s we saw Governments selling off crown corporations.

II. **Negotiated versus Tender Offers [p. 708]**

   A. Friendly versus unfriendly mergers

      1. .Most mergers are friendly and the officers and directors of the involved companies negotiate the terms.
      2. During the 1970s and 1980s, takeover tender offers occurred frequently and often were opposed by the management of candidate firms. The Air Canada attempted takeover by Onex in late 1999 would be a good example.

   B. Unfriendly takeover attempts have resulted in additions to the investment community's vocabulary. **[p. 709]**

      1. **Saturday Night Special:** a surprise offer made right before the market closes for the weekend.
      2. **Leveraged takeover**: the acquiring firm negotiates a loan based on the target company's assets (particularly a target company with large cash balances).

   C. Actions by target companies to avoid unwanted takeovers. Known sometimes as applying shark repellent.

      1. **White Knight** arrangements.
      2. Selling **crown jewels.**
      3. Targeted repurchase of shares.
      4. Voting in **golden parachutes.**
      5. Taking on more debt. Avoiding large cash balances.
      6. Adopting **poison pills** or other shareholders' rights plans
      7. Moving corporate offices to jurisdictions with protective provisions against takeovers.
      8. Buying the other firm first (a **Pacman defense**)

   D. Many mergers cause a domino effect resulting in further mergers.

   E. The Canadian Government regulates large takeovers that lesson competition and fair pricing.

III. **Motives for Business Combinations [p. 712]**

    A. Business combinations may be either **mergers or consolidations**.

        1. Merger: A combination of two or more companies in which the resulting firm maintains the identity of the acquiring company.
        2. Consolidation: Two or more companies are combined to form an entirely new entity.

    B. Financial motives **[p. 713]**

        1. Risk reduction as a result of the **portfolio effect**.
           a. Lower required rate of return by investors.
           b. Higher value of the firm.

        2. Improved financing posture
           a. Greater access to financial markets to raise debt and equity capital.
           b. Attract more prestigious investment dealers to handle financing.
           c. Strengthen cash position and/or improve debt/equity ratio.

        3. Obtain a tax loss carry-forward

        4. **Synergism:** 2 + 2 = 5

    C. Non-financial motives **[p. 715]**

        1. Expand management and marketing capabilities.
        2. Acquire new products.

    D. Motives of selling shareholders

        1. Desire to receive acquiring firm's stock which may have greater acceptability in the market.
        2. Provides opportunity to diversify their holdings.
        3. Gain on sale of stock at an attractive price.
        4. Avoid the bias against smaller businesses.

IV. **Terms of Exchange [p. 716]**

    A. Cash purchases **[p. 716]**

        1. Capital budgeting decision: Net present value of purchasing a going concern equals the present value of cash inflows including anticipated synergistic benefits minus cash outlays including adjustment for tax shield benefit from any tax loss carryforward.
        2. Many firms were purchased for cash in the 1970s and 1980s at prices below the replacement costs of their assets, but the rising stock market of the 1990s has made this difficult to duplicate.

    B. Stock for stock exchange **[p. 717]**

        1. Emphasizes the impact of the merger on earnings per share.
        2. If the P/E ratio of the acquiring firm is greater than the P/E ratio of the acquired firm, there will be an immediate increase in earnings per share.
        3. Shareholders of the acquired firm are usually more concerned with market value exchanged than earnings, dividends, or book value exchanged.

C. In addition to the immediate impact on earnings per share, the acquiring firm must be concerned with the long-run impact of the merger on market value.

1. An acquired firm may have a low P/E ratio because its future rate of growth is expected to be low. In the long run, the acquisition may reduce the acquiring firm's earnings per share and its market value.
2. The acquisition of a firm with a higher P/E ratio causes an immediate reduction in earnings per share. In the long run, however, the higher growth rate of the acquired firm may cause earnings per share and the market value of the acquiring company to be greater than if the merger did not take place.

D. Determinants of earnings per share impact of a merger

1. Exchange ratio.
2. Relative growth rates.
3. Relative sizes of the firms.

E. Ultimately it is the market value maximization of share price that is the goal of a merger.

F. Portfolio effect **[p. 718]**

1. If the risk assessment of the acquiring firm is decreased by a merger, its market value will rise even if the earnings per share remain constant.
2. Two types of risk reduction may be accomplished by a merger.
   a. Business risk reduction may result from acquiring a firm that is influenced by an opposite set of factors in the business cycle.
   b. Financial risk reduction may result from a lower use of debt in the post-merger financial structure of the acquiring firm.

V. **Accounting Considerations in Mergers and Acquisitions [p. 719]**

A. A merger is treated as either a **pooling of interests** or a **purchase of assets** on the books of the acquiring firm.

B. Criteria for pooling of interests treatment

1. Companies joined by exchange of shares in which none of the parties can be identified as the acquirer. This was the intent in the proposed bank mergers of 1999.

C. Purchase of assets

1. Necessary when the tender offer is in cash, bonds, preferred stock, or common stock with restricted rights.
2. Any excess of purchase price over book value is recorded as goodwill and written off for accounting purposes as impaired. For tax purposes three quarters (75%) can be amortized at a CCA rate of 7% (declining balance basis).

D. Pooling of interests versus purchase of assets

1. The exchange of stock under a pooling of interests arrangement is usually a tax-free exchange.
2. In the 1970s and 1980s, many proposed and actual mergers were purchases. Shareholders of the acquired firm were often disenchanted with the stock market in general and preferred cash to an exchange of stock. The 1990s saw a return to share exchanges, probably because investors were willing to accept shares that were valued higher in the equity markets of the 90s.
3. Although purchases tend to raise earnings per share, the cash required has a substantial capital cost associated with it.

VI. **Premium Offers and Stock Price Movements [p. 721]**

    A. The average premium paid over market value in mergers or acquisitions has been in the 40-45 percent range.

    B. High merger premiums are related to the belief that replacement value exceeds market value.

    C. Acquired companies apparently have superior risk adjusted returns, but it is uncertain whether or not the acquiring firms achieve superior results.

    D. Merger arbitrageurs (ARBS) have influenced the merger market, by buying potential takeover companies in hopes of selling when a higher takeover price is announced.

    E. The market for corporate control may act to align management with the shareholder goal of wealth maximization.

VII. **Holding Companies [p. 723]**

    A. A holding company has control over one or more other companies.

    B. Advantages of holding companies.

        1. Offers unusual opportunities for leverage.
        2. The isolation of legal risks.
        3. Dividends paid between companies are usually tax free.

    C. Disadvantages of holding companies.

        1. A poor year by one or more companies may result in a very poor year for the holding company as well.
        2. Coordinating the management of multiple companies is often expensive and difficult.

Chapter 20: Multiple Choice Questions

1. A surprise takeover offer made immediately before the market closes for the weekend is called a: [S.G. p. 228]
    a. White Knight.
    b. Saturday Night Special.
    c. Leveraged takeover.
    d. Poison pill.
    e. Pooling of interests.

2. The largest Canadian merger of 2002 was: [p. 708]
    a. Royal/ Bank of Montreal.
    b. CN Rail/ Nav Canada.
    c. Sun Life/ Clarica
    d. PanCanadian/ Alberta Energy.
    e. TransCanada/ Nova.

3. Which of the following may require goodwill to be written off for tax purposes? (Choose the best answer.) [p. 720]
    a. Merger
    b. Acquisition
    c. Purchase of assets
    d. Pooling of interests
    e. Consolidation

4. An acquisition attempt can be fought by a(n): [p. 709]
   a. Poison pill.
   b. Holding company.
   c. ARB.
   d. Goodwill offer.
   e. Saturday Night Special.

5. Which of the following discourages takeover attempts: [S.G. & p. 709]
   a. Large cash balances of target firms
   b. Business risk reduction
   c. Financial risk reduction
   d. Increasing dividends of target firm
   e. Synergism

6. Which of the following is a financial motive for business combination? [p. 713]
   a. Expansion of marketing capabilities
   b. Acquisition of new products
   c. 2 + 2 = 5
   d. Expand into a more dynamic business
   e. Obtain a corporate jet

7. A merger is usually associated with: [p. 708]
   a. A tax-free exchange of stock.
   b. A proxy fight.
   c. Common stock with restricted rights.
   d. A cash tender offer.
   e. An unfriendly takeover.

8. The acquisition of a company that has a lower P/E ratio will: [p. 718]
   a. Not affect the current earnings per share of the acquiring firm.
   b. Raise the current earnings per share of the acquiring firm.
   c. Lower the current earnings per share of the acquiring firm.
   d. May raise or lower the current earnings per share of the acquiring firm.
   e. Raise the current earnings per share of the acquired firm.

9. The primary advantage of a holding company is: [p. 723]
   a. The elimination of taxes.
   b. Easier coordination of management of multiple companies.
   c. The assurance of financial success.
   d. Unusual opportunities for leverage.
   e. Cheaper management operations.

10. Which of the following statements about merger arbitrageurs is correct? [p. 721]
   a. Arbitrageurs have a long-run orientation.
   b. Arbitrageurs usually support the target company in a takeover attempt.
   c. The greatest risk to the arbitrageur is that the merger will be called off.
   d. In a stock-for-stock exchange, an arbitrageur is likely to short-sell the stock of the target firm while buying the stock of the acquiring firm.
   e. Arbitrageurs are usually the managers of the acquisition candidates.

Multiple Choice Answer Key: Chapter 20

1.	b	2.	d	3.	c	4.	a	5.	d
6.	c	7.	b	8.	b	9.	d	10.	c

Chapter 20: Problems

20-1. Gibraltar is considering the acquisition of Roller Coaster Corporation. Although Roller Coaster is expected to have a bright future, it has recently experienced large financial losses and has an operating loss carryforward of $2,000,000. Gibraltar's taxable earnings have varied only slightly in recent years and are expected to be $800,000; $815,000; and $825,000 for the next three years if the proposed acquisition does not take place. Gibraltar has a 40% tax rate.

(a) What will Gibraltar's taxes be for the next three years if the proposed acquisition is accomplished (assume Roller Coaster operations break even during this period)?

(b) What will be the tax savings to Gibraltar from the acquisition?

(c) If Gibraltar has a cost of capital of 14%, what would be the value of the tax savings available from the acquisition?

(d) Rework (a) under the assumption that Roller Coaster operations will generate $500,000 per year in taxable income.

20-2. The Cain Corporation can expand by acquiring Abel Corporation for $1,500,000 cash. The Cain Corporation would be able to lower its taxes as a result of Abel's $500,000 tax loss carryforward. Cain officials think that Abel would contribute $200,000 aftertax cash flow per year for a period of 10 years. Cain is expected to have $250,000 per year in taxable income if the merger is not consummated. Cain is in a 40% tax bracket and its cost of capital is 12%. Should Cain acquire Abel for $1,500,000?

20-3. The management of the Block Corporation are considering a cash purchase of Hirt Corporation for $3,000,000. Hirt has a $300,000 tax loss carryforward that could be used immediately. The expected cash inflows and synergistic benefits to be derived from the purchase of Hirt are:

Years	1-5	6-10	11-15
Cash inflow	$450,000	$300,000	$150,000
Synergistic benefits	30,000	25,000	10,000

Block has a cost of capital of 10% and a 44% tax rate. Should Block acquire the Hirt Corporation?

20-4. Officials of the North Corporation and the South Corporation have been negotiating the terms of a merger of the two firms. The financial information for the prospective merging firms is as follows:

	North	South
Total earnings	$500,000	$700,000
# shares of stock outstanding	200,000	350,000
Earnings per share	$2.50	$2.00
Price-earnings ratio	10	13
Market price per share	$25.00	$26.00

(a) If one share of South Corporation is traded for one share of North Corporation, what will postmerger earnings per share be? (Assuming earnings remain the same.)

(b) If South Corporation pays a 20% premium over market value of North Corporation, how many shares will be issued?

(c) With a 20% premium, what will postmerger earnings per share be?

(d) Suppose a 10% synergistic increase in total earnings is affected by the merger. What will postmerger earnings per share be if a 20% premium is paid?

20-5.   Apple Corporation has agreed to a 40% premium over market value exchange of stock with Possum Corporation. The financial information for the two firms is as follows:

	Orange Corp.	Apple Corp.
Total earnings	$8,000,000	$20,000,000
# of shares of stock outstanding	2,000,000	8,000.000
Earnings per share	$4.00	$2.50
Price-earnings ratio	12	8
Market price per share	$48.00	$20.00
Projected annual growth rate for next 10 years	14%	4%

(a)   Compute postmerger earnings per share.

(b)   Compute the postmerger growth rate for the combined firms for the next 10 years.

(c)   Project no-merger and postmerger earnings per share for Apple Corporation for the next 10 years.

(d)   Compare the premerger and postmerger position of a shareholder in Orange Corporation. Assume that the postmerger P/E ratio is 10 and the shareholder owns 100 shares prior to the merger.

(e)   Compare the with-merger and without-merger position of a shareholder in Apple Corporation at the end of years 1 and 10. Assume that the shareholder owns 100 shares and the postmerger P/E ratio is 10 and the premerger P/E ratio is 8.

Chapter 20: Solutions

20-1.   **Gibraltar**

(a)   *Gibraltar's Taxes with Acquisition*

	Year 1	Year 2	Year 3
Before tax earnings	$800,000	$815,000	$ 825,000
Tax loss carryforward	800,000	815,000	385,000
Taxable income	$ 0	$ 0	$440,000
Taxes (40%)	$ 0	$ 0	**$176,000**

(b)

Gibraltar's Taxes Without Acquisition

	Year 1	Year 2	Year 3
Before tax earnings	$800,000	$815,000	$825,000
Taxes (40%)	$320,000	$326,000	$330,000

Tax Savings from Acquisition

	Year 1	Year 2	Year 3
Taxes without acquisition	$320,000	$326,000	$330,000
Taxes with acquisition	0	0	176,000
Tax savings	$320,000	$326,000	$154,000

Total tax savings = $320,000 + $326,000 + $154,000 = **$800,000**

Total tax savings can also be found in the following manner:

Tax loss carry forward × *tax rate*
$2,000,000 × .40 = **$800,000**

As will be shown in (c), the **value** of the tax savings, however, differs from the amount of the tax savings.

(c) *Value of tax savings*
= $320,000 ($n = 1, i = 14\%$) + $326,000 ($n = 2, i = 14\%$) + $154,000($n = 3, i = 14\%$)
= $280,702 + $250,846 + $103,946
= **$635,494**

(d) *Gibraltar's Taxes with Acquisition and $500,000 Profit/Year from RC*

	Year 1	Year 2	Year 3
Before tax earnings	$1,300,000	$1,315,000	$1,325,000
Tax loss carryforward	1,300,000	700,000	0
Taxable income	$ 0	$ 615,000	$1,325,000
Taxes	$ 0	$ 246,000	$ 530,000

20-2. **Cain Corporation**

Tax savings from the tax loss carryforward of $500,000 ($250,000 in each of first two years since Cain has $250,000 taxable income annually):

Year 1	Year 2
$250,000	$250,000
.40	.40
$100,000	$100,000

Value of Abel Corporation to Cain Corporation
Value of Abel = $200,000 ($PV_{IFA}, n = 10, i = 12\%$) + $100,000 ($PV_{IFA}, n = 2, i = 12\%$)
Value of Abel = $1,130,045 + $169,005 = **$1,299,050**

The value of Abel Corporation to Cain Corporation is $1,299,050 and **should not be purchased for $1,500,000**.

20-3.   **Block Corporation**

Cash Outflow

Purchase price	$3,000,000
Less tax shield from tax loss carryforward	264,000
(.44 × $600,000)	
Net cash outflow	$2,736,000

Cash Inflows

	Years 1-5	Years 6-10	Years 11-15
Cash inflow	$450,000	$300,000	$150,000
Synergistic benefits	30,000	25,000	10,000
Total cash inflow	$480,000	$325,000	$160,000

Present value of inflows
= $480,000 ($PV_{IFA}$, $n = 5$, $i = 10\%$) + $325,000 ($PV_{IFA}$, $n = 10 - 5$, $i = 10\%$)
+ $160,000($PV_{IFA}$, $n = 15 - 10$, $i = 10\%$)
= $1,819,578 + $764,979 + $233,842 = $2,818,399

Net present value = $2,818,399 − $2,736,000 = **$82,399**

Block Corporation should acquire the Hirt Corporation.

20-4.   **North and South Corporations**

(a)   Postmerger earnings per share
Total earnings = $500,000 + $700,000 = $1,200,000
Number of shares outstanding = 200,000 + 350,000 = 550,000

$$New\ eps = \frac{\$1,200,000}{550,000} = \textbf{\$2.18}\ (rounded)$$

(b)   If a 20% premium is paid, shareholders of North Corporation would receive [$25 + $25(.20)] = $30 worth of South Corporation stock for each share of stock held.

Total value of stock paid to North Corporation shareholders will be;
200,000 × $30 = $6,000,000.

Number of shares issued = $6,000,000/ $26 = **230,769** (rounded)

(c)   Postmerger earnings per share with a 20% premium will be:
Postmerger EPS = $1,200,000/ 580,769 = **$2.07** (rounded)

(d)   Postmerger earnings with a 10% synergistic increase in total earnings will be:
Postmerger earnings = $1,200,000 + $1,200,000 (.10) = $1,320,000
Postmerger EPS with a 10% synergistic effect and a 20% premium equals:
$1,320,000/ 580,769 = **$2.27** (rounded).

20-5. **Apples for Oranges**

(a)   Number of shares issued

        Value paid per share of Possum = $48 + $48 (.4) = $67.20
        Total value paid = $67.20 (2,000,000) = $134,400,000
        Number of shares issued = $134,400,000/ $20.00 = 6,720,000

        Postmerger earnings per share
        $28,000,000/1 4,720,000 = **$1.90** (rounded)

(b)   Postmerger growth rate
        8/ 28 (14%) + 20/ 28 (4%) = **6.86%** (rounded)

(c)   *Expected Earnings Per Share for Apple Corporation with and without Merger*

	Without Merger			With Merger		
Year	Beginning EPS	Growth Rate	Expected EPS	Beginning EPS	Growth Rate	Expected EPS
1	$2.50	4%	$2.60	$1.90	6.86%	$2.03
2	2.60	4	2.70	2.03	6.86	2.17
3	2.70	4	2.81	2.17	6.86	2.32
4	2.81	4	2.92	2.32	6.86	2.48
5	2.92	4	3.04	2.48	6.86	2.65
6	3.04	4	3.16	2.65	6.86	2.83
7	3.16	4	3.29	2.83	6.86	3.02
8	3.29	4	3.42	3.02	6.86	3.23
9	3.42	4	3.56	3.23	6.86	3.45
10	3.56	4	3.70	3.45	6.86	3.69

(d)   *Value of premerger shares* = $48 × 100 = **$4,800**
        Total premerger earnings = $4 × 100 = **$400**

$$\# \ of \ postmerger \ shares \ per \ premerger \ share = \frac{\$48 + \$48(.4)}{\$20} = 3.36$$

        Total number of postmerger shares = 100 × 3.36 = 336
        Price of postmerger shares = 10 × $1.90 = $19.00
        Value of postmerger shares = 336 × $19 = **$6,384**
        Amount of postmerger earnings = 336 × $1.90 = **$638.40**

(e)   *Without Merger*

Year	EPS	Number of Shares	Total Earnings	P/E Ratio	Price Per Share	Market Value of Stock
1	$2.60	100	**$260**	8	$20.80	**$2,080**
10	3.70	100	**370**	8	29.60	**2,960**

                             With Merger

Year	EPS	Number of Shares	Total Earnings	P/E Ratio	Price Per Share	Market Value of Stock
1	$2.03	100	**$203**	10	$20.30	**$2,030**
10	3.69	100	**369**	10	36.90	**3,690**

Chapter 21

International Financial Management

Summary: This chapter deals with the international dimensions of corporate finance and provides a basis for understanding the complexities of international financial decisions.

I. **Introduction [p. 736]**

    A. Many factors have contributed to greater economic interaction among the world's nations.

        1. Advances in communication and transportation.
        2. Adaptation of political systems.
            a. Post World War II rebuilding programs.
            b. European Common Market (ECM or EU).
            c. Political, social and economic changes in Russia.
        3. International flows of capital and technology.
        4. International currency: U.S. Dollar.
        5. Interdependence for scarce resources.

    B. International business operations are complex, risky and require special understanding. Canada and Canadian corporations are particularly dependent on international trade as emphasized by Figures 21-1 and 21-2. Figure 21-3 demonstrates Canada's close trading relationship with the United States. Canada's preponderance of merchandise trade is evidenced in Figure 21-4.

II. **The Multinational Corporation (MNC) [p. 740]**

    A. Basic forms of MNC.

        1. **Exporter**: exportation to foreign markets of domestically produced products.
        2. **Licensing Agreement:** granting of a license to an independent local (in the foreign country) firm to use the "exporting" firm's technology.
        3. **Joint Venture**: cooperative business operation with a firm (or firms) in the foreign country.
        4. **Fully Owned Foreign Subsidiary**.

    B. International Environment versus Domestic Environment.

        1. More risky: in addition to normal business risks, the MNC is faced with **foreign exchange risk** and **political risk**. The portfolio risk of the parent company, however, may be reduced if foreign and domestic operations are not correlated.
        2. Potentially more profitable.
        3. More complex: the laws, customs, and economic environment of the host country may vary in many respects:
            a. Rates of inflation.
            b. Tax rules.
            c. Structure and operation of financial institutions.
            d. Financial policies and practices.
            e. Work habits and wages of labourers.

III. **Foreign Exchange Rates [p. 741**

    A. To facilitate international trade, currencies must be exchanged. For example, and exporter will usually desire payment in the currency of the home country. The importer must swap the domestic currency for the currency desired by the exporter in order to pay the bill.

B. Factors affecting exchange rates

1. Supply of and demand for the currencies of the various countries.
2. The degree of central bank intervention.
3. Inflation rate differentials **(Purchasing Power Parity Theory)**.
4. Interest rate differentials **(Interest Rate Parity Theory)**.
5. **Balance of payments**.
6. Government policies.
7. Other factors
    a. Capital market movements.
    b. Changes in supply of and demand for the products and services of individual countries.
    c. Labour disputes.
    d. Political turmoil.

C. Many variables affect currency exchange rates. The importance of each variable or set of variables will change as economics and political conditions change throughout the world.

D. Spot Rates, Forward Rates, and Cross Rates **[p. 747-748]**

1. **Spot rate**: he exchange rate between currencies with immediate delivery.
2. **Forward rate**: the rate of exchange between currencies when delivery will occur in the future.

$$Forward \ \ premium \ \ (discount) = \frac{Forward \ - \ spot}{spot} \times \frac{12}{contract \ \ length \ \ (months)} \qquad \text{(21-1; page 748)}$$

3. **Cross rate**: the exchange rate between currencies such as Danish Krone and British Pounds based on their exchange rate with another currency such as Canadian Dollars.

IV. **Managing Foreign Exchange Risk [p. 749-753]**

A. Foreign exchange risk is the possibility of experiencing a drop in revenue or an increase in cost in an international transaction due to a change in foreign exchange rates.

1. Three types of foreign exchange risk exposure
    a. **Economic exposure** identifies market value of net investment subject to change in economic value due to currency fluctuation.
    b. Accounting or **translation exposure**: depends upon accounting rules established by CICA accounting recommendations. This is often an unrealized gain or loss.
    c. **Transaction exposure**: the foreign exchange gains and losses resulting from international transactions, when foreign funds are converted to Canadian dollars.

2. There are three strategies used to minimize transaction exposure:
    a. Hedging in the forward exchange market: the recipient (seller) of foreign currency in an international transaction sells a **forward contract** to assure the amount that will be received in domestic currency.
    b. Hedging in the money market: the recipient borrows foreign currency in the amount to be received and then immediately converts to domestic currency. When the receivable is collected, the loan is paid off.
    c. Hedging in the currency futures market: **futures contracts** in foreign currencies began trading in the International Monetary Market (IMM) of the Chicago Mercantile Exchange (CME) on May 16, 1972.
    d. Hedging in the currency options market: options contracts on foreign currencies are traded on the CME.

V. **Foreign Investment Decisions [p. 753]**

A. Canada invests abroad.

1. Canada held $778 billion in assets abroad, primarily by way of direct investment ($301 B).
2. The primary locale of Canadian investment abroad is the U.S., then the EEC, and the U.K.

B. Reasons for Canadian firms to invest in foreign countries:

1. Higher rates of return;
    a. Resources readily available
    b. Lower production costs particularly with regard to labor costs
    c. Tax advantages
    d. Ease of entry because of advanced technology
2. Strategic considerations:
    a. Trade Blocs
    b. Proximity to market
    c. Competition
3. International diversification

C. Foreign firms are expanding their investment in Canada.

1. Foreign investments in Canada reached $1,023 billion in 2000 with the United States dominating followed by the EU and Britain. Bond holdings were $379 billion and direct investment was $286 billion.
2. The great foreign control of Canadian assets and industry is a continuing concern.
3. The reasons for investment in Canada include:
    a. International diversification.
    b. Strategic considerations.
    c. Saturated markets.
    d. Labour restrictions overseas.
    e. Access to advanced technology.
    f. Political stability.
    g. Closeness to U.S. market.
    h. Advance economic structure.

D. Analysis of Political Risk **[p. 757]**

1. The structure of the foreign government and/or those in control may change many times during the lengthy period necessary to recover an investment. "Unfriendly" changes may result in:
    a. Foreign exchange restriction.
    b. Foreign ownership limitations.
    c. Blockage of **repatriation of earnings**.
    d. Expropriation of foreign subsidiary's assets.
2. Safeguards against political risk.
    a. A thorough investigation of the country's political stability prior to investment.
    b. Joint ventures with local (foreign) companies.
    c. Joint ventures with multiple companies representing multiple countries.
    d. Insurance through the federal government agency, the Export Development Corporation (EDC).

VI. **Financing International Business Operations [p. 759]**

A. **Letters of credit**: in order to reduce the risk of non-payment, an exporter may require an importer to furnish a letter of credit. The letter of credit is normally issued by the importer's bank and guarantees payment to the exporter upon delivery of the merchandise if the specified conditions are met.

B. Export credit insurance: the Export Development Corporation may provide insurance against non-payment by foreign customers.

C. Funding of transactions

    1. **Export Development Corporation [p. 759]**: facilitates the financing of Canadian exports through several programs.

    2. Loans from the parent company or sister affiliate.

        a. **Parallel loans**: an arrangement where two parent firms in different countries each make a loan to the affiliate of the other parent. The procedure eliminates foreign exchange risk.

        b. **Fronting loans**: loans from a parent firm to a foreign subsidiary via a bank located in the foreign country.

    3. **Eurocurrency loans [p. 761]**: loans from foreign banks that are denominated in dollars.

        a. There are many participants in the Eurodollar market from throughout the world particularly the U.S., Canada, Western Europe and Japan.

        b. Lower borrowing costs and greater credit availability have enabled these markets to become an important source of short-term funding.

        c. The lending rate is based on the **London Interbank Offered Rate (LIBOR)**.

        d. Lending in the Eurodollar market is almost exclusively done by commercial banks. Large Euro-currency loans are frequently syndicated and managed by a lead bank.

    4. **Eurobond market [p. 762]** long-term funds may be secured by issuing Eurobonds. These bonds are sold throughout the world but are denominated primarily in U.S. dollars, Deutsche marks, Swiss francs and Japanese yen.

        a. Disclosure requirements are less stringent.

        b. Registration costs are lower.

        c. Some tax advantages exist.

        d. Caution must be exercised because of the exposure to foreign exchange risk.

    5. **International equity markets [p. 763]**: selling common stock to residents of a foreign country provides financing and also reduces political risk. See Table 21-2, page 764.

        a. Multinational firms list their shares on major stock exchanges around the world. Half the stocks listed on the Amsterdam stock exchange are foreign.

        b. Marketing securities internationally requires firms to adjust their procedures. For example, chartered banks have a dominant role in the securities business throughout Europe.

    6. **International Finance Corporation (IFC) [p. 764]**: the IFC was established in 1956 and is unit of the World Bank. Its objective is to promote economic development in the 119 member countries of the World Bank.

        a. A multinational firm may be able to raise equity capital by selling partial ownership to the IFC.

        b. The IFC decides to participate in the venture on the basis of profitability and the potential benefit to the host country.

        c. Once the venture is well established, the IFC frees up its capital by selling its ownership interest.

VII. **Global Cash Management [p. 765]**

A. Government restrictions, volatile interest rates, differing inflation rates, technological constraints, and other variables increase the complexity of managing cash globally.

VIII. **Unsettled Issues in International Finance [p. 765]**

A. The complexity of the multinational business environment generates questions for which there are no easy answers.

    1. Should a foreign affiliate design a capital structure similar to that of the parent firm or one that fits the acceptable pattern of the host country?

    2. Who should determine the dividend policy of a foreign affiliate? The affiliate management or the parent management?

B. Successful participation in the international business environment requires cohesive, coordinated financial management.

IX. **Appendix 21A: Cash Flow Analysis and the Foreign Investment Decision [p. 772-774]**

A. Cash Flow Analysis

B. Tax Factors

C. Foreign Exchange Considerations

D. Present Value Analysis

E. The Risk Factor

X. **Review of Formulas**

See text page 767 or insert card.

Chapter 21: Multiple Choice Questions

1. The_____ is the exchange rate between currencies with immediate delivery. [p. 747]
   a. Cross rate
   b. Transaction rate
   c. Spot rate
   d. Forward rate
   e. LIBOR

2. Which of the following may provide insurance against nonpayment by foreign customers? [p. 759]
   a. OPIC
   b. IFC
   c. IMM
   d. EDC
   e. CICA

3. Which of the following is a loan from a parent firm to a foreign subsidiary via a bank located in the foreign country? [p. 760]
   a. Parallel loan
   b. Letter of credit
   c. IFC loan
   d. Fronting loan
   e. LIBOR loan

4. The most widely used currencies in the Eurobond market are: [p. 762]
   a. U.S. dollars and British pounds.
   b. Deutsche marks and Canadian dollars.
   c. Canadian dollars and Japanese yen.
   d. British pounds and Japanese yen.
   e. U.S. dollars and Deutsche marks.

5. In order to reduce the risk of nonpayment, an exporter may require an importer to: [p. 759]
   a. Furnish a letter of credit.
   b. Obtain a parallel loan.
   c. Repatriate earnings.
   d. Pay with foreign currency.
   e. Expropriate assets.

6. Foreign exchange risk exposure that is associated with existing accounting rules is called: [p. 749]
   a. Transaction exposure.
   b. Translation exposure.
   c. Economic exposure.
   d. Political risk.
   e. Repatriation risk.

7. Which of the following is most useful in reducing political risk? [p. 758]
   a. A forward contract
   b. A futures contract
   c. A joint venture with a foreign company
   d. Hedging in the money market
   e. Exchanging currency in the spot market

8. Which of the following statements concerning international business is correct? [Chapter 21]
   a. Currency exchange rates tend to vary inversely with their respective purchasing powers.
   b. The relationship between interest rate differentials and exchange rates is called the purchasing power parity theory.
   c. The balance of payments is the difference in a countries exports and imports.
   d. United Nations' member countries are prohibited from intervening in the foreign exchange market.
   e. Currencies always sell forward at a discount from the spot rate.

9. Which of the following statements is not correct? [p. 737-740, 754, 836]
   a. Over 40 percent of Canada's production is from international trade.
   b. About 80 percent of Canada's merchandise trade is with the United States.
   c. Canada imports over 10 percent of its merchandise from Japan.
   d. About 40 percent of Canada's international debt is held as bonds.
   e. About 50 International firms have listed their shares on the TSX.

10. The rate on Eurodollar loans is usually based on the: [p. 761]
   a. Forward rate.
   b. Cross rate.
   c. London Interbank Offered Rate.
   d. Spot rate.
   e. Interest rate parity theory.

Multiple Choice Answer Key: Chapter 21

1.	c	2.	d	3.	d	4.	e	5.	a
6.	b	7.	c	8.	a	9.	c	10.	c

Chapter 21: Problems

21-1.   Referring to Table 21-1 in the text (page 743) compute the amount of each of the following currencies that could be bought with $5,000 in March 2002.

    (a)   Sudanese dinars

    (b)   British pounds

    (c)   Japanese yen

    (d)   Indian rupees

21-2.

    (a)   Which of the currencies in *21-1* above weakened relative to the Canadian dollar from April 1996 to March 2002? Which strengthened?

    (b)   What was the percentage change in the value of each of the currencies, from a local perspective?

21-3.   Stacy Johnson is planning a trip to Europe. A local bank sells a Euro for $1.4212 (asking price).

    (a)   What is the euro exchange rate expressed in Canadian dollars?

    (b)   How many euros will Stacy be able to buy for $1,000?

    (c)   The banks' bid price (what they pay for euros) is $1.3705. If Stacy charges all of her Euro purchases on credit cards and brings all of the euros (from *b*) home, how much will the bank pay for the euros in Canadian dollars?

21-4.   Suppose *The Globe and Mail* reports the following exchange rates for the British pound:

Spot	$2.2854
30-day forward	$2.2795
90-day forward	$2.2686
180-day forward	$2.2530

    (a)   Was the British pound selling forward at a premium or at a discount?

    (b)   What was the 180-day forward premium (or discount)?

    (c)   If you exchanged 1,000,000 British pounds in the spot market based on these rates, how many Canadian dollars would you receive?

    (d)   If you executed a 180-day forward contract to exchange 1,000,000 British pounds for Canadian dollars, how many dollars would you receive in 180 days?

21-5. Courtney Walker has forecasted that the Swiss franc will rise in value relative to the Canadian dollar over the next 365 days. Suppose the Swiss franc is currently being exchanged in the spot market for 0.97 Canadian dollars per franc.

    (a)   If Courtney converts $1,000 to francs and deposits the francs in a Swiss bank earning 3% interest annually, how many francs will she have at the end of the year?

    (b)   If the exchange rate of Swiss francs increases to 1.05 dollars per franc, how many dollars will Courtney have after she exchanges?

    (c)   What rate of return will she earn?

    (d)   If Courtney's forecast proves to be incorrect and the exchange rate at the time she exchanges is .95 dollars per franc, what will her rate of return be?

21-6. Suppose the spot exchange rates of the Danish krone and the Brazilian real were $0.1858 and $0.6794, respectively (in $ Canadian). On the same date, the cross rate between the Danish krone and the U.S. dollar was 8.5837 (krone to U.S. $).

    (a)   What was the rate of exchange (cross rate) of Danish krone to the Brazilian real?

    (b)   What was the Canadian dollar value of the U.S. dollar?

21-7. Dee Lane is considering visiting Switzerland where she visited as a teenager. She recalls that the exchange rate in 1984 was $0.42/ franc. She does not have access to current exchange rates, but he knows that the price indices for the Canada and Switzerland relative to 1984 are 458 and 180, respectively. Using the purchasing power parity theory, provide Dee with an estimate of the current exchange rate (2003).

21-8. The Jonah Corporation is evaluating a joint venture with a Jamaican firm (Whale, Inc.). Jonah would be required to contribute 100,000,000 Jamaican dollars to the construction of a plant in Jamaican. The current exchange rate of Canadian dollars/ Jamaican dollar is $0.0288. Jonah's estimated aftertax (Jamaican and Canadian) cash flows from the project are 40,000,000 Jamaican per year for five years. Jonah's required rate of return on international projects is 16%.

    (a)   Assuming that the exchange rate remains constant over the five years, should Jonah enter into the joint venture? Use the NPV method to make your determination.

    (b)   Assuming that the aftertax cash flows are repatriated each year and the following exchange rates are expected, should Jonah participate in the joint venture.

Year	Exchange Rate
1	.030
2	.032
3	.028
4	.024
5	.021

Chapter 21: Solutions

21-1.   **Spot rates**

    (a)   Sudanese dinars: $5,000 × 162.075 =   **810,375**

    (b)   British pounds: $5,000 × 0.4418 =   **2,209**

    (c)   Japanese yen: $5,000 × 83.6120 =   **418,060**

    (d)   Indian rupees: $5,000 × 30.5064 =   **152,532**

21-2.   **Exchange rates changes over time**

    (a)   The Indian rupee, Sudanese dinar and Japanese yen weakened relative to the dollar. The British pound strengthened.

    (b)   % Δ in currency value: express first in local currency

Canadian dollar/ Sudanese dinar: $\dfrac{1}{110.0} = 0.009091$ $\dfrac{1}{162.075} = 0.00617$

$$\%\Delta \ in \ value = \frac{0.00617 - 0.009091}{0.009091} = -0.3213 = \textbf{-32.13\%}$$

Canadian dollar/ British pound: $\dfrac{1}{0.4842} = 2.0653$ $\dfrac{1}{0.4418} = 2.2635$

$$\%\Delta \ in \ value = \frac{2.2635 - 2.0653}{2.0653} = 0.0960 = \textbf{9.60\%}$$

Canadian dollar/ Japanese yen: $\dfrac{1}{78.6782} = 0.01271$ $\dfrac{1}{83.6120} = 0.01196$

$$\%\Delta \ in \ value = \frac{0.01196 - 0.01271}{0.01271} = -0.0590 = \textbf{-5.90\%}$$

Canadian dollar/ Indian rupee: $\dfrac{1}{25.1572} = 0.03975$ $\dfrac{1}{30.5064} = 0.03278$

$$\%\Delta \ in \ value = \frac{0.03278 - 0.03975}{0.03975} = -0.1753 = \textbf{-17.53\%}$$

21-3.   Stacey Johnston

(a) $Exchange\ rate = \dfrac{1}{1.4212} = 0.7036$ I Canadian dollar will buy **0.7036 euros.**

(b)   *Euros purchased with* $1,000 = 1,000 × 0.7036 = **703.60**

(c)   *Dollars received* = 703.60 × $1.3705 = **$964.28**

21-4.   **Forward rates**

(a)   British pound selling at a discount.

(b)   180-day discount

$$Forward\ premium\ (discount) = \dfrac{Forward - spot}{spot} \times \dfrac{12}{contract\ length\ (months)}$$

$$= \dfrac{2.2530 - 2.2854}{2.2854} \times \dfrac{12}{6} = -0.0284 = \mathbf{-2.84\%}$$

(c)   *$ received* = 1,000,000 × $2.2854 = **$2,285,400**

(d)   *$ received* = 1,000,000 × $2.2530 = **$2,253,000**

21-5.   **Courtney Walker**

(a) $Swiss\ francs\ deposited = \dfrac{\$1,000}{\$0.97} = 1,030.93$
Interest earned = 0.03 × 1,030.93 = 30.93
Total francs = 1,030.93 + 30.93 = **1.061.86**

(b)   *Dollars received at time of exchange* = 1,061.86 × 1.05 = **$1,114.95**

(c) $Rate\ of\ return = \dfrac{\$1,114.95 - \$1,000}{\mathbf{\$1,000}} = 0.1150 = \mathbf{11.50\%}$

(d)   *$ received at time of exchange* = 1,061.86 × .95 = $1,008.77

$$Rate\ of\ return = \dfrac{\$1,008.77 - \$1,000}{\mathbf{\$1,000}} = 0.0088 = \mathbf{0.88\%}$$

Note that two thirds of Courtney's 3% return on the Swiss franc deposit was eroded by the unexpected drop in the value of the Swiss franc.

21-6. **Cross rates**

(a)

$$\text{Rate of exchange Danish krone into Brazilian real} = \frac{\$0.6794}{\$0.1858} = \mathbf{3.6566}$$

This suggests 3.6 Danish krone to receive 1 Brazilian real.

(b)　　1 $ U.S. buys 8.5837 Danish krone
1 Danish krone buys $0.1858 Canadian
Therefore 1 $ U.S. buys 8.5837 × $0.1858 = **$1.5949 Canadian**

21-7. **Purchasing power parity**

$$\text{Comparative rate of inflation} = \frac{458}{180} = 2.544 = \mathbf{254\%}$$

$/ Swiss franc (now) = $0.42 × 2.54 = $1.0668

21-8. **Jonah Corporation**

(a)　　*Initial investment* = 100,000,000 × .0288 = $2,880,000

Annual aftertax cash flow in $ = 40,000,000 × .0288 = $1,152,000
$NPV = \$1,152,000 \; PV_{IFA} \; (n = 5, i = 16\%) - \$2,880,000$
$NPV = \$3,771,986 - \$2,880,000 = \mathbf{\$891,986}$

On the basis of the expected net present value, Jonah should enter into the joint venture.

(b)　　　　　　　　　　*Annual Cash Flow in Canadian Dollars*

Year	Exchange Rate	Jamaican dollars	Canadian Dollars
1	.030	40,000,000	$1,200,000
2	.032	40,000,000	1,280,000
3	.028	40,000,000	1,120,000
4	.024	40,000,000	960,000
5	.021	40,000,000	840,000

NPV = $1,200,000 (n = 1,i = 16%) + $1,280,000 (n = 2,i = 16%) + $1,120,000 (n = 3,i = 16%) + $960,000(n = 4,i = 16%) + $840,000 (n = 5,i 16%) − $2,880,000
= $1,034,483 + $951,249 + $717,537 + $530,199 + $399,935 − $2,880,000
= $3,633,403 − $2,880,000
= **$753,403**

The joint venture is acceptable even with the declining exchange rate in the latter years. If the exchange rates declined earlier, however, the situation could change significantly.